PIZZA TIGER

PIZZA TIGER

Tom Monaghan

with Robert Anderson

RANDOM HOUSE NEW YORK

Grateful acknowledgment is given for permission
to use the drawing of the Harold McCormick house,
copyright © 1955 by The Frank Lloyd Wright Foundation.

Library of Congress Cataloging-in-Publication Data

Monaghan, Thomas S., 1937-
Pizza tiger

1. Monaghan, Thomas S., 1937- . 2. Domino's
Pizza (Firm) 3. Restaurateurs—United States—
Biography. I. Title.
TX910.5.M59A37   1986   338.7′6479573′0924 [B] 86-10131
ISBN 0-394-55359-4

Manufactured in the United States of America

24689753

FIRST EDITION

Book design by Carole Lowenstein

To Margie,
whose help and support sustained me
in the struggle to build Domino's Pizza
and whose love
makes it all worthwhile

PIZZA TIGER

MY MOST VISIBLE ACCOMPLISHMENT in life has been the building of Domino's Pizza from a single store into the world's largest pizza-delivery company. But my story is more than an account of a struggle for success. It's also a chronicle of the pursuit of dreams.

I have a lot of dreams, and I don't think I'll ever achieve them all. I hope not. I don't like having to think about a day when I might stop having new ones.

I'm an entrepreneur, but I'm also an idealist. So while I thoroughly enjoy the things money can buy, such as private jets, a helicopter, a yacht, a big-league baseball team, an Indy race car, some of the world's finest classic cars, and a northwoods resort, they are all just frosting. To me, the real substance of life and work is in a constant battle to excel. I am determined to win, to outstrip our company's best performance and beat the competition. But to my mind, winning in business is nothing unless you do it strictly according to the rules.

That idealistic attitude has often struck others as naïve or vain or foolhardy, especially during periods of crisis in the early years of Domino's, when the odds against the company's survival seemed overwhelming. But in fact, ideals are what saved the company. They kept hope alive. Eventually, they provided the fuel that propelled our corporate growth.

I was twenty-three years old, with no college degree and virtually no business experience, when I opened the restaurant that was the beginning of Domino's, on December 9, 1960. It was a small, ungarnished pizza shop at the edge of the Eastern Michigan University campus in Ypsilanti. My brother, Jim, and I went into hock up to our eyebrows to buy the place, and our sales in that wintry first week were only $99. Our partnership proved to be stormy, and my brother pulled out of the venture after about eight months. For some time after that, it seemed like he had made a very wise decision. But when Domino's celebrated its twenty-fifth anniversary in December 1985, we had 2,600 stores. We were represented in all fifty states and six foreign countries. Our growth continued to accelerate. It was clear from our performance in the first three quarters of 1986 that we would end the year with 3,600 stores and sales of $2 billion.

Two billion dollars! That's an awful lot of pizza! To be specific, we would sell at least 189 million pizzas in 1986. And that, I'm happy to say, represents a 40 percent increase over the previous year.

Momentum is an awesome force, and Domino's Pizza Inc. had it as we continued our push into new markets across the country during 1986.

Our nearest competitor in 1986 was Pizza Hut. But about one third of Pizza Hut's business is in non-pizza items. Domino's has no non-pizza items except Coke, and I think it's safe to say that we sell more pizza than Pizza Hut. Our figures show that we sell

19 percent of all the pizza sold in the United States, which is a pretty exciting statistic when you think of the future, given the current surge in pizza's popularity. A Gallup poll of American teenagers in 1984 showed that pizza is far and away their favorite food. Sorry, Colonel Sanders, and watch out, Big Mac: The pizza revolution is at hand.

The sweep of this change in the nation's eating habits is clearly reflected in Domino's growth chart. Our sales line in the early years is way down at the bottom, a jagged series of peaks and valleys; in some years it goes off the chart and into the basement. Then comes a long, gradual climb to 1980, when the line spurts straight up to the top of the chart. Everything we established in our first twenty years was merely a foundation. The rest, the entire superstructure of the company, was built in six short years.

I'll never forget the meeting of the Ann Arbor President's Club in 1980 at which members were asked to state the five-year goals for their organizations. I stood up and said mine was to make Domino's Pizza a household word in America. Eyebrows shot up like window shades all around that room. I heard loud groans of protest and a few snickers. I couldn't blame the members for being skeptical. Most of them knew that Domino's, with 290 stores, was pretty small change in the franchising field. And several in the group were aware of the massive business problems I'd had in the past. A few also knew that we had just lost a lawsuit brought by Amstar Corporation to protect its Domino Sugar trademark. Even though we were appealing the decision, it seemed certain that we were going to have to pour a lot of money into changing our company's name and that a confusion of corporate identity and consequent loss of revenue undoubtedly would follow. After the meeting, one of the members came up to me and said, "A household word, eh? You've got to be kidding, Monaghan."

"No," I replied. "I'm not kidding. We're going to continue growing at a rate of forty to fifty percent a year, just as we are now. That means we'll have at least two thousand stores by 1985, and we'll be a truly national company with nationwide recognition."

We did maintain that rate of growth during the next five years. Furthermore, we exceeded our projections for new stores, and our per-unit sales volume grew every year. Our profits have been growing faster than our sales, and an independent survey showed that in 1985 fully 90 percent of the people in the United States recognized the name Domino's Pizza.

Of course, that public awareness was given a tremendous boost by the company's association with the Detroit Tigers. I bought the Tigers, the realization of one of my long-standing dreams, in 1983. I knew they had the makings of a great team, but I had no idea they would play as they did in that incredible 1984 season. They roared into first place in the American League at the outset of the season with nine straight wins. They won thirty-five of their first forty games, the best start in baseball history. And they stayed in first place throughout the season. Only six other teams in the annals of baseball have led the league wire-to-wire. The last ones to do it were the legendary New York Yankees of 1927, the year Babe Ruth and Lou Gehrig were at their peak and Ruth hit sixty home runs. In team play, the 1984 Tigers outdid those storied Yankees, and they capped their fabulous summer by winning the World Series.

To commemorate that championship season, I was awarded a World Series ring. It's big and a bit gaudy, but for a long time I wouldn't leave home without it. I wore it on the same finger as my wedding band, and I enjoyed the contrast. The plain wedding ring cost me $12, and I guess you could say the World Series ring cost me $53 million, which is what I paid for the Tigers.

In many ways, that contrast is symbolic of me and my life. The wedding band reflects the simple and enduring values that are my greatest strength. The World Series ring represents my flamboyant side, the part of me that thrills to bidding against a lot of high rollers for a classic car. My flamboyance isn't an ego trip, it's showmanship. It gives me the kind of public relations benefit Bill Veeck used to get from his stunts.

Once, when Veeck owned the Chicago White Sox, he needed to rebuild a gate in Comiskey Park so it would be high enough to admit some large pieces of maintenance equipment. But Veeck knew fans would object to the construction if he did it only for that purpose, so he held a Nellie Fox Day at which a sailboat was to be presented to the immortal Fox. In order to get the boat with its tall mast into the park, of course, Veeck had to rebuild the gate, and fans acepted the construction enthusiastically. He killed two birds with one stone, and that's the kind of promotion I love. Veeck and P. T. Barnum are heroes of my flamboyant side. At the same time, men like Pope John and Abraham Lincoln appeal to my straitlaced standards.

I never confuse these sides of my makeup. So I see no contradiction between, on the one hand, sitting down at home to a simple meal that my wife spoons out of the pots it was cooked in and, on the other, insisting that meals in the executive dining room at Domino's headquarters be of five-star quality, impeccably served, with white linen tablecloths, fine china designed by Frank Lloyd Wright, silverware, and crystal glasses.

I read somewhere that Freud said the two most important things in human existence are love and work. I agree with that. And I think people are at their best when they combine the two and *love* their *work*. Life is too precious to be wasted in doing work you don't love. The saying "love is blind" can also be extended to work, and I've sometimes had difficulty seeing flaws in

Domino's. Yet if I had loved it less, I might have given it up years ago.

The management techniques I applied in building the company were developed mostly by trial and error. But all of them were based on a homemade philosophy I call my five personal priorities. I first came up with this list during a voyage from the Philippines to Japan while I was in the Marine Corps. I had plenty of time aboard that troopship to reflect on my life and goals, and I haven't changed my list in any way since. My five priorities are: *spiritual, social, mental, physical,* and *financial,* in that order. I don't pretend to be a philosopher; I don't know enough big words. In fact I don't *want* to know any big words. I don't like them. The only ones I'm able to stomach are those used by architects. I'm an action guy. I believe in deeds, not words. But I'll do my best to explain what these priorities mean to me.

SPIRITUAL

My background makes concern about spiritual matters as natural to me as breathing. I grew up in a Catholic orphanage, and for a short time I attended a seminary, with every intention of becoming a priest. My religious faith is strong. I know I can never be a success on this earth unless I am on good terms with God. I know I would not have been able to build Domino's without the strength I gained from my religious faith. In the earlier years, I was hit by a long series of difficulties. Each one seemed like a knockout blow. But I was able to get off the floor every time and come back stronger than ever. That's the power of faith. I use it every day. No matter how tense or tired I get, I can take time out to pray or say a rosary and feel refreshed. That's a tremendous asset.

It's also a fact, though, that I got kicked out of the seminary.

So I have a very clear understanding of the line between religious and secular interests. When it comes to strictly secular matters of business, my spiritual priority is expressed in the Golden Rule: *Do unto others as you would have others do unto you.*

I've always told Domino's employees and franchisees that all they have to do to be successful is have a good product, give good service, and apply the Golden Rule. Those elements alone will make any company stand out above its competitors and will generate better public relations than high-powered PR campaigns. Dramatic newspaper stories and TV interviews are great. We've had our share of them at Domino's in recent years. But the most important PR is the kind that's spread by customers, word-of-mouth, because you're doing the little things right, day in and day out.

The biggest little thing you can do is simply be nice to people. I've often remarked in speeches that my objective is to have everyone say that Domino's Pizza people are nice. Not brilliant or charming or models of efficiency, just *nice*. How can that be achieved? Simply by getting employees to take every opportunity to be friendly, to smile at the customer and say "please" and "thank you" and "sir" and "ma'am." I am very serious about the proper technique for taking telephone orders, how to say the right words and get as much friendliness into your voice as possible. It sounds very basic, and it is. But it's one of those fundamentals you have to stress over and over again, like a football coach harping on blocking and tackling. And though it's a little thing, it pays off big and in unexpected ways. If you are nice to other people, they'll be nice to you. Not only will your business prosper, but your customers' return of courtesy will bolster your self-image and you'll become a happier person.

To be nice to others, to think of the needs and interests of others, is the way to start putting the Golden Rule into action.

Unfortunately, most people don't have the importance of being nice to others instilled in them by their parents. I had only a brief taste of it myself, from a nun named Sister Beralda in the orphanage. But I never forgot it, and I don't think it's ever too late to learn.

Honesty and ethical behavior can be taught. Managers can sometimes do it by example, and it's an uplifting experience for both manager and employee when it happens. But if a person lacks integrity, attempting to work a character change is tough.

I've been surprised on a couple of occasions to learn that a trusted executive was guilty of some sort of unethical behavior. It's difficult to fire a person for some relatively minor infraction, especially when you have a lot of time and money invested in his training and when his performance otherwise has been terrific. The temptation is to go along with promises to reform. But my experiences in doing so have been unhappy. Part of the fault in these situations was mine. I am slow to recognize dishonesty in others because I prefer to trust people. I look for the good in others, not the bad. But I've learned my lesson. Whenever I find a bad apple now, no matter how bright or appealing he is, I know he'll wind up spoiling the barrel. I toss him out immediately.

SOCIAL

A loving wife and family are, to me, essential for a happy and productive life.

My wife, Margie, was in my corner through all those tough battles of the early years in Domino's. To say I couldn't have succeeded without her would be a tremendous understatement.

We met in February 1961, fourteen months after I got into the pizza business. I was making my first personal delivery from a new store I'd opened in Mount Pleasant, Michigan. The address on the order was Sweeny Hall, a dormitory at Central Michigan University, and Margie was working the switchboard at the reception desk when I walked in. She was cute, and I started a conversation with her while waiting for my customer to come down and pick up the pizza. Margie wasn't unfriendly, but she wasn't very talkative either. To cover my shyness, I asked her which companies were doing the most pizza business there. All I remember her saying is, "An awful lot of pizza is delivered up here."

I was smitten with her right off the bat. I sang and hollered as I drove back to the store. I told Frank Sukovich, my manager in training, about the cute chick I had seen. Then I asked him if he was ready to run the store without me so I could take a night off. He said, "Sure, that's cool." I went to the pay phone up front—I didn't want Sukovich to hear me, and I didn't want to tie up our phones—and I called Sweeny Hall. I told the girl on the switchboard that I was the guy who just delivered a pizza up there and asked her if she would go to a movie with me.

"Oh, I just came on duty," she said. "You must have been talking to Bonnie."

She gave me Bonnie's number, and I repeated the whole spiel. But she wasn't the girl either. She had asked a girl named Marjorie Zybach to substitute for her on the switchboard. So I had to get up my nerve for a third time. But I knew as soon as Margie answered the phone that I had the right girl, the vibes were so intense. I was certain she'd agree to go out with me, and she did.

After our second date, I gave Margie a heart-shaped pizza for Valentine's Day. It was a big hit with her friends in the dorm. On our third date, I looked into those big blue eyes and realized I was in love.

We were married on August 25, 1962. At first, we lived in house trailers. I was only taking a salary of $102 a week out of the business, and we lived very simply. Margie worked as a waitress for a while and then as a school librarian. After our first two daughters were born—Mary in May 1963 and Susie in May 1965—Margie helped me in the Ypsilanti store. Our babies slept in cardboard boxes in the corner while Margie answered telephones and did the bookkeeping. She still works in Domino's accounting department, and personally hands out paychecks to every employee in our headquarters. Our four daughters have grown up with Domino's as a sort of extended family. They've done baby-sitting for franchisees, worked at various jobs in stores and around the office, and they've shared some of the heartbreaks and triumphs of people in the company.

After family on my scale of social relationships come friends. Nobody can succeed in business without the help of friends. And that probably goes double in franchising, where trust is the grease that keeps the working parts from binding. Friendships with franchisees are as varied as the individuals involved. Some are like stone walls: You have to keep working at them to keep them standing, and they may fall apart for no apparent reason. Others endure despite all kinds of problems. This is the kind of friendship I have with Steve Litwhiler, who established the first Domino's franchise outside the state of Michigan. I took money out of my own pocket to set Steve up in business in Vermont, and he later saved my neck when I was in trouble with the IRS by lending me ten thousand dollars without question—without even asking for an IOU.

I hardly know how to classify my friendship with a franchisee like Harold Mitchell in Zanesville, Ohio. Mitch has always been one of my most vocal critics; we've had some hot arguments in franchisee meetings. In fact, Mitch got me so upset at one session in 1978 that I told my assistant, Helen McNulty, "This job is just too exasperating; it's worth more than I'm making. I'm going to give myself a raise!"

The next time I saw Mitch, I walked up to him and said, "I want to thank you. You got me to increase my salary by five thousand dollars a year."

Our differences of opinion haven't prevented Mitch and me from being good friends. He owns 41 percent of our Ohio commissary, and in 1982 he helped me get a $500,000 loan from the commissary so I could buy an office building for Domino's.

Community involvement is another important part of my social priority. I believe a business has an obligation to participate in programs to help the community that supports it. The Jaycees have provided a reliable vehicle for me to get involved in community work over the years, and that relationship also has been a great help to me in times of need. For example, in 1968, after fire destroyed our headquarters, the Ypsilanti Jaycees pitched in and donated many hours of manual labor to clean up the mess, and they helped me find temporary office space.

MENTAL

The key factor in maintaining a healthy mind is a clear conscience. This means you have done your best to live up to your own expectations. A clear conscience fosters self-esteem, a positive attitude, and an optimistic outlook, all of which promote success in business. I believe the mind needs exercise, that it will grow in capacity and thinking ability if it is forced to by constant questioning and the desire for new information.

I've always been curious about the way I think. I did well enough in school whenever I was motivated to apply myself, but I'm not a good student in the academic sense. I get impatient with classroom teaching. I don't want someone else's answers to problems; I want to find my own. When I took the aptitude tests given by the Marine Corps, there was a section on pattern analysis that was supposed to be very difficult. But I breezed through it in half the allotted time. Then I looked around and saw that everyone else was still scribbling away, so I went back through my paper, found a couple of small mistakes, and corrected them. I was still the only one finished. I learned later that I was the only guy in the outfit and maybe the only one in the Corps who had a perfect score on that test. I was reminded of that some years afterward, when a psychologist told me that I tend to think in patterns.

My friend and mentor Eugene Power, founder of University Microfilms International and originator of the concept of printing single editions of scholarly volumes, "books on demand," has told me that my thinking process is much like his. "I have watched you at board meetings, Tom," he said, "and you think intuitively. You do not go step by step through a logical consideration of facts, you go from problem to solution in a single leap."

That's often true. But just as often, my conclusions come only after drawing a line down the middle of a sheet of paper and writing down all the pros of a decision on one side, all the cons on the other, and weighing them against each other.

In doing that kind of thinking, though, I have to be sure I know the facts surrounding all the pros and cons. Otherwise I'll go off on some tangent. Reading is one way of getting the facts, of course, and I read a lot of books. But for me, the best way to find things out is by asking questions. One of the most important words in the English language is *why*. When I'm in a restaurant, I like to get into the kitchen to see how they do things. If I see a new twist, I'll ask *why* they do it that way. Good chefs take pride in their operations, so they're usually happy to explain. When I was thinking about buying Domino's first corporate jet, I took every opportunity to talk to mechanics who service private planes. They can give you the real scoop on how well various aircraft hold up and which engines are mechanically the best.

My questioning sometimes irritates people. A former top executive in Domino's used to get red-faced and say I was driving him crazy, because no matter what he told me, I would always ask "Why?" or "Why not?" I was just trying to learn from him, and I'll do that with anyone who has something worth knowing, and that's everybody.

PHYSICAL

It may sound corny, but I subscribe to the idea that the body is the temple of the soul. As a living edifice, it needs proper fuel and good maintenance. If I lost my health, I'd give every penny I had to get it back, and I don't know anyone who wouldn't.

I know how tough it is to lose weight because I'm naturally a big eater. If I let myself, I could polish off a large pizza and any dessert put in front of me and ask for seconds. But I'm religious about counting calories. Every Friday and Monday, or on any day that my weight has moved up over 163 pounds when I get on the scale in the morning, I limit myself to 500 calories. I eat dessert only eleven times a year: Christmas, Easter, Thanksgiving, just before Lent, St. Patrick's Day, and six family birthdays. I call these my "pig-out" days. But despite my calorie counting, I couldn't keep my weight under control without exercise.

Six days a week, I do forty-five minutes of floor exercises, including 150 consecutive pushups, followed by a six-and-a-third-mile run. Twice a week, I end my run in the fitness center at our new headquarters, Domino's Farms, and work out for an hour. I do repetitions on the progressive-resistance weight machines as fast as possible and have a trainer help me work each muscle group to exhaustion.

People magazine has called me a "fitness freak." But I don't think I'm fanatical about fitness; I've made my routine a habit now and I don't want to break it. I admit, though, that over the years I've harassed some of my employees and franchisees to lose weight. One of them was Dick Mueller, a franchisee who for a time was our vice-president of operations. I went so far as to put a clause in his franchise contract giving him a higher percentage of royalties if he lost a specific amount of weight and a lower percentage if his weight increased. He dieted for a time but couldn't stick with it. He estimated that our agreement cost him $4,000 in lost royalties. Finally, I told him, "Dick, if you complete a marathon within a year, and I mean *run* it, not *walk* it, I'll give you fifty thousand dollars." That did it. He lost nearly a hundred pounds in a little less than a year and finished the twenty-six miles of a marathon in Baton Rouge, Louisiana. I was at the finish line cheering him on with a check for $50,000.

I wanted to grab all the publicity I could get for Domino's, of course, so the check I was waving was a blow-up, two feet wide and six feet long. It did the trick. A wire-service reporter was intrigued, and newspapers all around the country picked up the story he dispatched about the "pizza executive who lost a hundred pounds and ran to get a fat check." The piece mentioned Mueller's affiliation with Domino's, which I found doubly satisfying, since it failed to say that the marathon was sponsored by Burger King!

Even without the public-relations benefit, though, I considered that $50,000 dollars well spent. Mueller's health meant that much to me. He's no longer quite as skinny as he was when he ran that race, but he's still moving plenty fast. He now has more than 200 Domino's stores, making his company, RPM Pizza, Inc., our largest franchise operation.

FINANCIAL

The financial priority is last on my list, because it arises from the others. I know that if I attend to the first four properly, financial success will follow as surely as day follows night.

I view money in much the same way P. T. Barnum did: it's

important only for the things it can allow you to do. Hamilton Basso wrote of Barnum that he wanted money because it allowed him to reach for "the larger hope, the more compelling dream," which for him was fame. My dreams are different, but achieving them is the reason I want to make more and more money.

Barnum is one of my heroes, and the general opinion that he was a con man is unfortunate. It's based mostly on the saying he supposedly coined that "there's a sucker born every minute." Of course, he did enjoy using the title he gave himself: Prince of Humbugs. But Barnum actually was a very scrupulous, honest man. He was an advertising genius, too, and his business principles are as sound today as they were in 1859, when he described them in an essay called "The Art of Money Getting." He stressed the importance of economy, the value of maintaining a balanced budget, of being systematic, and of "being polite and kind to your customers." Barnum took huge enjoyment in ideas like the one for getting slow-moving crowds to walk out of his American Museum on a particularly busy day by putting up signs stating "This Way to the EGRESS." To make sure people read his outdoor advertisements, he put them on the back of signs saying "Don't Read the Other Side." He had an elephant at Iranistan, his estate near Bridgeport, Connecticut, and to advertise his circus, he hitched the elephant to a plow and had it walked out at times when it would be seen from passing railroad cars.

Barnum had a keen interest in money. In fact, he may have carried it a bit too far; his dying words were, "What were yesterday's receipts?" But an entrepreneur could do a lot worse in forming his financial philosophy than to base it on the example set by Phineas Taylor Barnum.

There you have an overview of my five personal priorities. How I used them in building Domino's will be a major theme of the rest of this book.

. . .

Another important principle I've stressed over the years is: *Have fun in the work you do.* I enjoy being a pizza man as much as P. T. Barnum enjoyed being a showman. This ties in, of course, to the idea of loving your work. I believe that if you've chosen the career that's right for you, it will give your life a feeling of purpose; you'll love it. And if you love your work, it will be fun.

Having fun starts right at the heart of our business, which is not in corporate headquarters in Ann Arbor but out in our stores. We promise our customers that they will get free delivery of a hot, tasty made-to-order pizza in thirty minutes or less. The fun comes in fulfilling that promise. We call it "handling the rush."

The rush is defined as any time a store has an order that hasn't been put in the oven. Everything in our system is calculated to expedite production and get that pizza to the customer within thirty minutes. I was involved in every step of the design of Domino's system, and I worked it so hard for so long that I know every nuance of its operation. At one time I thought I was the world's fastest pizza maker, and my ability to handle the rush will always be a source of pride and satisfaction for me.

Our system is simple. Each step is clearly defined and logical. Its real beauty, though, is in the thrill of working as a team when the pace gets really frantic, when the phones are ringing without letup and the drivers are running back out the door right after they come in. Each member of the team has to employ manual dexterity, economy of movement, speed, and quick thinking. If you make a mistake, confuse an order, have a driver unable to find an address, or forget any of the little details that go into making a perfect pizza, you can mar a whole night's work. People respond to that kind of challenge. It's a game, and the ones who have a knack for it can go a long way in Domino's. They're the ones we call Dominoids, and we say they have pizza sauce in their veins.

Personally, I miss making pizzas. Sometimes my fingers itch to slap out dough, and I wish I could get back into that furious make-line rhythm. But part of the price I've had to pay for success is being removed from all that.

I should add, though, that there isn't an executive in Domino's, including me, who will stand by and look on if a crew is working short-handed. We jump in and help until the rush is handled. A spot of pizza sauce on your suit during store inspections isn't a sign of bad grooming at Domino's; it's a badge of honor.

My talent for pizza making was always my ace in the hole in the process of building Domino's. I knew that even if the worst happened and the company went under, Margie and I could always make a good living by opening a small pizza shop.

Facing the threat of bankruptcy was never much fun, of course, and neither was the process of learning the techniques of business administration. I had to do it the hard way. Frequently, I was put behind the eight ball by business partners and others because I was trusting and I assumed that they would be as ethical in their dealings with me as I was with them. I just wanted to learn from them. Well, I learned all right, but at tremendous cost.

Executives who never worked out very well in Domino's were Ph.D.'s or MBA's who criticized me for not being "professional," or were contemptuous of our lack of organizational structure and procedures. They worried because we didn't have clear-cut policies on this or that. It pained them that our lines of authority were unclear. In most cases, I discovered, their criticisms were just smoke screens to hide the fact that they weren't getting their job done. If something is messed up, I believe in taking corrective action immediately. But I want to be certain it *is* messed up. It may just *seem* messed up to some people because it isn't being done according to the textbook.

I don't mean to downgrade the value of a college degree. I have a high regard for education, and I used to feel somewhat inadequate because I didn't have a degree.

But I've learned that if you are out in front creating something new and different in business, such as a delivery-only pizza restaurant chain, no degree is going to help you much. No textbook is going to fit your needs exactly. You have to design the organization as you go along. And since no model exists for it, you have to persuade people to share your vision of what it will be like.

The reason this task appealed to me, I think, is that I am an architect at heart. I love the challenge of building the organization I see in my mind's eye. To make that vision come alive and grow and prosper is one of the greatest thrills I can imagine.

I've studied Frank Lloyd Wright's work and his ideas ever since I was twelve years old, and I think he was the greatest architect who ever lived. Great as he was, however, he had one concept that he was never able to realize. This was to merge technology and nature by building a skyscraper in a rural setting. None of Wright's clients could be persuaded to do it. But now I am making it happen, finally, through construction of Domino's new international headquarters, Domino's Farms. We moved into the first phase of this five-year project on December 9, 1985, with a ceremony celebrating the start of the company's twenty-fifth anniversary year. When the rest is completed, it will be a $300 million complex that, in addition to the long, low, Wright-style office building, incorporates a farm and a lake at the base of the Golden Beacon, a tower designed by Frank Lloyd Wright. The farm will be open for the public's enjoyment; it will be a place where families can come for picnics and tours of the grounds. Kids will be able to pet the animals, which will include a lot of unusual ones, like Shire horses, the biggest horses in the world, and pygmy goats, miniature horses, huge white Chianina cattle from Italy, and peacocks. My collection of classic cars will be on display, as will a museum of steam farm equipment. The farm will cover fifteen hundred acres and eventually may include a working "you-pick" farm developed by the renowned horticulturist Booker T. Whatley. Jogging trails laced through the property will lead to a $750,000 health center operated by the University of Michigan Hospital.

There are lots of architectural problems yet to be solved in our plans, but when we are finished, I hope that workers in Domino's offices will be able to look out a window and see a cow or a horse looking in at them.

The Golden Beacon, which will be the crown jewel of the complex, was conceived in 1957 for a site on Chicago's Gold Coast, but it was never built. I purchased the design from Wright's Taliesin Foundation and had the architects there rescale it to the same height, but with thirty stories instead of fifty. Thirty is a magic number at Domino's—we deliver to the customer's door in thirty minutes. So it seems fitting that when someone wants to get to the top of our tower, he'll push the elevator button marked 30.

The view from the top of the Golden Beacon will be meaningful to me in a very personal way. To the east, though not quite visible in the distance, is Detroit, home of the Tigers. In the opposite direction, just a couple of miles away, is the house where my parents lived when I was born. That house, then a very humble little place and now much changed by additions, holds in its dry old walls dusty reminders of my earliest childhood. It also recalls to me the agony I felt at the death of my father, a loss that left a permanent mark on my life.

MY FATHER DIED ON CHRISTMAS EVE, when I was four years old.

Mother took me with her to the funeral home and held my hand as we walked up to his casket. I was frightened. It didn't seem right for Dad to be lying there. I pulled away from her grip and jumped up on the casket. I grabbed him and hugged him tight, crying: "Wake up, Daddy! Wake up, Daddy!"

Our little house in the country near Ann Arbor, Michigan, seemed empty to me from then on. I have many memories of that place and the yard around it, where I used to play. My earliest recollection is of running after Dad when I was about two years old; I wanted to be with him wherever he went. I remember watching him at work outside the house and wondering why he used three nails instead of one to fasten a board.

Beyond my childish impressions, most of the things I know about my father are from my mother's diary, which she has kept daily since she was twelve years old. A few years ago, she made photocopies of all the pages that pertained to me and gave them to me for Christmas. My mother came from Chelsea, a small town near Ann Arbor. Her father, Warren Geddes, had been a promoter, traveling by train from town to town around southeastern Michigan to show two-reel movies that were followed by vaudeville acts. He later owned the Princess Theater in Chelsea and the Electric Theater in Almont. Perhaps I got my entrepreneurial instincts from him.

My mother was a junior in high school when she met my dad, in December 1932, at a party. She was attracted to him, she wrote, because of his curly hair and quiet manner. He had a good mind and a subtle sense of humor, though he had only an eighth-grade education. His parents were separated, and his father, who had custody of the seven children, died at age thirty-nine. Dad, who was only thirteen at the time, quit school to help support the family. When he met my mother, he was working on a dairy farm. Later, while courting her, he baled hay for local farmers, using equipment he'd inherited from his father. Dad also worked for a time at a Ford Motor Company generator plant.

Dad married my mother on April 14, 1936. She was in nurse's training and she worked as a nurse's aide until that July, when she became ill and the doctor told her she was pregnant. That's when she and Dad decided they needed a house instead of the two rooms they were renting. My Grandmother Monaghan owned a parcel of land on Newport Road near the Huron River about four miles from Ann Arbor, and she sold one corner of it to my parents on what amounted to an interest-free loan. Dad's original idea was to build what he called a mobile garage home, twenty-four by twenty-six feet. Then he decided instead to put the house on a permanent foundation. My mother didn't like the change of plan; she didn't think they could afford it, but Dad won out. They managed to buy the cement blocks for the foundation, but they were $50 short of the $236 they needed for lumber. Dad tried to get a bank loan for $50, but was refused. Finally, Grandmother loaned them $45, and my mother made up the rest by working as a domestic.

My mother's diary notes that on October 16, 1936, she and Dad had gone to a Mr. Hall's farm to pick up the hay baler he had left there as security on a loan. Mr. Hall wouldn't let them take the machine without getting his money, so Dad had to give up baling hay and look for odd jobs to keep bread on the table. He couldn't work much because he was ill even then with the ulcers that eventually would cause peritonitis and kill him at age twenty-nine.

I was born on March 25, 1937. My mother likes to tell about how my father came to see her in the hospital, and held me for the first time. She says he stood there by her bed looking down at me and said, "He's worth a million dollars."

By this time, Dad had found a fairly steady job driving a tractor-trailer rig for the Interstate Company, and he and my mother had moved into the tiny three-room house he'd built. Dad never did finish that house, though he kept working on it whenever he could. I remember him talking enthusiastically about how someday he would build an addition for a bathroom and an extra bedroom.

At first they used water from a nearby creek for washing and hauled drinking water from a neighbor's well. Then they had a well dug, and my mother felt she was living luxuriously when she got a hand pump installed in the kitchen sink. During their first few nights in the house, they slept on a pile of cellotex wallboard. Then my grandmother gave them a bed and my aunts donated other pieces of furniture. My mother prepared meals on a two-burner electric hot plate. She had only three cooking pans (cream-colored graniteware with green trim, she noted). But even though the house must have been drafty and uncomfortable and its little rooms must have been crowded after my brother, Jim, was born in August 1939, it remains in my memory as warm and spacious as a mansion.

Dad was a gentle man. He was very patient with me, though my mother says I was a "holy terror" who needed watching every minute. I guess she is right, because I still have a big scar on my forearm from the day I tugged on an electric cord and brought a hot electric teakettle down on myself. But Dad only punished me once that I can recall, and that was when I was about three years old. He intended to drive down to some neighbors' house with a block of ice for their icebox. My mother said I couldn't go, but I believed Dad would want me with him and made up my mind to go anyhow. When Dad pulled out of our yard in our '37 Pontiac, I jumped onto the rear bumper beside the block of ice and clung there as we lurched along the deeply rutted gravel road. It never occurred to me that I might fall off and be injured or killed. After Dad parked in the neighbors' yard, I went running around the car to surprise him, shouting "Here I am!" I'll never forget the stricken look on his face. And I'll never forget the spanking he gave me, either.

I was fascinated by our car. I loved to get in it and pretend I was driving. This got me into trouble with Dad again one day, when the car was parked in our yard and I must have unwittingly knocked it out of gear or released the parking brake. Suddenly, I was hanging on for dear life as the car rolled toward a four- or five-foot drop-off at a retaining wall, beyond which was a long slope running down to the Huron River. Luckily, the front wheels dropped into a shallow ditch that stopped the car just before the drop-off. I got a good lecture from Dad, and I was more hurt that he didn't seem to believe me when I told him I didn't do anything intentionally than if he had whipped me.

Dad had two brothers who were bricklayers. I was told that they were the best, that they always won the bricklaying contests at the annual Labor Day picnic. Dad got upset with them when they drank a lot of beer, but they joshed him, saying he was just jealous because he couldn't drink on account of his ulcer. But he had high principles. My mother said he told her he would have become a priest if he had been able to continue his education.

When Dad died in 1941, my mother got $2,000 in insurance. Half of it went to pay off the house and property. She put the other half in the bank as an emergency fund. She couldn't see how she could support my brother and me: She was earning only $27.50 a week, and her expenses were $30 a week. Besides, she'd always had a difficult time managing me. She says that even when I was a baby, before I could walk, which I did at seven months, she couldn't leave me alone for a minute because I was so strong and restless that I'd pull the safety pins right out of my diapers. So she decided to put us into a foster home. Her plan was to go back to school and become a registered nurse. Then, after she got a good job, she would take us back to live with her again. That's what happened, but it took a long time. For me, it was too long.

Jim and I were sent to live in a couple of different homes, each for a period of a few weeks. Then we were taken in by an old German couple, Mr. and Mrs. Frank Woppman. They were fine people, but they had strict rules. For example, you had to remove your shoes before you entered their house. This kept the house neat and clean, but it was a nuisance for a hyperactive little kid like me. I enjoyed living there, though. Uncle Frank, as I called Mr. Woppman, liked to tease me. He'd tell me I was ugly, and his favorite name for me was *Dummkopf.*

When I was halfway through the first grade, Jim and I were sent to Jackson, Michigan. I soon discovered there were two prisons in Jackson: the Michigan State Penitentiary and the one I was put in, St. Joseph's Home for Boys, a Catholic orphanage run by Felician nuns. The orphanage was in a huge old mansion, and though I hated the institution, I loved its architecture. It had grand Victorian lines topped by a marvelous cupola that commanded a view of the vast, terraced front lawn. The grounds were surrounded by a wrought-iron fence and had a giant beech tree that was a landmark in the community. I learned how big that yard was when I had to push one of the dozens of lawnmowers the nuns kept stored behind the latticework of the rambling old porches. I learned a lot of other things in the orphanage too: how to scrub and polish floors and iron shirts and trousers by the hundreds. I became the fastest ironer in the place. In addition to these chores, every boy had an assigned duty. Mine was to clean the carved banisters of the soaring main staircase. I was fascinated by the way the stairs were constructed. They were at least eight feet wide; they would accommodate all the boys in the orphanage as a grandstand from which to watch movies. But their most striking feature was a tall newel post topped by a large statue of St. Joseph.

Life in the orphanage was stifling. In the six and a half years I spent there, I never got over the feeling that my existence was abnormal, that my lot in life was unjust. I didn't brood about it and, except for the first day, I didn't rebel. I'm not even sure it was rebellion I was expressing then. I only remember feeling intensely unhappy about my strange new surroundings. I confronted one boy who seemed repulsive to me. I'm not sure why, but he had some sort of cap or bandage on his head and I found that so offensive that I hit him. That boy later turned out to be one of the best athletes in the orphanage. We all called him Eightball, and despite my unhappiness at being in St. Joseph's, I made friends with him, as I did with many of my fellow inmates.

My best friend was Roy Morris. He shared my feeling of being an outsider, not belonging in the orphanage. But Roy had even more reason; he wasn't a Catholic. His parents had put him in the orphanage for a few years while they took care of some crisis in the family business. He recalls that he got off to a bad start, just as I had with my fighting. After his admission interview, he was walking up to the second floor with his mother and a nun and he noticed Jesus Christ on the wall. Pointing to it, the six-year-old Roy exclaimed, "Mom, that's the same Indian they have downstairs!"

It seems the nuns never trusted him after that. He remembers being awakened in the middle of the night and being whipped for allegedly stealing a small chain. "I didn't do it," he says. "But my pleas of innocence were ignored." Roy also remembers having his mouth washed out with soap, and I got that treatment more than once myself for making some wisecrack. He recalls, too, that to polish the oak floors, we had to rub them with bread wrappers, which had a wax coating. Then we'd buff them by having one kid sit on a blanket while others pulled him around till his backside got so hot he'd fall off.

Roy left the orphanage several years before I did, and I missed him a lot. But we were so young, we had no way to keep in touch. Forty years later, Roy happened to read about me in a *Newsweek* story on the incredible winning streak of the 1984 Tigers. He telephoned my office the next day, and it was a thrill to hear his voice again. Roy lives in New Jersey now. He and his wife have five children, and he is chairman of the board of two large companies that produce personalized computer letters for direct-mail promotions: Scanforms, Inc., and Cybermatics, Inc.

I kept in touch with only two other guys I grew up with in the orphanage, John Franklin Curry and Jim Bryson, though I met a lot of the others at a reunion in 1985. Curry and I walked to

school together and were teammates in various school sports for
five years. He was a good guy to have on your side in any situation, because even as a sixth-grader, he weighed nearly three
hundred pounds, and he was amazingly quick and agile. From
the orphanage, Curry went to high school at Boys Town, and I
was proud when I read that he'd made the Nebraska all-state
football team in his junior and senior years. He became a boring-
machine operator in Grand Haven, Michigan.

Jim Bryson went on to a career with Consumers Power Company in Jackson. He was one of the older boys. He used to referee
our basketball games, which we played in a gymnasium so cold
in the winter that we could see our breath. Bryson would pick up
the newspapers for the nuns each morning and would read the
sports pages on his way back from the store. He'd tell the rest of
us about the important current events, such as the Tigers games.
We would scream excitedly and punch one another when they
won. When they lost, we'd go into mourning.

The first two grades of school were taught in the orphanage,
but from third grade on, boys walked in groups to attend various
schools in the area. Curry and I went to St. Mary's. We were
accounted for by number, and for years I was number 25 on the
list. I liked that because 25 was the uniform number of Hal White,
the Tigers' pitcher. My schooling in the orphanage had begun on
a high note, thanks to the inspiration of a gentle, loving teacher,
Sister Berarda. She became my surrogate mother, and I flourished
under her care. I was an absolute star at everything I did. I was
the best jigsaw puzzle solver, the best Ping-Pong player, the best
marble shooter. I stood out in every team sport, too. But most
interesting to me in retrospect is the fact that I was also an outstanding student. There was talk of advancing me a grade because
I did so well in class. But that was probably the last time I was
noted for scholarship. I did well then, I think, because Sister

Beranda always encouraged me, even when my ideas seemed far-fetched. I remember telling the class that when I grew up I wanted to be a priest, an architect, and shortstop for the Detroit Tigers. The other kids laughed and said that was impossible. I couldn't be all three. Sister Beranda quieted them down and said, "Well, I don't think it's ever been done before, Tommy, but if you want to do it, there's no reason you can't." That was inspiring.

Unfortunately, when I entered third grade, the encouragement of Sister Beranda, who had been both teacher and house mother, was replaced by the impersonal atmosphere of classes at St. Mary's and the stern rule of a different house mother in the orphanage. She ruled by the strap. We were whipped for the slightest infraction; there was no leniency, never a reprieve. That house mother was as tough as the strictest drill instructor I ever had in the Marine Corps. We would have to pull down our pants and she'd swing her strap with every ounce of strength she had. Under her regime, I lost interest in outside activities. My school grades slid and other kids started surpassing me in sports. I went into a gradual slump. I managed to keep about a B average, as I recall, but I never regained the enthusiasm for classwork that Sister Beranda had given me.

My mother visited Jim and me fairly often. She always said she was trying to bring us to live with her, but she never seemed able to make the right arrangements. So life in the orphanage dragged on, with school year following dreary school year. I often wondered what life would be like outside that place, but I thought I had no real hope of experiencing it until I grew up.

After my mother finished her schooling, she moved to Traverse City, a resort community in northern Michigan, where she hoped to find relief for her hay fever. I knew nothing about Traverse City except that it was far away and was called the state's cherry capital. Then one day when I was in sixth grade, my mother told me she was taking Jim and me back to live with her. I could hardly believe it. But sure enough, the following August we went north to join her in the house she was buying from a woman she worked with on the nursing staff of Munson Hospital.

I can recall how exciting it was to be free, to be able to go into stores by myself and look at the merchandise, to be allowed to have money in my pocket, to be able to make money. The transition from the regimentation of the orphanage to complete freedom with my mother was exhilarating.

One of my first forays into town was to seek a job at a car dealership. I felt I knew a lot about cars. Observing them had been a chief interest of mine on our twice-daily walks between school and orphanage. I read everything about them and kept a scrapbook of cars. So I wanted to work in a place where I could be around cars. I knew a dealer wasn't likely to hire a twelve-year-old, but I was willing to work without pay. I went to every dealership in town and asked the managers to let me sweep the floor or wash cars—anything. I'm sure they thought I was a bit nuts. At any rate, they didn't let me hang around.

After our years apart, it seemed like my mother and I couldn't be together for more than a minute without getting into an argument, so I stayed away from her as much as possible. After I completed seventh grade, I worked at different summer jobs that kept me out of the house. A boy named Paul Steffes and I picked cherries for a while. I thought hand-picking was too slow and said there should be a machine to shake the trees so the cherries would fall onto tarps. That, of course, is exactly the way it's done today. Paul and I also used to go fishing off the docks on Lake Michigan, and we'd sell our catch door-to-door. I'd do the same with vegetables I grew in a little garden patch at home. I also sold the *Traverse City Record Eagle* on the corner in front of Milliken's department store.

I spent a week or so that summer visiting my "rich uncle" Ed Monaghan, who owned a construction business in Ann Arbor, and when I returned to Traverse City, the problems between my mother and me worsened. We fought constantly. She said she just couldn't handle being both mother and father to me anymore, and she applied to the state Children's Home and Aid Society to have me placed in a foster home. This time I was sent to the farm of a family named Beaman in Interlochen. I liked Mr. Beaman and enjoyed working with him on his gravel truck, but I decided that what I really wanted was to be on a real farm, where I could drive a tractor and milk cows. I stayed on the Beaman place for the rest of the school year and most of the following summer. When I returned to Traverse City, I spent as little time at home as possible. A boy named Alan Gray and I spent days on end playing Ping-Pong in his basement. We must have played thousands of games, and I think I won every single one.

When school resumed that year, both my brother and I were sent to live on the farm of a family named Johnson. It was more of a working farm than Beaman's, and I enjoyed it. Even better was the next place I landed a few months later, this time without Jim. He went back to live with my mother. My new home was a farm owned by Mr. and Mrs. Edwin Crouch, a very humble but, to my way of thinking, wonderful place. I liked everything about farm life. I liked getting up early in the morning and helping with the chores. I learned to milk cows, pitch hay, chop wood for kindling, and shovel manure as well as any farm kid.

Looking back now, I understand that part of the reason the Crouches took in foster children like me was to supplement the meager income they could wrest from their land. It was a rocky, hilly, hard-to-plow tract along the Boardman River. It didn't have a real barn, just some cow sheds, and the hay was kept outdoors in stacks. The house was a simple two-story frame with weathered gray siding that probably had never seen a coat of paint. There were two small rooms on the second floor; one of them my bedroom. The other room was vacant except during occasional visits by one or another of Mr. and Mrs. Crouch's three daughters, who lived in Traverse City.

I don't remember much about my room, though I recall being able to see daylight through the cracks in its walls. On cold mornings there would be frost on the wall, because the only heat in the house was from a space heater downstairs in the living room. I don't think we ever used that room. The kitchen was the center of our family life. I did my homework and read by the light of a kerosene lamp. The arrival of a gas lantern Mr. Crouch had purchased was a grand occasion for us. I was dazzled by its power: "equal to that of a forty-watt electric bulb," the salesman had said.

One book I remember reading by the light of the new gas lantern was about the boyhood of Abraham Lincoln. His story inspired me to dream big. If a poor farm boy from Illinois could work hard and become President of the United States, why should I put limits on myself? Catalogues were good for more materialistic dreaming. I loved those big, thick Wards and Sears "wish books." Looking through them gave me a special kind of knowledge, a sense of what things cost and what made one item more valuable than another. I would dream of having things— not the *good* or the *better*, but the *best*—and I could visualize them so perfectly, it was like actually possessing them. I would picture my house or cabin and sometimes I would even build it in my imagination, which was hard work. Then I would furnish it completely with things illustrated in the catalogues.

My mental construction projects led me to seek a more detailed knowledge of architecture. I'd always been fascinated by buildings, but through books in the Traverse City Library I now learned about Frank Lloyd Wright. I read everything I could find about him. I was particularly impressed by one statement: that of the ten greatest architectural masterpieces of the half century from 1900 to 1950, seven were by Frank Lloyd Wright.

My dreams were important to me, and my favorite time of day was in the frosty mornings, when I walked a mile and a quarter to the main road to catch the bus to St. Francis High School. I'd fill every step of the way along that muddy lane with dreams about Tom Monaghan the brilliant architect or Tom Monaghan teenage tycoon. In my dreams, I was also sought after by the prettiest girls in the school. I was fascinated by them. My obsession with girls was kind of odd, considering the fact that I was so shy I could scarcely say hello to the ones I liked, not to mention that they seemed to have no interest at all in me. But, of course, that didn't deter me from dreaming about them. My morning reveries were sometimes interrupted by the thunder of a frightened partridge taking off from the ditch or a deer bounding away across the field. I dawdled on the way to school, but when the school bus dropped me off in the afternoon, it felt so great to be free and I was so full of energy that I ran all the way home.

During this period, religion became increasingly important to me. I found I missed the clockwork of rituals I had grown accustomed to in the orphanage. Not that I was devout—I wasn't. But I felt that religion was the one thread of continuity in my life. I never missed mass on Sunday. My faith was strengthened by the friendship I'd developed with our parish priest in Traverse City, Father Passeno. I had learned enough Latin to be an altar boy when I was in second grade, and I became one for him. Father Passeno often acted like a real father to me, giving me encouragement and helping smooth out my misunderstandings with my mother. I had tried to show my appreciation to him when I was in the eighth grade by using seven dollars I'd saved from summer jobs to buy him a beautiful Lalique glass statue of the Virgin Mary.

In the spring of my freshman year at St. Francis, I decided I was not being true to myself. I'll never forget that moment of revelation, because it came when I was on the Crouch farm shoveling manure. The symbolism of the situation was overpowering: Standing up to my ankles in muck, I saw that I had been wallowing in crass, wordly thoughts when I should have been concentrating on my spiritual quest. I decided then and there that I would become a priest. I remembered what I had told Sister Beralda, and I intended to make good on it. I knew I'd be a year behind the other boys in the seminary, but I had no doubt that I could make it up.

Father Passeno listened to my story of self-discovery and promised to help me apply to the seminary in Grand Rapids. I was elated when I was accepted and could hardly wait to go. Father Passeno warned me that I might find it difficult to adjust to life in St. Joseph's, but neither he nor I had any inkling of what a disaster I would be as a seminarian.

I lasted less than a year. Never before or since have I felt so crushed. I am no stranger to failure, but no other setback devastated me as this one did, because it was so final. I can recall the ominous silence as I approached the rector's office that last day. It was only one of many trips I had made to be reprimanded by him, but I had a sense of foreboding about this one. I reflected on my recent experiences and wished I hadn't been in hot water so often.

The problem, as I see it now, was the similarity between the discipline of the seminary and that which I had disliked so much in the orphanage. I had grown adept at sidestepping rules in the orphanage, and I didn't take the regulations of St. Joseph's seriously enough. I couldn't avoid getting involved in pillow fights in the dorm or whispering during the "Grand Silence." These were viewed by the seminary faculty as major transgressions. Part of my downfall, too, was that upperclassmen acted as proctors, and once they got it in for you, you couldn't look cross-eyed without getting put on report. All a proctor had to say was, "See the rector in the morning." You could be dismissed if you were sent to see the rector four times, and I stretched the limit. Even so, I thought of myself as a dedicated seminarian.

But Rector Monsignor Falicki thought otherwise. He told me bluntly that I "lacked the vocation." He was a large man, six feet six, and I admired him because he had been a catcher for a farm team of the New York Yankees before he was ordained. He was also a tough man, unaffected by the tears that burst from my eyes when he told me I was being kicked out. "When you pack your bags for Easter vacation, you'll be packing them for good," he said. I pleaded for another chance. I called upon my grades, which were good (except in Greek). I told him about the goals I'd had since I was in second grade. But he had made up his mind. I was out.

It was a sorry young failed seminarian who dragged himself back to Traverse City. My mother was incredulous. She had thought her problems with me were over when I went off to become a priest. Now here I was on her doorstep again, and we got right back into our constant bickering. I decided not to be bothered by the discord at home or my problems in joining classes at St. Francis High in midyear. I found at least one small satisfaction in being back: I was among girls again. However, I was still afflicted with paralyzing shyness, and I couldn't get up the courage to ask one of them for a date.

Instead of doing homework, I spent my evenings setting pins at Conaway's bowling alley. This was my kind of work. I could scoop up the ball before the pins stopped flying around the pit. I'd grab six pins at a time—three in each hand—and spot them in one continuous motion. I could handle four lanes at a time all night long. I had to walk three miles to get to Conaway's, and I would often skip dinner to avoid my mother. Marion Conaway, who ran the alley with her husband, John, took it on herself to look after me. She'd ask me if I had eaten. When I'd say, "No, but I'm not hungry," she'd say, "Well, I'm hungry and I don't like to eat alone, so you'll have to join me." She'd set a big bowl of stew in front of me, followed by a slab of cake. I managed to make them disappear pretty fast.

The situation between my mother and me grew steadily worse. Nothing I said or did seemed right to her. We quarreled often about her car, a 1948 Nash, which she'd bought with the thousand dollars saved from my father's insurance money. I borrowed the car at every opportunity. It was just a normal sixteen-year-old's desire to drive, but she couldn't understand that.

My brother didn't get involved in these disputes. He and I had never gotten to know each other well because of the two-year difference in our ages. In the orphanage he had looked to me for protection sometimes, but that was about it. He developed an interest in ham radio and was big on working with machinery. The other kids in the orphanage used to call him Professor Mike Monaghan because he was always talking about how mechanical or electrical things worked. We got along well enough.

One day I borrowed my mother's car without telling her where I was going, and she got frantic with fear. She called the police, and the situation seemed so unreasonable that I really lost my temper. I let them put me in jail overnight rather than apologize to my mother, because I didn't believe I'd done anything wrong.

Even after that, though, as long as I kept to myself and was around the house as little as possible, I thought things at home were tolerable.

But one day on my way home from school, a car pulled over and the driver rolled down his window and called to me:

"You Monaghan?"

"Yeah," I said. "What's up?"

He flashed a badge that said County Sheriff and told me to get in the car.

"We're going to your house to get your clothes," he said. "You're going to the detention home."

I was in shock. It was like some awful nightmare. I had committed no crime. I had never been delinquent in any way. Yet here I was being locked up like a common thief. The custodian's wife told me my mother had signed the order; she just couldn't put up with me any longer. I was ashamed. I didn't know how I would face the other kids at school after they learned I was in the detention home with a bunch of juvenile delinquents and some real criminals. If I were confronted with the fact, I certainly wouldn't lie about it. On the other hand, I reasoned, there was nothing wrong in trying to keep it from becoming general knowledge. So each day I walked to and from school in a circuitous route that took me near my mother's house. My classmates never caught on.

The only person at school who knew about my situation was the basketball coach, Joe Kraupa. After I failed to show up for practice and missed a game, he found out what had happened. But he kept my secret and he treated me decently. I was grateful for that because life among my fellow inmates at the detention home was void of compassion. I was appalled at the stealing that went on there. The other kids seemed to accept it, and I quickly learned to hide every personal item that wasn't carried with me. I didn't hesitate to protect my property with my fists. The custodians, a policeman and his wife, were nice people. They liked me, and a couple of times, when they had problems making other boys behave, they'd ask me to "talk to the kid by hand." I obliged. I had always been a pretty good boxer; my best punch was a left jab that seemed to snap out on its own. I frankly enjoyed a good fight.

After I had been in the home for about six months, my aunt Peg found out about the situation. It riled her Irish temper, and she went to court and got custody of me. I had spent a few weeks with her and my uncle Dan Mahler in Ann Arbor nearly every summer. I really enjoyed being with them and my cousin Maureen. It was a very warm family situation. I loved it when Aunt Peg would tell me stories about my father's boyhood. So I was delighted when Uncle Dan arrived in Traverse City to take me home with him. He and Aunt Peg were extremely kind to me in the months that followed. I was treated like a member of the family, and that's what I had craved ever since I first went to the orphanage. I had come close to a family feeling on the farm with Mr. and Mrs. Crouch, but this was really the first time since my father's death that I felt I was leading a normal life. My uncle Ed gave me a summer job in the office of his construction company and my own Jeep to drive.

I went to St. Thomas High School in Ann Arbor for my senior year. My record there was unremarkable. The caption under my picture in the class yearbook, *The Shamrock*, says, "The harder I try to be good, the worse I get; but I may do something sensational yet."

For some reason I could not buckle down and study at St. Thomas. I barely cracked a book all year. I just played sports and went through the motions in my classes. After school, I worked at a drug-store soda fountain—I thought I was the fastest soda jerk in town—making fifty-five cents an hour. I also continued setting pins and worked weekends as a busboy in the exclusive Barton Hills Country Club, where my aunt Peg was a part-time waitress.

Years later, I felt great triumph when I moved to Barton Hills and was able to join that club.

I graduated from St. Thomas by the skin of my teeth, and I was upset with myself. Even though I couldn't afford to fulfill my dream of studying architecture at the University of Michigan, my grades alone were bad enough to keep me out. I decided to try Ferris State College in Big Rapids, which had an architectural trade school. If you went through it and then worked in the field for nine years, you could take a test and become a licensed architect. But first I had to earn enough money to get me through a school year.

I was on my own immediately after high school. Aunt Peg and Uncle Dan had been more than kind to me, but they made it clear that they needed my room and it would be nice if I would find a place of my own. I did, a single room for $6 a week. What I really wanted was a piece of land in the country, where I could build an A-frame house, but that was impossible. I got a job delivering newspapers and magazines for a local distributor. I made $1.25 an hour, $1.87 for overtime. I tried to be the hardest worker in the place, the fastest stripper, the fastest bundler. I did everything on the run, and I put in a lot of overtime. I lived on $30 a week and banked the rest. By summer's end, I had saved $500. Maybe I put in too much overtime, or maybe my hustle got on somebody's nerves. At any rate, the boss called me in one day and said, "I'm not going to use you anymore." I was completely baffled. I said, "Why?" He just turned away and said, "I don't want to talk about it." That's the only time I've ever been fired, and I still don't know why.

There's a saying that in every adversity there's the seed of a greater opportunity, and it really was true in this case. Being fired seemed like a terrible blow at first, but it worked to my advantage because I got another job right away at better pay: $2.29 an hour with a construction crew. That was big money for an eighteen-year-old kid in 1955. When the project I was hired for was finished, I had to find another job. This time it was digging ditches for sewer pipe for the city water department. It paid only $1.65 an hour, but even that was a lot of money to me.

I decided I could probably begin school and support myself through the final quarter at Ferris on what I'd saved. But I was just getting well established in my classes when along came another setback. I got a terrible toothache, and the dentist I happened to go to, Dr. Wally Niemann, told me my teeth were in bad shape. It would cost $220 to fix them. I didn't want to spend the money, but I decided I had no choice. By the time I paid Dr. Niemann, having already laid out fees for tuition and books, I was down to just over $100 to get me through the quarter. I had moved into an upstairs room of a house with several other guys. My share was $5 a week for rent and $6 a week for food. We took turns doing the shopping and cooking. After about a month, I ran out of money. I found some stale popcorn in the corner of a cupboard and part of a bottle of wine, and that's all I had to eat for a week. At times I felt so weak I could hardly stand up. But I managed to struggle through the balance of the year. Luckily, the landlord allowed me to work out my share of the rent by doing yard work.

My grades at Ferris were excellent, and I asked the registrar to forward them to the University of Michigan because I intended to enroll there the following fall. I believed that somehow I would get a job that would see me through a year at Michigan. It would be more expensive there than at Ferris, so I figured I'd have to earn at least $2 an hour. There were no jobs like that to be found in Ann Arbor that summer of '56. I hitchhiked to Detroit and pounded the pavement there. Nothing. I was honest with interviewers and told them I was only going to be available for the summer, so I suppose that immediately blew any chance of getting a good job. I hitchhiked to Chicago and landed in the southern suburb of Harvey. I got a room in a rundown hotel for $10 a week, which I paid for by setting pins in a bowling alley at night while looking for other work during the day. Again, nothing. By this time it was the end of June, and I didn't have time now to save the kind of money I'd need to go to school in Ann Arbor.

One day I was walking past the Harvey post office and noticed what I thought was an Army recruiting desk inside. This reminded me of a conversation I'd had with an Army recruiter in high school. He'd told me it was possible to get a college education if you joined the Army. So I walked into the post office and talked to the man at the desk.

"Is it true that if I join the Army, I'll get some of my college paid for?" I asked.

"Absolutely," he said.

He explained that if I enlisted for three years, I would get two years of college free, with credits that would be transferable to the University of Michigan or any school I desired. That sounded good to me, and I told him I would join.

I spent the next day or so going through written tests, taking a physical, and signing a lot of forms. As I filled out these papers, I noticed for the first time a little ball-and-anchor symbol in one corner. I turned to the recruit next to me and pointed to the symbol.

"Is this the Marine Corps or the Army?" I asked.

He looked at me in disbelief and said, "It's the Marines, you dummy!"

'M AN OPTIMIST AT HEART. Even in my darkest moments, such as when I was sent to the detention home or dismissed from the seminary, I had hope for the promise of the future. That was my feeling as I signed my name on those enlistment papers.

I was sore about the way that recruiter had led me on. He hadn't set me straight when I kept referring to the Army. On the other hand, I couldn't fault him any more than my own ignorance—I associated the Marine Corps with its dress-blue uniforms, and since the recruiter had been wearing khaki, I assumed he was Army. It was a good object lesson for me about the danger of making assumptions. As an old top sergeant at a Marine brig used to tell the men on his guard details, the word *assume* has three parts: *ass-u-me,* because it "can make an ass of *you* and *me.*"

Anyhow, I decided to make the best of the situation, saying to myself, "Army or Marines, what's the difference?" I soon found

out there was a very great difference, and there were times, especially during the first few months, that I hated the Marine Corps
with a passion.

My perspective has changed. If I had a son, the best advice I
could give him would be to serve a hitch in the Marines before
going into business. Now I can appreciate the character-building
aspects of the Corps' approach, but it's hard to see merit in a
system when it is in the process of grinding you down, humiliating and harassing you.

In boot camp at Camp Pendleton, near San Diego, I was appalled at the foul language our drill instructors used. It was a rude
awakening for me. I wasn't a candidate for sainthood myself, but
I thought that these men, who were in a position of authority,
ought to be setting a good example. I was too naïve to understand
that they were acting out a planned program of humiliation
aimed at getting rid of our egos and our dependency on others.
Only when we were reduced to raw, quivering awareness of our
ignorance could we appreciate in our gut this great truth: *Each
man is responsible for his own actions.* Once we understood that, our
tormentors would begin the process of building us up, giving us
an individual feeling of self-worth. This is what leadership is built
on. The Corps appears to be *powering over* individuals when, in
fact, it is *empowering* them, teaching them self-motivation. This is
the source of the Marines' famous *esprit de corps.*

One reaction of the recruits to the constant harassment by
their superiors was to lash out at each other. Fights would break
out in the barracks for no apparent reason. I got in a few myself.
Once, after some jerk punched me, I made matters worse by
going to headquarters and spouting off about what a disgrace I
thought the outfit was. In my opinion, it was full of hoodlums, I
said, and I couldn't see how the taxpayers' money could be used
to support it. That complaint brought me to the attention of all

the drill instructors. From then on, they tried to outdo each other in hazing me. I once stood at attention naked (I'd been in the shower when I was called out for some trumped-up infraction) while two drill instructors took turns berating me, shoving my rigid body back and forth between them. I was sick with humiliation, but I was determined to take whatever they dished out.

It became a point of pride for me never to drop back or fall out on marches. In fact, I would volunteer for marches because I wanted to step up my personal exercise program. I was determined to be the most physically fit Marine in my outfit.

After boot camp and advanced infantry training, I was sent to Okinawa. While there, I decided that my hitch in the military would be time completely wasted if I didn't improve my mind as well as my body, so I launched an intensive self-improvement program. I read just about every book in the base library that I thought might help me, especially inspirational ones, by authors such as Norman Vincent Peale and Dale Carnegie. I also read a lot of biographies and practical books on subjects I thought might be useful to me someday: things like how to build log cabins and the techniques of farming, animal husbandry, and forestry. Though my status was lowly, I could build empires in my mind and imagine myself as wealthy and successful. My dreams had improved over my schoolboy visions, which dealt mostly with impressing girls. I was now able to place myself in a situation so realistically that I could visualize all the problems that might come up and figure out ways to deal with them. I was also learning to assimilate information of all kinds and bring it together in a planning process. For example, there was my plan to launch my new life in Bemidji, a small town in north-central Minnesota.

I figured that when I got out of the Marines I would have at least $2,000 dollars in savings, and I'd be able to make a completely fresh start at going to college and building something. So as long as I was starting over, I might as well live in the ideal place. I pored over books about different parts of the country, comparing their climates and business, political, and social environments. One thing I wanted in my ideal place was a college. Another was land on which I could build a cabin and raise most of my own food. I wanted to be totally self-sufficient. After considering factors like the cost of land, availability of building materials, and the kind of crops I could grow, plus the fact that I find a northern climate invigorating and I wanted to be able to hunt and fish, I finally concluded that my ideal place was Bemidji.

I wrote to the Bemidji chamber of commerce and got all kinds of brochures and maps from them. I subscribed to the Bemidji daily newspaper and to the area's weekly paper. I began thinking of myself as a citizen of Bemidji. I wrote to real-estate companies about property I saw for sale in the papers, and received a lot of listings. There was one forty-acre site for $1,200 that included a log cabin, and I darn near bought it. But I decided to wait until I got a furlough back in the States so I could go up there and look the place over.

I wouldn't get a furlough for at least a year, however, and after six months in Okinawa, I got orders for Japan. I was elated, because this would give me a chance to see Frank Lloyd Wright's Imperial Hotel. My interest in Wright's work had become almost a devotion, so a trip to the Imperial Hotel would be like a visit to a shrine. Many of my dreams continued to revolve around architecture and furnishings. I subscribed to *Architectural Forum* magazine and kept up with what was going on in the field. One of my favorite pastimes was to study specialty catalogues and come up with ideas on how to take artifacts designed for one use and adapt them to some completely different purpose: I envisioned taking pieces of farm implements and making them into furniture, like using tractor seats as breakfast-bar stools. I did this with industrial equipment, too, long before high-tech became fashionable in design.

When I got to Japan, I was based at a camp at the foot of Mount Fuji. It was beautiful. Even guard duty was a pleasure when you could look up through the branches of the cherry trees and see that graceful snow-capped volcanic cone aglow in the moonlight. It was only a short train ride to Tokyo, and of course, I went to visit the Imperial Hotel at every opportunity. I couldn't afford to stay there, but I looked into every nook and cranny of it. It was a great building; I felt like an old friend had died when they tore it down in 1967. Apart from my few outings to the Imperial Hotel, a Kabuki show at the Kokusai Theater, a Japanese Giants baseball game, and a visit to the University of Tokyo's architecture school, I spent my off hours in various base libraries and working out in the gym. I felt I was marking time in the Marines. I tried taking some night-school classes, but they proved to be just another frustration because my duty assignments kept preventing me from completing them.

Near the end of my tour of overseas duty, my outfit went on amphibious maneuvers to the Philippines. On the long, slow voyage back to Japan, I came up with my five personal priorities. The feeling that gave rise to thinking them out was much the same as I'd had back on the farm in Traverse City when I decided to go to the seminary. During the time I'd been in the Marines, my dreams had been of wealth and success. Now I was pulled up short by the realization that the exciting scenerios I'd been creating—which, I had no doubt, would someday be realized—could turn out to be empty and meaningless if they lacked consideration for others and for God. I asked myself what good a lot of money would be to me if I didn't have friends, a good marriage, continued good health, or if I didn't go to heaven.

I was certain that no matter how elaborate or grandiose my

daydreams got, I would never get to the point where I would violate my Catholic upbringing. I couldn't knowingly do things that were wrong. From these kinds of thoughts I developed my priorities.

After that, my dreams of success became even richer because I was comfortable in the knowledge that they had a strong ethical foundation.

By the time I arrived back in the States, with a little over a year remaining on my hitch, I was twenty-one years old and I felt like a seasoned veteran. As events would prove, however, I was still pretty naïve and gullible.

I went home on furlough—my planned trip to Bemidji was aborted when the military flight I took was diverted from Minneapolis to Detroit—and walking around the University of Michigan campus again made me realize that Ann Arbor was where I really belonged. I had enough money saved to get through my first couple of years of school, and I was confident that now I would find work to carry me the rest of the way. I could always go to Bemidji when I finished college.

For the remainder of my hitch, I was assigned to guard duty at a brig at Camp Pendleton, in Southern California. I made several new friends there, among them a guy whose father worked in a Las Vegas gambling casino. We used to go to Vegas on weekend passes. One Sunday I was hitchhiking back to the base and I was picked up by a big happy-go-lucky character driving a shiny '59 Buick. He introduced himself as John Patrick Ryan and told me he was in the oil business. "I'm a promoter," he said, and went on talking about all kinds of fascinating big-money deals he had made.

"It's a great life if you don't weaken," John Patrick said. He laughed as he described several dry holes he had just finished drilling in Texas. They had wiped him out of cash, but he was confident that he would be able to line up several wealthy investors for a new project he had his eye on. I wondered why wealthy investors would be willing to take such a big risk, and John Patrick explained how depletion allowances made his ventures such great tax shelters. "Fat cats need deep caves," he said. He explained in detail how he would go into an area and tie up leases, line up investors, and go about drilling. He knew all the technicalities of drilling for oil: what it cost and what the potential problems were. I found it intriguing; it was a whole new world to me.

"After I wind up some business in Los Angeles, I'm going up to Carson City and do some groundwork," he said. "All I need is five hundred dollars for seed money. Then I'll be able to get started again."

"Well, heck, I've got five hundred dollars in the bank back home," I said.

"You do?"

"Sure. I've been saving a chunk of every paycheck since I joined the Marines."

He moved right in on that. He said that if I gave him $500 and would take his promissory note for $1,500, payable in ninety days, he would give me a sixteenth of a share in the well and he would also teach me the tricks of investing in the oil business. In addition, he would pay me $400 a month while I was learning.

I was elated. This seemed like an ideal investment, an easy way to pay for my college education. Ryan clearly had the know-how, and I was certainly willing to work hard and learn from him. So I agreed.

When we got to Barstow, California, John Patrick pulled over to a pay phone and suggested that I call and arrange to have the money sent to me. I telephoned the trust officer at the Ann Arbor bank and told him what I wanted to do. He tried to talk me out of it, but I insisted. Finally, he said he would wire it to me in Los Angeles. We drove to the Western Union office there and picked up the money. I handed it to John Patrick, and he gave me a promissory note stating all the things we had agreed on.

So now I was an investor in the oil business. Trouble was, I heard nothing from my new mentor for weeks. I was getting worried. Then one day he showed up on the base with a big smile and a briefcase full of leases, thirty-day options and all kinds of other papers that he pulled out and waved at me excitedly. We were on the verge of breaking through to big money, he said. He just needed a little more capital to get us over the hump. I had a sinking feeling in my stomach about this, but I was committed and I didn't want to lose what I'd put into it over a few dollars more.

"How much do you need?" I asked.

"I figure fifteen hundred dollars will move us to where we need to be," he replied.

I was reluctant, but he was so darned self-assured that I finally said, "Okay. That's about what I have left in the bank."

I called Ann Arbor again and closed out my account. I handed the money, about fifteen hundred dollars, to John Patrick and he gave me another promissory note. A few days later, I started my processing out of the Marines, and John Patrick asked me to come out to Las Vegas and meet him when I finished. I agreed without much enthusiasm. The oil business didn't seem nearly as attractive now as it had a few weeks earlier. But after I got my discharge papers on July 2, 1959, and collected three hundred dollars in mustering-out pay, I headed for Las Vegas.

John Patrick picked me up in a battered old station wagon; his wife's car, he explained. He drove me over to the house he'd rented and introduced me to his family. It sure didn't look like the home of a budding oil tycoon. But he said he'd had an incredible streak of bad luck. Some of his investors had backed out, and his kids had been sick. Now his wife had to have an operation. It was a really sad story.

However, he said he had a big opportunity to show me. We drove out to a well someone had drilled a mile or two west of the strip, and John Patrick said he was certain the drilling had been stopped only a short distance from hitting oil. He had a chance to take it over cheap, and we agreed to go ahead and buy the well. I was worried, but I let myself be persuaded. John Patrick was still optimistic, which made me ashamed of my doubts. Besides, I felt sorry for him. So I gave him the rest of the money I had, keeping only fifteen dollars to buy food while I hitchhiked back to Michigan. He assured me he would pay off the notes on schedule, and I said I would be counting on that because I was soon going to be enrolling at the University of Michigan.

I got a ride that took me all the way to Salt Lake City, but I didn't enjoy the scenery much. I couldn't stop worrying about Mr. Ryan. In Salt Lake City, an Air Force sergeant and his wife picked me up. They were heading for Lowry Air Force Base in Denver, where he was stationed, and as we drove along, they asked if I could kick in some money for gas. They were broke. Well, that seemed fair enough. But then we had a blowout several miles from a service station and had to drive to it on the rim, which ruined what was left of the tire. The station had a used tire for ten dollars. The sergeant promised to pay me back when we got to Denver, so I spent my last cent to buy gas and that used tire. We made it to their apartment on the air base that night, and I slept on the sofa. The next morning when I woke up, the sergeant was gone and his wife told me tearfully that they had not been able to get any money. She was wearing only a thin negligee, which made it difficult for me to stand there and argue with her, so I took off.

Denver is a pretty nice town. Domino's is big there now. But for me, back then, it was a Rocky Mountain low. I didn't know where to turn. The only job I knew was setting pins, but it appeared to be an obsolete skill: All the bowling alleys I checked out in the telephone directory had automatic pinsetters. Finally, a kind soul told me about some lanes he thought still used pin-boys—in Littleton, about seventeen miles from town.

By this time it was dark, and I didn't have a place to sleep, so I went to Traveler's Aid and they sent me to a mission. It was on skid row, in the vicinity of Laramie Street, and was full of derelicts, mostly old men who seemed to be alcoholics. I wanted to leave the minute I saw the condition of the place, but it was too late; the man at the desk said the door was locked and I would have to stay until morning. What a horrible night! First they made us take a shower in some filthy stalls and handed us hospital-type nightgowns. That's when it got really creepy, because there apparently were a lot of homosexuals in the place and they started hollering at me, "Hey, baby . . ." Boy! I was ready to break down the door with my fists, but all I could do was wait out the night. I didn't move around on the bunk much because the sheets were so dirty, I didn't want to let them contact my bare skin, so I just lay there until morning tensed up and ready to lash out at anyone who touched me. No one did, but still I didn't sleep a wink. They opened the front door at 6 A.M. and I was outside by 6:01. Hungry as I was, I didn't even wait around for breakfast. I'll never forget that experience, and I feel sorry for people who are so down and out they have to go to a place like that.

I couldn't afford a toll call to Littleton, so without knowing whether there'd be a job for me or not, I walked all the way out there. I don't know what I would have done if they had turned me away. Luckily, the manager had an opening, and after listening to my story, he said I could sleep in a room behind the pits. There was a separate business in the basement of the bowling alley; preformed concrete fireplaces and other things of that sort were made there. The owner gave me some work, too, pushing wheelbarrow loads of cement around.

One of the men I worked with in the basement was a horse-racing fanatic. He took me to the track with him one afternoon and I watched him bet. I was reluctant to get involved myself. The odds didn't seem right to me. But this guy was amazing. He picked the winning horse every time. He doubled his money. I was convinced that he really knew what he was doing. So the next week, after I got a paycheck, I went to the track with him and followed his betting advice. You guessed it. I lost. And I felt like a first-class fool.

I have nothing against gambling if it's done for fun and in moderation. I enjoy a good game of poker for ten-cent stakes as much as anyone. But that experience taught me not to believe in any sure-fire systems for winning.

Another memory I have of Littleton was my brush with a union enforcer. He was the scrowliest guy I've ever seen in a pin-striped suit. He said I would have to join the union if I worked beyond the second two-week pay period. I didn't plan to stay there anyhow, but that helped me make up my mind to leave for Ann Arbor as soon as I collected my next paycheck.

My mother had remarried and moved back to Ann Arbor by this time. My brother, Jim, had an apartment in town, actually just two attic rooms, but he invited me to move in with him. He also gave me a rusted-out '49 Plymouth, for which I was grateful. Jim was working for the post office and had various other jobs, including occasional work at a pizza place owned by a man named Dominick DiVarti.

I started looking around for work, but I had a hard time concentrating on it because I was so upset about John Patrick Ryan. There had been a letter from him waiting for me at my mother's house when I returned. But it was just another promise that things would work out fine, and I heard nothing further from him. Here I was in a position to enter the University of Michigan—I'd been accepted and everything—but the money I'd saved for it was gone. I can remember sitting in that little apartment literally fuming about not hearing from Ryan. I got depressed and had terrible headaches and painful earaches. Finally, the ninety days were up, and I had to face the fact that Ryan was not going to contact me as he'd promised. I went to the FBI in Ann Arbor to see if something could be done about it. No soap. I was told that since the amount was less than five thousand dollars, it was out of the FBI's jurisdiction, and besides, there are so many people using the name John Patrick Ryan that the likelihood of finding him was small. That made me even more depressed. I still planned to enroll at Michigan, and I had to have some sort of job to support myself. I found one at the Washtenaw News Agency, owned by a wily old character named Harry Genova. As it turned out, the news agency would be my substitute for business school and Harry Genova was my professor. He had to start by explaining the most rudimentary things, because *accounting* and *bookkeeping* were meaningless words to me. In fact, when Harry told me to write a memo introducing myself to the carriers, I didn't know what the word *memo* meant.

I was hired as home-delivery manager for out-of-town papers, and I had to learn quickly how to recruit, train, and motivate carrier boys, in addition to mastering the fundamentals of the business. I enjoyed it, and Harry's no-nonsense way of outlining how and why he handled things gave me a useful model for dealing with all kinds of business problems. He talked rough, but he had a heart of gold. I got to be good friends with Harry's son, Nick, who also worked at the agency, and he would sometimes cool his old man down when he got mad at me.

I started my classes at Michigan with mixed feelings of expectation and apprehension. My earaches kept getting worse. At times the pain was so bad I couldn't think straight. I worried that I wouldn't be able to do both the course work and my job at the news agency. I also began to have misgivings because I couldn't afford to buy most of the required textbooks. At first, I thought I'd be able to get by if I paid extra-close attention in class, used the library diligently, and borrowed books from other students. But I couldn't keep up. After about three weeks and several visits to the student health center, where a doctor treated me for a ruptured and infected eardrum, I decided my best course of action would be to drop out without prejudice and enroll for the second semester, when both my eardrum and my bank book would be in better shape.

Thanks to Harry Genova's tutelage, I mastered the basics of newspaper distribution and was eager to expand. I heard that a newsstand was for sale at the corner of Huron and Main, a terrific location in downtown Ann Arbor. The owner wanted five hundred dollars for it. All I had was my tuition refund from Michigan, but I managed to arrange to buy it over time, with no money down. Now I was in business for myself in addition to my job at the news agency, and I charged into it like a baserunner trying to beat out a double play. I'd get up at 5 A.M. every day to supply my stand with the morning papers. After the rush ended there, I'd go to the news agency to do my bookkeeping and get ready for carrier delivery of the afternoon papers.

After a few weeks of working my stand, I discovered that because there were so many college professors in town, there was a great demand for *The New York Times*. This looked like opportunity to me, so in every spare moment, I would put on my one suit and tie and go knocking on doors in the finer residential sections of town. I'd ask the homeowners if they would like to have the

Sunday *New York Times* delivered, and enough of them did to make up the first home-delivery route the paper had west of the Allegheny Mountains. That one route netted me twenty-five dollars every Sunday morning, which I thought was pretty darn good. But it covered the entire town, and I had to drive hard and run to every door to complete it by noon.

I enrolled at U of M again in February, but once again, I lasted only three weeks. I couldn't give up my work because I had purchased a '55 Ford station wagon and the payments were forty-nine dollars a month. Besides, I discovered that courses like calculus were way over my head; I simply was not up to speed with the other students. So I dropped out and enrolled in several night courses at Ann Arbor high school. They gave me a lot more confidence in my ability to succeed in the classroom.

That winter I spent a lot of time on campus, mingling with students at the Newman Club. I wanted to be identified with the U of M rather than as a townie, so I dated coeds and took them to Red's Right Spot, a favorite student hangout. The cook there was a witty little Irishman named Jim Gilmore, and there was something about him that made me want to get to know him better. As it turned out, I later learned far more about him than I really wanted to know. Gilmore had a twinkle in his eye and gift for one-liners that kept his customers chuckling.

By the time September rolled around and I was in the process of enrolling at Michigan again, my brother came up with a terrific proposal for a business partnership. He had a chance to buy a pizza place in Ypsilanti from Dominick DiVarti. Jim had been doing some carpentry in DiVarti's Ann Arbor restaurant when he chanced to overhear a conversation between DiVarti and a man Jim described as "an older guy who was very intense." About three years earlier, DiVarti had expanded his operation to Ypsilanti with a store called DomiNick's. But it had been closed for about six months and he now wanted to sell it. After the other man left, Jim asked DiVarti, "What's this about a pizza shop in Ypsi?" DiVarti tossed him the key to the place and told him to go look it over.

Jim had seen enough of DiVarti's operation in Ann Arbor to make him excited about the possibilities for the Ypsilanti store, but he didn't want to give up his secure job at the post office. He proposed that we buy DomiNick's together and take turns operating the place. The selling price was five hundred dollars, plus assumption of a few thousand dollars in debts. That seemed to me like a mighty big obligation, but the store only operated seven hours a day, from 5 P.M. until midnight, and that seemed perfect. I would work three and a half hours, Jim would work three and a half hours, and the income would be enough to put me through college. I could see myself becoming an architect and a wealthy pizza entrepreneur at the same time. I rented out my newsstand for twenty-five dollars a month. I also gave Harry Genova notice that I was quitting Washtenaw News.

I always thought we started to run DomiNick's without getting a receipt for our down payment, but twenty years later I learned that DiVarti had scribbled a note on a little piece of paper: "Received $75 Jim Monaghan to hold up sale of store. This amount is for December rent. 12/1/60." We got a loan for the rest of the money we needed to buy the store and get it open—a total of nine hundred dollars—from the post office credit union. So now we were the proud owners of DomiNick's Pizza.

DiVarti allowed us to continue to use his name on the place, which was good since we didn't think Monaghan's Italian Pizza had the right sound. DiVarti had come up with the idea of selling individual six-inch pizzas for thirty cents each. The story was that he did it to compete with McDonald's, but he said it just seemed like a good gimmick. He had painted the outside of the store white with green polka dots sprinkled at random all over it, which he thought would convey the impression of small pizzas. It wasn't my idea of terrific restaurant decor, but I had too many other things on my mind to consider changing it.

DiVarti took Jim and me to his Ann Arbor store and gave us a few lessons in pizza making. I found that the manual work of rolling out the dough and slapping it into shape appealed to me, and I was captivated by his description of the recipe for the sauce. His statement "The secret of good pizza is in the sauce" made a lasting impression on me. I vowed right then that I would have the best pizza sauce in the world. I spent more than a dozen years seeking it in all kinds of kitchens across the country, starting the very next night at Harry Genova's house. Harry had invited me over for dinner to celebrate my entry into the pizza business, and we talked a lot about my new career. "You know who makes the best pizza in the world?" Harry asked, and pointed to his wife, who had just served us a terrific spaghetti dinner. We all wound up in the kitchen—Harry, Nick, and I—with Nick's mom going through the steps of putting her homemade sauce together and writing it down for me. I appreciated it, though I never did use it. It was too complicated.

I moved into an apartment right across the street from our new business. Since I no longer needed my Ford station wagon and couldn't afford it anyhow, I gave it to Jim and he took over the payments. I made a deal with two unemployed factory workers, Carroll Teboe and Jay Phillips, to deliver for us using their own cars. They would get a commission of 10 percent of what they collected and a minimum of ten cents per delivery. If it hadn't been for their willingness to work on commission, our business would never have gotten off the ground.

I had been introduced to pizza in high school. I didn't care for it at first; its appearance—the orangish color and stretchy cheese—didn't seem appetizing to me. But after I tried it a few times, I developed a liking for it. By the time we opened Domi-Nick's, I had come to *love* pizza and could eat a ton of it. There were several competing pizzerias in Ypsilanti, and in the early days of our operation I would often buy their products to test them. I'd eat slowly and analytically, to see what I was up against. My aim was to make the best possible pizza, so I used the best ingredients I could buy and piled them on. But I felt the competition had better sauce than we did, and I didn't know what to do about that. Jerry Garber, a salesman for our supplier, Paul Fata & Sons, told me about an old Italian place in Lansing that had the best pizza sauce he'd ever tasted. I paid the place a visit, and sure enough, I liked its sauce much better than the Di-Varti creation we'd been using. To my surprise, the owner didn't hesitate to give me the recipe, and it was a big hit with our customers.

Our store didn't cater to the sit-down trade. We had only two small tables in the front part, and I don't think more than four customers could sit there comfortably to eat. We had to depend on delivery and carry-outs. But we got very few calls at first for the simple reason that we didn't have a telephone. DiVarti had taken a quarter-page ad in the Yellow Pages, which cost $68.50 a month, and we didn't think we could afford that. However, the phone company wouldn't give us the same number unless we continued the ad. I thought their policy was too strict. It had a dampening effect on new enterprise. But all my arguments might just as well have been delivered to a telephone pole. The phone company manager was unwilling to give me the slightest break. After about a month, I could see this was a no-win situation for me, so I capitulated, paid for the big ad, and got the phone hooked up.

Meanwhile, the fifty-fifty deal my brother and I had decided on was falling apart. He didn't want to jeopardize his job at the post office, and I tried to be understanding about that. Yet it seemed to me that he was coming in less and less, and I was doing more and more of the work. I was committed to this pizza thing. I had given up my newspaper enterprises; I had no other source of income, and I was feeling the weight of the debts we had to pay off.

Jim and I had completely different approaches to work. We discussed remodeling the store and agreed on taking down a partition and making a pass-through window to speed up making pizzas. He said he'd bring his Shopsmith over some day and do it. But several days passed with no action, so I finally started hammering that partition apart with my bare hands. Jim was amazed when he came in and saw what I was doing. He went right home and got his tools, and we remodeled the place overnight.

We had some brotherly disagreements, and sometimes, I'm ashamed to admit, they were punctuated by thrown plates and assorted other objects. One time I burned a pizza and got so exasperated that I tossed it over the top of the oven. It hit the wall and stuck there, creating an incredible mess oozing down to the floor. Jim claims to this day that I threw the pizza at him, but it's not so.

We always patched up our differences with promises to do our best to work together, and we'd get high on handling the rush, making pizzas like mad. Afterward, we'd just collapse, look at each other, and laugh. One day Jim found a huge stainless steel bowl in a junkyard. It must have come out of some kind of commercial washing machine. He took it to a tinsmith's shop and did a little soldering on it and it made a great container for hand-mixing batches of pizza dough.

I thought Jim cared about the business as much as I did, so I was surprised when one day, about eight months after we'd formed our partnership, he came around and said he wanted out.

He said he didn't want anything for his share, but I suggested that he take the old Volkswagen Beetle we had bought to use for a delivery car, and he agreed.

With Jim stepping out of the picture, my hope of running the pizza business part-time and going to the U of M full-time flew out the window for good. It was a setback, but I took it in stride and was optimistic, just as I'd been about my recruitment into the Marine Corps. I told myself I would just accept the situation as it was and turn what seemed to be a negative into a positive.

In that instant, I made the decision to commit myself heart and soul to being a pizza man. And I felt a tremendous sense of relief. My purpose was clear, and the knowledge that the future success—or failure—of the business rested on my shoulders alone was welcome. I thought of all the dreams I'd had of being wealthy and successful, and I told myself, "If it is to be, it is up to me."

MY CONFIDENCE ROSE QUICKLY during those early months in the warm kitchen of DomiNick's. I was learning something new with every pizza I shoved into the oven, and it was gratifying to watch our sales climb to $750 a week.

I had lived down that $99 first week. But I'll never forget how inadequate I'd felt on opening day, when that first customer walked in and gave me his order. I stared at him like a fool. At that point I had made only two or three pizzas in my life, and the thought of him standing there watching my fumbling efforts was paralyzing.

Fortunately, he let me off the hook by saying, "I'll come back in about twenty minutes and pick it up." I smiled and croaked, "Yessir!"

In our fourth and fifth months, I was beginning to get a bit euphoric about our progress, envisioning DomiNick's as the most dynamic business in Ypsilanti. Then the bottom dropped out. The school year ended and almost all the Eastern Michigan University students left town for the summer. I had anticipated a decline in sales, of course, but not a disaster. And what else can you call a sales decrease of 75 percent? There were nights in the middle of the week when we were lucky to take in nine dollars. On weekends, it was fifty or sixty dollars. I suppose the slump heightened the tension between my brother and me. In August, when we dissolved our partnership, I was practically living in the store. Although I didn't open until five o'clock in the afternoon, there was a lot of what I call *backroom work* to be done first. I made the sauce and the pizza dough fresh every day. Then the meat and vegetable toppings had to be prepared and sliced. The most tedious and time-consuming job was dicing the cheese. I vowed I would find a way to do that mechanically, but there was nothing suitable in the restaurant equipment catalogues I pored over. There were always errands to be run: supplies to pick up, bills to be paid. And any extra time I had went into making improvements in the store. My chief concern was with the layout of the oven and counters. I kept rearranging them, trying to cut a few steps and shave fractions of seconds off the time it took to make pizzas. Given the oven I had, there was nothing I could do to reduce cooking time. But I could control the assembly of raw materials, and I was obsessed with finding ways to speed up this end of the process. I was constantly on the run.

I wouldn't have been able to function if it hadn't been for Carroll Teboe and Jay Phillips making deliveries. A few times when they weren't around, I'd take an order on the phone, make the pizza, then lock the door and do the delivery myself. It was a crazy situation.

If I ran out of something, I would take money out of the till and run to the grocery store next door. The couple who owned it felt sorry for me, and they'd sell me stale fruit pies for a dime. I'd go back to my kitchen and eat a whole darned pie. I was always hungry. Much as I loved pizza, I couldn't afford to eat my own product, unless it was a burned one or an order someone hadn't picked up.

When September arrived, there was a gratifying surge of business. I hired my first hourly employee, Steve Levinski, who later became a cop, and then another, Ron Braugh. I went through the dorms at Eastern putting up menus; this and the cartop signs I put on our delivery cars got our phones ringing steadily. Weekly sales averages nearly doubled from their peak of the previous year, and I was pocketing four hundred dollars a week in profit. If I could sustain that, I'd be making twenty thousand dollars a year. That seemed to me like a decent income, though not nearly enough to satisfy my ambitions.

Part of the reason my profits were better was that I dropped six-inch pizzas from the menu. Although these individual pizzas were a popular item with students, they were a pain in the neck to make, and as I inadvertently discovered, their food cost was higher than that of the larger pies. The scales fell from my eyes one night when we were shorthanded and needed to streamline production so we could handle the rush. Reluctantly, I decided to eliminate small pizzas. I was afraid this move would hurt our business, but the complaints weren't serious, and I was astonished to discover that I made more money. This was the first night in a long time that we'd handled the business—we didn't get bombed—and we ended up with 50 percent more sales than we'd ever had before. I realized then that it took just as much time to make a small pizza as a large one, and it took just as long to deliver a small pizza. This revelation was a major breakthrough in the history of Domino's Pizza.

A similar situation caused me to drop submarine sandwiches

from the menu. One Sunday, our busiest night, we had only half a crew and something was going to have to give. We decided to eliminate subs, and the effect this had of increasing the amount we made was astonishing. Less, in this case, gave us more, and it was one of the most important lessons I ever learned.

My instincts told me I had something unusual going in Domi-Nick's, though I wasn't quite sure what it was yet. I felt that if what I was doing worked this well in Ypsilanti, it would work in other college towns. I began looking through the enrollment figures and other information on colleges and universities in the *World Almanac,* mulling over where I might want to open another store. One of my customers told me he thought I should open a place near the Central Michigan University campus in Mount Pleasant. He said pizza stores there didn't have free delivery, which was common in Ann Arbor and Ypsilanti. "You'd do great up there," he assured me, and that stuck in the back of my mind.

One day shortly before my brother and I split up, a man who looked very familiar came into the shop and ordered a pizza.

"Say, aren't you the cook at Red's Right Spot?" I asked.

"Yeah, Jim Gilmore," he said, giving me that elflike smile and extending his hand. "I'm not working for Red Shelton anymore, though," he added. "I'm working days now as a cook in the U of M dormitories."

That comment led to a long discussion about the restaurant business, and I discovered that he had founded Pizza from the Prop, Ann Arbor's best-known pizzeria, possibly the first one in the country to offer free delivery, certainly the first I'd ever heard of. I was impressed.

Gilmore came in often after that, and I looked forward to our conversations. He had seen the restaurant business from just about all sides, and I was fascinated by his stories of how various operations worked. I felt I was learning a lot from him.

Jim was a real character. He came from Decatur, Illinois. His father had been a whiskey salesman, and Jim inherited his gift of gab and an unfortunate weakness for alcohol. The booze had caused Jim to go bankrupt in a couple of restaurants and had given his face a ruddy, broken-veined roughness that made him look older than his fifty-two years. But he made no secret of his past problems. He said Alcoholics Anonymous had straightened him out, thank God, and he was off the sauce forever.

As I got to know him better, Jim's appreciation of the potential in my pizza business seemed to grow. His speech took on a conspiratorial tone, he obviously relished plotting deals.

One day he said in his stage whisper, "Hey, I have the secret pizza-sauce recipe I invented for the Prop. Wanna buy it?" I didn't. I didn't like the Prop's sauce. I believed my sauce—the recipe from the place in Lansing—was better. But I told him that what I really wanted was for him to come to work for me. I thought we would make a winning combination.

He thought about that for a few minutes and said he agreed, we could do big things together. But the only way he would come in was as an equal partner.

I tried to get him to agree to 49 percent or less, but he knew he had me on the line. He held firm and finally wore me down. He agreed to pay me five hundred dollars for his 50 percent interest, though he said he didn't have the cash at the moment. I said, "Okay, sure, pay me at your convenience."

I was really excited about the deal. I felt that Jim's experience would be the key to a rapid expansion of the business. He and I made a trip to Mount Pleasant together and found a location where we could open a shop there. It wasn't much—a tiny cement-floored place in an alley. I bought a used refrigerator, a used oven, and an old stainless steel counter. My total investment was twenty-two hundred dollars. I kept wondering when my new partner would mention the five hundred dollars he was to put into the business, but he didn't mention it, then or ever. With Jim Gilmore, as I was to learn, the only convenient time to pay a debt would be when the devil gave him a choice between that and playing goalie on hell's hockey team.

Many years later, my brother told me that ironically enough, the man he'd overheard Dominick DiVarti talking to about the sale of DomiNick's had been Gilmore.

"After you and I split up, I mentioned to DiVarti that you were going into partnership with Gilmore," Jim added. "He said, 'Holy Jesus, you'd better tell your brother not to get hooked up with that guy. He's a three-time loser!' "

Gilmore had told me about his past problems, of course, and I wanted to believe he had overcome them. I was naïve, I admit, but I don't think there's anything wrong with being naïve. I was willing to trust him. I don't think DiVarti's view would have influenced me much if I had known about it, though it might have made me a little more cautious. Gilmore had his attorney draw up a partnership agreement. They felt that since he had been bankrupt, it would be better to put everything in my name. That was okay by me, too. I just wanted to get up to Mount Pleasant and get going on our second place while Jim went to work in our Ypsilanti operation.

Somewhat to my surprise, Jim said he didn't want to give up his job at the university. He assured me he could do that and still manage our store easily by coming in for a while each night and on weekends. I argued with him about it in a friendly way, but I didn't push it. I figured he had enough experience to know what he was talking about. I was so confident about his ability that I just knew DomiNick's would get much better after I left and Gilmore took over.

Opening the Mount Pleasant place was exciting. I knew what

I wanted, and I was able to put it together quickly. I even knew exactly what I'd call it. Various names had been on my mind for some time. But one day a customer had come into DomiNick's and said, "Hi there, pizza king!" *Pizza King;* I really liked that.

Pizza King was an immediate success in Mount Pleasant. I hired a good crew and brought one employee from Ypsilanti, a guy named Frank Sukovich, to train as manager. Before long, Pizza King was surpassing the Ypsilanti store in sales, which gave me a terrific shot of confidence. I was on a roll. I had met a wonderful girl, Marjorie Zybach, and business was really humming. I felt ready to conquer the world.

More and more, my world was revolving around Margie. And between being so wonderfully distracted by her and working seven nights a week at Pizza King, I wasn't paying as much attention as I should have to what was happening back in Ypsilanti. I rationalized this by reminding myself that my partner had a lot more experience than I did. We had daily telephone conferences in which Gilmore would tell me what was happening, and we'd discuss the best way of handling day-to-day problems. Most of the time, I went along with his ideas. Our chats were cordial. But I was nettled by his constant complaints about being short of cash. On the other hand, I was willing to do whatever was necessary to build up the business, so I kept sending him money.

Monday was just about the only day I felt I could take part of an evening off from Pizza King. I'd leave Sukovich in charge and drive up to the campus to see Margie. I knew after our second date that she was the girl I wanted to marry. She was wholesome and decent and unpretentious, and those blue eyes of hers were absolutely electrifying. So I went to a jewelry store and bought a four-hundred-dollar engagement ring, the most expensive one I could charge with no money down. The diamond was only half a carat, but it looked bigger because it had a lot of ornamentation around it. The jeweler assured me that if my girl didn't accept it, I could bring it back.

I had the ring in my pocket when I picked Margie up for our third date. I drove to Big Rapids, about forty miles away, where I was considering opening a store. We went to a pizzeria and sampled its pizza, which I made some derogatory comments about. Margie said it didn't compare to the heart-shaped pizza I had given her. Then we drove around the city and campus to scout out possible store sites. I kept up a stream of nervous talk about the kind of place I was looking for. Margie seemed interested in the business details I was pointing out, so I got more and more expansive about my plans. I wanted to convince her that I was a substantial and worthwhile person, and I told her I was going to be a millionaire by the time I was thirty. She chuckled and said something about me having a good line. I could tell she was just kidding, and I hoped she didn't think I was. I was dead serious. There was absolutely no doubt in my mind that I would attain my dreams. I was shy, but I had plenty of self-confidence.

When we got back to her dorm, I didn't ask her to marry me. I didn't know how to get the words out. I just handed her the ring.

"I can't take it," she said.

"Yes," I said.

"I can't."

"Please."

"I'll think about it . . ."

Finally, she realized I wasn't going to take no for an answer. She said she would take the ring with her, but she wouldn't wear it. Well, she might wear it while she was sleeping, but she wouldn't show it to anybody. I considered that a victory. And sure enough, a week later, she said yes, she would marry me.

I was on cloud nine from then until the day I put on my best clothes, a suede sport coat and a plaid shirt, which I still have, and drove to Bay City to meet Margie's parents. To my dismay, her mother treated me like dirt. She seemed to think I was some kind of hoodlum.

I was crushed. I was sure that was the end of it for me with Margie. But to my relief, she told me she didn't intend to be influenced by her mother's opinion. She later showed me a seven-page letter her mother had written that cut me to ribbons in every paragraph. At one point she wrote: "He is a scruffy beatnik . . ." I was amazed. I was as square as a checkerboard, and she calls me a *beatnik*!

I was particularly hurt because I always felt I got along well with older people. Margie's father and I understood each other better. He was a power-plant supervisor for Bay City, and he'd spent forty years working his way up through the system. He was a nice guy, but very conservative. His favorite topic of conversation was how tough things were during the Depression. And he seemed convinced that another one was right around the corner. Yet he was a little more free-spirited than Mrs. Zybach, who was a negative sort of person. Her response to anything Margie or I did before we were married was critical. Afterward, our relationship steadily improved, and she actually grew to like me.

Had I known Margie then the way I do now, I would not have feared that she'd be influenced by her mother. Margie knows her own mind, and she has a will of iron. I got an inkling of that in her reaction to changing her religion. Margie was brought up in the Lutheran Church. She had to take Roman Catholic instruction so we could get married in the Church. I had hoped to persuade her to convert; in fact I just assumed it would happen. I respect her right not to change, but I still hope and pray that one day she will.

In her final semester, that spring of 1962, Margie got a practice-teaching assignment at a school in Dearborn, which is near

Ypsilanti. That gave me a good opportunity to drive down and visit my partner's operation. I was looking forward to showing my future wife our flagship operation. With all the money I'd been sending down, I expected to see a real class act, but what I got was an incredible shock. The store was a shambles. Gilmore had bragged about how much emphasis he put on cleanliness, and he had pointed out things about my approach that he said were sloppy. So if nothing else, I expected his operation to be a model of cleanliness. But it was crummy. To add insult to injury, he had a pinball machine in the store! The worst thing, though, was that the pizzas were awful. They were nowhere near round.

I was irate. Gilmore was very apologetic. He had misjudged his own capacity, he said. He wasn't so young anymore, and he just didn't have the energy he'd thought he had to handle two jobs.

It was clear that he must have been taking money, but I had no hard evidence. Besides, I felt sorry for the old rascal. His battered features looked stricken, and his contrition seemed genuine. I still valued his knowledge; I didn't want to lose that. So I took a deep breath and made a decision: "If he's dishonest, that's his problem," I told myself. "I will live up to my end of the bargain regardless."

Jim said, "I want to be a good partner to you, Tom. I know a great location on campus at U of M, and if we bought that, the volume would justify my quitting the cooking job and concentrating on our business full-time. We'd both be a lot better off, because you know how fantastic the potential is at the University of Michigan."

He was singing the kind of song he knew I wanted to hear. I just couldn't help liking the guy even though I no longer had the illusion that he was a genius who could guide me to lofty heights. I would be pleased if he'd just pull his share of the load. Anyhow, we went over to the campus and looked at the location he had in mind. It really was excellent. We didn't have enough money to rent it and buy the equipment, however, so I drove back to Mount Pleasant and made a deal with Sukovich, my manager, for him to buy half interest in that store. His dad loaned him four thousand dollars, and we made the deal. In May 1962, we opened Pizza King in Ann Arbor. We agreed that Gilmore would run it and I would return to Ypsilanti and whip DomiNick's back into shape. This worked out well. I could keep a better handle on things, and Margie could drive over from Dearborn and visit me in the 1960 Rambler I had bought her. We had set our wedding date for August 25, before the colleges were back in session and our business started booming.

Margie got a job at a pancake house in Dearborn, and I was busy moving the Ypsilanti store. Our lease was up and I'd found a better location, two blocks east, at 310 Cross Street. It takes a powerful amount of work to open a store. In Domino's we say it's like having a baby, even though now we open nearly three new stores every day and have it down to a science. You have to do a lot of careful planning. You have to negotiate the lease, then get the plumbers and electricians in there, deal with the health department and various other inspectors, and handle all kinds of unforseeable details.

One of the things I hadn't anticipated in this case was the telephone call I got from Dominick DiVarti soon after we moved. He said he didn't want me to use his name anymore. "It's confusing my customers," he said. We got into a heated argument about it, and the next call I got was from his attorney. I had a pretty wild temper at that time and carried a bit of a chip on my shoulder, so I got into a shouting match with the attorney, too. Later, after I cooled down, I could see it was useless to argue. I hated to lose the name DomiNick's because we had built it into something meaningful; it was well respected in the community. But done was done. We had the right to keep the name for three months, and I vowed I'd come up with something better by then. No, not just better, our new name would be superlative! I asked my employees to come up with suggestions.

Business took off immediately in the new DomiNick's location. Gilmore's Ann Arbor store, which we called Pizza King, was doing only fair. Jim was keeping it clean, though, and the quality of his product was much improved with him on hand full-time. Profits were so poor at Jim's store, and it had cost so much to get the two places open that we weren't putting much in the bank at that point.

The Ypsilanti store jutted out of the front of a big old Victorian house, and I thought it would be great if Margie and I could just move in there after we were married. But she wanted no part of it, and nothing I said could budge her. That was my first taste of her remarkable ability to stonewall. When she has made up her mind on something, it's useless to try and budge her. I guess the reason she didn't want to live behind the store was that I would spend even more time working. I'd be so accessible to the business that we'd have no privacy whatsoever. In retrospect, I think she was absolutely right. But I couldn't see it at the time. The upshot, after a lot of discussions, was that we agreed to buy a used house trailer as our first home. We found an old thirty-nine-footer, eight feet wide, for fourteen hundred dollars. The interior was all dark wood paneling, which gave it a warm, cozy feeling. I think that trailer was the most comfortable place we've ever lived. Maybe that's nostalgia talking because it was our first home, but I really did enjoy it.

I liked the whole idea of trailer living. It's a lot like living aboard a yacht in that it requires an orderly and methodical approach—a place for everything and everything in its place. I even thought I might get into the business of operating trailer parks. I visited a good many of the parks in the area while driving to and from my store, and I made sketches of how I would lay one out. I told myself I wouldn't mess around with the kind of second-rate facilities many of the parks provided. I was sure that people would pay a little more to get a location that was really clean, comfortable, and pleasing to the eye. Chances are, I might have invested in a trailer park at that time, but Jim Gilmore co-opted any such move and tied up all my capital-raising potential with his scheme for expanding Pizza King in Ann Arbor.

Gilmore was of the opinion that there was a lot of wasted space in his store. Of course, his experience had been with traditional types of restaurants, and I think he liked the idea of playing host to people. At any rate, he said he thought we could get more productivity per square foot on our lease and take better advantage of the density of the student population if we would broaden our appeal. He wanted to put in a bunch of tables and add a sandwich line—hamburgers, hot dogs, chicken, barbecue, and submarine sandwiches—and make the store into a combination between a McDonald's and a pizza place.

I believed Jim was as eager to build the business as I was, but he was even more impulsive than I. He was a loose cannon. He'd buy just about anything anyone tried to sell him, probably because he was afraid someone else would get it if he didn't. His attitude always was "let the devil take the hindmost." One day he talked over his idea of expansion with Howard Miller, an equipment supplier. Miller drew up some nifty plans to show how the place could be redesigned. Naturally, the drawings included all kinds of new equipment and Jim just had to have everything in them. But his projections for the business persuaded me to go along with his ideas. It looked like a sure winner, and I figured it probably would be a better investment than a trailer court. To come up with my share for the remodeling, we sold the remainder of our interest in the Mount Pleasant Pizza King. But we still were short of money, so we brought in a third partner, a friend of Gilmore's named Clark "Red" Shelton, the owner of Red's Right Spot. Shelton put in about four thousand dollars.

Meanwhile, Margie and I got married and set up housekeeping in our little trailer. She had landed a job in the library of Palmer Junior High School in Wayne, Michigan. Our plan was to live off my salary and bank hers. Basically, that's what we did, but it was a lean existence. I was putting every cent I could spare into building the business, so the check I took out of the restaurant partnership was only $125 a week, which left $102 after taxes. Then Margie went for a routine dental checkup and came back with the news that she had to have about $700 worth of work done on her teeth. That was a shocker, because her teeth looked perfect.

I couldn't complain, though, because Margie was a champion at saving money. Even with the unexpected bills, she managed to add a little to our savings account each month. And thank God she did, because about three months later we learned she was pregnant. We had no insurance to cover having a baby, which was going to cost about five hundred dollars, and we also had to start thinking about getting a larger trailer.

I had made a study of house trailers, as is my habit with any subject that interests me. When I get thinking about something like that, I want to know everything I possibly can about it, down to the last detail. So I did a lot of reading about trailers and talked to a lot of trailer owners, and I knew that the Vagabond was considered the Cadillac of the field. It had all copper plumbing, dovetailed drawers, hand-rubbed oak paneling, and the chassis was real sturdy. It also had heating in the floor similar to Frank Lloyd Wright's radiant heating. I wanted a Vagabond because it was the best. So I talked up that brand with Margie when we'd go driving through various trailer parks looking for "For Sale" signs. I was elated when we found a nice Vagabond selling for thirty-eight hundred dollars. I knew it had cost the original owner at least eight thousand dollars. The Ann Arbor Bank financed it for us; they said it was the first house-trailer loan they'd ever made. But we put two thousand dollars down on it—which Margie had saved from her teaching job—so they had a secure deal. We came out all right on it, too, because we held on to the small trailer and rented it out to one of my managers.

Our first baby was born on Memorial Day 1963. I had two names picked out—John for a boy, because I'd always liked the sound of *Jack Monaghan*. I was a big fan of President John F. Kennedy, and my Uncle Jack Monaghan, the bricklayer, had been a charismatic guy to me. If it was a girl, we'd name her Mary, after the queen of all the saints. Mary it was, the first of four girls, and I was delighted.

In that same month, May 1963, we opened our third restaurant, in a former diner on Ecorse Road on the east side of Ypsilanti. Looking back on it now, I wonder how we did it, because Gilmore's expanded operation in Ann Arbor wasn't making money yet. DomiNick's was carrying the whole load. But I was eager to get a location on the east side of Ypsi. The Huron River splits the town and made delivery over there difficult from Domi-Nick's west side location on Cross Street. I could see that having a store on the east side would not only improve delivery in the area, it also would make DomiNick's better in serving the west side. Divide and conquer: It's an ancient military concept that applies perfectly to the logistics of pizza delivery. It would be important throughout the growth of Domino's, and it's crucial in fighting the emerging pizza wars of 1987.

I was eager to put this strategy into action, so we bought the diner, a small, ten-stool location, and named it Pizza King. We made space for a pizza oven, a cooler, and a counter. There was no room to do the back-room work for the pizza making, but I saw a way to turn that disadvantage into a positive: We'd simply bring the food over from the Cross Street store every day. I got the idea from an article about Bill Knapp and the commissary system he used in his well-known Michigan chain, Bill Knapp's Restaurants. He said it gave him better quality control, and it seemed to apply perfectly to our situation. Each day we made extra dough-balls and toppings for Ecorse Road. The dough was stacked in bun pans, which we strapped into the back of a pickup truck. I didn't realize it then, but that would be the beginning of Domino's commissary system.

I felt that things were really coming together for us now, and so did Gilmore. In addition to running Pizza King in Ann Arbor, he was supervising the diner part of our store on Ecorse Road in Ypsi while I ran the pizza operation there. Late in the summer of '63, we bought back Red Shelton's interest. In October, we incorporated as DomiNick's Pizza King, Inc., as a stopgap measure until we came up with a new name for DomiNick's. Then, sometime after New Year's of '64, Gilmore got another one of his great ideas. There was a full-service restaurant in Ann Arbor called the Golden Butterfly, which he saw as his golden opportunity. "I can make this place hum, Tom," he said. "It will be the best restaurant in Ann Arbor." As usual, he persuaded me he was right, so we formed a separate corporation, Gilmore's Restaurant, Inc, also as fifty-fifty partners, though everything was still in my name. We bought the place for ninety thousand dollars, assuming the note on it, and he changed the sign to Gilmore's Restaurant. It was a terrific deal for him, but too bad for me, as I discovered too late.

I was working my tail off, putting in about a hundred hours a week, and once he opened the new place, Gilmore slacked off completely. I doubt he worked more than ten or twelve hours a week. He'd show up to check the cash registers, slap a few customers on the back and chat with them, and possibly do a little book work. But much of the time he was traveling or supervising construction at his home. He made a lot of lavish improvements on that house. He put a chain-link fence around the property, bought expensive new furniture, put on a new roof and siding, built kennels for his dogs, and filled his basement with new power tools, which I don't think he ever used. He also bought five acres of additional land around the house and bought a series of five new cars during the time we were partners. Meanwhile, I was driving a rusted out old Rambler. Had I thought about it, I suppose I would have surmised he was living high on the hog from some inheritance of his wife's. He certainly wasn't doing it on his salary from our businesses, which were all losing money except for DomiNick's. We were both supposed to be taking out $125 a week in salary. Margie and I weren't even cashing half the checks I brought home. We were living on $55 a week.

When people tried to clue me in that my partner was taking me for a ride, I told them, "Well, Jim knows the food business and he's a tremendous help." I didn't want to confront him with accusations, because I had my mind set on growing, not squabbling or breaking up. I told myself, "Some day, some way, everything will work out. I can't really get hurt too bad if I play it straight." That's what I believed, and I tried to make enough money to cover his losses.

In July 1964, despite our cash problems, we bought Pizza from the Prop. The owner approached me about it, and I saw it as another opportunity to divide and conquer—break up the U of M campus area and improve the service of our Ann Arbor Pizza King. I also wanted the store because it came cheap—no money down—and an operation that's already going is better than a startup; it's like jumping on a moving train. I figure that if I can get hold of a business, I can make it prosper. The name Pizza from the Prop was so well established that we decided not to change it. In fact, we considered putting it on our other places. But the whole name situation was too much of a jumble. We were registered to do business as Ypsilanti DomiNick's, yet we were incorporated as DomiNick's Pizza King. Now there was Pizza from the Prop. I would have given more thought to straightening out this tangle if I hadn't found myself in the midst of a bigger problem.

JIM GILMORE got sick in the fall of 1964. I went to the hospital to visit him, full of sympathy for his failing health. His alcoholic past had damaged his liver; he apparently had pneumonia and jaundice, and he looked awful. But he brushed aside my pleasantries and told me he wanted to break up our partnership.

"Tom, I want to run sit-down restaurants and you want to deliver pizzas," he said. "So you pay me thirty-five thousand dollars and take the pizzerias, okay?"

I didn't comment, but my mind was racing. He's got to be kidding, I thought. We have 80 or 90 percent of our investment in his two restaurants, Gilmore's and Pizza King, and he thinks the other three stores are worth $35,000? He's sicker than I thought. He must be delirious.

Then he said, "You told me yourself, Tom, that you thought DomiNick's alone was worth thirty-five thousand dollars."

I didn't argue, not with him lying there looking like something the cat dragged in and the kittens couldn't eat. But I knew what he was referring to, and it got my hackles up. One time when he was feeling depressed about how bad things were going, I tried to cheer him up by saying, "You know, DomiNick's is probably worth thirty-five thousand dollars." He said, "Do you really think it is?" I said, "Sure." So now he was using that against me, and it made me mad.

For the first time, I hardened my heart toward Jim. I decided I would take him up on his proposal to split—no matter how much it cost me. It was time. We sure couldn't keep going as we had been. But I was going to hire my own attorney. Up to this point, old Jim's attorney had handled all the legal matters and old Jim's accountant had done our books. But from now on, young Tom was going to look out for himself.

I checked around Ypsilanti and found an attorney named Larry Sperling, who got good recommendations everywhere. He came across in person as a quiet, fair-minded guy. As it turned out, he was splitting away from a partner himself, so he had an appreciation for my situation. But I didn't like his initial advice. After going through my financial statements and considering my tangled business setup, he told me I ought to declare bankruptcy and start over again.

"I hate the word *bankrupt*," I said. "So you can forget that. I want to work my way out of this thing. I know I can do it."

While Sperling went to work straightening out my legal situation, I was busy screwing up my home life. I'm not sure why it happened, though I guess all the uncertainty about the debts and the Gilmore situation had something to do with it. Anyhow, I took a bunch of employees out after work to celebrate a record night. The Christmas season had started and everybody was cheerful. I bought beer for everybody and drank more myself than I could handle. I never did have much tolerance for alcohol. Usually, I nursed my drinks while joining in the spirit of a party.

When I got home to the trailer and went into the bedroom, Margie rolled over and looked at me, and for some reason the question in her eyes made me mad. I yelled at her, and she got scared.

She had no idea what I might do, so she went in and got our baby to protect her from me. That made me even madder.

I was lunging around and accidentally knocked over the Christmas tree, scattering ornaments all over the floor. I felt like an idiot. I got down on my hands and knees and crawled around for about half an hour picking up ornaments and putting them back on the tree.

Margie sat on the couch the whole time, with the baby on her lap, watching me. When I finished, she said, "Well, that certainly looks nice."

That made me mad all over again. I knocked the tree back down and jumped up and down on it like a maniac. Then I went slamming out the door and went to the motel next door to the trailer park. By the time I got there, I knew this was the stupidest thing I'd ever done in my life. I just lay in that motel room staring at the dark the rest of the night. I'd alternate between fits of shame and remorse and fear that Margie would never forgive me.

Next morning, I went back to our trailer. Margie didn't say much; she just looked me over quizzically. I was relieved, because I sensed she would forgive me. I followed her around, helping to straighten the place up and telling her how sorry I was, how ashamed I was. She finally let me kiss her and said she wasn't mad at me.

"I just hope you won't come home like that again," she said.

"You don't have to worry about that, honey," I replied. "I'll never have another drink the rest of my life."

I've kept that promise. I don't even have a glass of wine with dinner. I used to drink a lot of colas, but I quit them to cut down my calorie intake. My favorite drink now is soda water, and I consume gallons of it every week.

I think Margie knew I meant it when I said I'd never take another drink. She'd already seen me demonstrate my self-discipline when I quit smoking. When we first met, she had no idea I smoked cigarettes because I had given them up for Lent. It never occurred to me to mention the habit. After we'd been engaged for a couple of weeks, I took her to lunch at a coffee shop in Mount Pleasant to celebrate St. Patrick's Day. Technically, of course, St. Patrick's Day is still in the middle of Lent, but it's not Lent for me. My pride in being Irish allows me to break Lent that day.

So I casually pulled out a cigarette and lit up, and I'll never forget the look of shock and surprise on Margie's face. I was taken aback. But I could understand her reaction. She had no idea the guy she was engaged to had what she considered to be a vile habit. So I said, "I'll tell you what I'll do: I'll quit smoking the day we get married."

That's exactly what I did. I knew I'd be able to do it, even though I'd tried to quit smoking several times before and was unsuccessful. The difference was that this time I told other people I was doing it. Once I did that, there was no alternative; I couldn't go back on my word.

The day before our wedding, I told all my friends that I was smoking my last cigarette, and that was that. Cold turkey. This was before cigarette advertising was banned from TV, and those commercials must have had some subliminal message, because they bothered me for about six months. Whenever I watched one, I'd find myself unconsciously reaching for a cigarette. But I would not have smoked one, no matter what.

The same went for drinking. I never wanted to experience another episode like that Christmas-tree disaster.

St. Patrick's Day 1965 was an especially festive one for me, because two days earlier Gilmore and I signed the agreement that said: "Whereas Monaghan and Gilmore find that for the business and personal benefit of each and for the benefit of the corporations involved, that any business relationship between them be severed and they hereinafter operate separately and independently of one another . . ."

The deal Larry Sperling had worked out was that I was to pay Jim twenty thousand dollars. I would get DomiNick's, the Pizza King in Ypsilanti, and Pizza from the Prop. Jim would retain two of our five places—Pizza King in Ann Arbor and Gilmore's Restaurant.

Jim had incurred some heavy debts on his places. He had bought all that equipment in his Pizza King, and he had installed completely new fixtures and accessories throughout Gilmore's. He'd made Gilmore's into a nice, homey place. But nothing in it was paid for, not even the ashtrays. The twenty thousand dollars I gave him in our dissolution got him out from under that. It left him free and clear and gave him a running start.

I had to scrape to get the money. I borrowed ten thousand dollars from one of my major suppliers, Paul Fata. The bank loaned me another five thousand, and the rest came from Margie's piggy bank.

Making a complete break was impossible, since all his obligations were in my name. So if he got back into debt and failed to pay debts, I'd have to assume his obligations. Sperling had Jim sign a security agreement that would give me control of all his assets if he defaulted. But that was a situation I devoutly wished to avoid. I told him, "Jim, I am wishing you the best, and I want you to be sure and stay healthy."

While all the legal maneuvering and negotiation with Gilmore was going on, I had been brainstorming with my employees on a new name for our business. I needed to have one before the dead-line for the 1965 telephone directories.

I would have used the name Pizza King, except for the fact that Gilmore owned one of the Pizza Kings. Pizza from the Prop didn't sound right, maybe because it was so strongly identified with Ann Arbor and originally with a broader menu. For a while I considered using the name Pinocchio's. It had an Italian sound, and I remembered reading a statement by one of President Eisen-hower's speechwriters that he used a lot of words containing p's because the letter sounds pleasing to the ear. When I get started on something like that, I tend to harp on it continuously, and that's what I did as we went about our daily tasks in the Cross Street store. We must have gone through hundreds of different names. Most of them weren't even close.

One day in February, Jim Kennedy, who later became my top manager at Cross Street, came back from a delivery and burst in the door shouting, "Hey, Tom, I've found our new name!"

"Yeah?" I said. "What is it?"

"Domino's."

"That's it! That's it!" I yelled. I was so excited, I danced around like a kid. I knew it was exactly right because it met all our criteria for a name: It was Italian, it was unique—I didn't know of another pizza place in the country using the name, though I later found out there were a number of them—and it was close to DomiNick's both in sound and spelling, so if some-one were looking up our old name in the phone book, the new name would be in the same vicinity.

I had already talked to an advertising man named Sam Fine who was just launching his own agency in Ann Arbor. I'd out-lined to him my plans to concentrate on pizza only, with free delivery and no sit-down service. He seemed intrigued by the concept. He also struck me as a very creative guy. So when Ken-

nedy came up with the name Domino's, one of the first things I
did was to call Sam Fine. He immediately began designing a logo
for us. I had envisioned a black logo, because dominos are black.
But he came up with a red domino and put three white dots on it,
which he said represented our three stores.

"You can add a dot every time you add a new store," he said.

That didn't seem so wildly impractical at the time. I wasn't
thinking of being a national chain; I simply wanted to have the
best pizza business in Ypsilanti and Ann Arbor. Now, I suppose,
we might consider having a dot for every thousand stores, but
that would eventually become impractical, too.

We ordered illuminated cartop signs with our new logo, and
they looked snazzy. We also did some radio advertising and
bought space on a billboard. But we didn't have enough money
to do a big advertising campaign. In fact, technically, I was broke.
All the money for advertising had to come out of daily receipts.

But once I was free of the Gilmore partnership, I felt like I had
been shot out of a cannon. I could see the system of production
I'd designed for the stores beginning to function like clockwork,
and I was on fire with plans to extend our service throughout
Ann Arbor and Ypsilanti.

I sold the diner portion of the Ecorse Road Pizza King to a
woman who was working there. She named it Marty's Diner, and
we continued delivering from it as Domino's.

One of the keys to becoming dominant in our two-city area, I
believed, was to offer the highest quality in our product. So I laid
down strict standards about the ingredients we'd use. Domino's
pizzas would be made with nothing but high-gluten flour, the
most expensive flour I knew of, made from the hard wheat of
northern climates like the Dakotas or Canada. We used nothing
but full-cream cheese, made from whole milk rather than from
skim milk. I put an absolute ban on processed cheese made from

powdered milk. All our toppings had to be top grade: mushrooms from the caves of Illinois, pear-shaped tomatoes from California, Canadian bacon for ham, and only one brand of pepperoni, which I personally selected as the best.

But probably the most important element of our standards was that our dough was made fresh every day and stretched by hand to make individual orders. Pizza is a complicated product— part chemistry, part artistry. The dough that forms its foundation is important to both. There are gasses in the raw dough that will escape if it is stretched more than a few seconds before it goes into the oven. That's why a preformed shell produces a crust that's tough and flat-tasting. The last-minute stretching of the dough is vitally important. Spinning dough and tossing it overhead, by the way, is pure showmanship. It does nothing to improve the taste of the pizza, and it takes extra time. I enjoy doing it, and I might toss one occasionally to entertain little kids, but there's usually no time for showmanship in a Domino's store.

Though my standards of quality were pretty sophisticated, my approach to management in 1965 was strictly seat-of-the-pants. I had no manual or file of operating procedures. There was no personnel code and not much need for one, because even though I had about eighty employees, most of them were part-time drivers. I didn't even have an office. My briefcase was an old cardboard box.

I'd get together with my managers once a week. I'd buy their lunch, and they'd give me their reports. Then we'd discuss any problems we had. Keeping cars repaired and running was always a major item, and everyone shared mechanical information on a continuing basis. Sometimes I wondered whether I was in the pizza business or the used-car business. I never let one of those meetings break up, though, without discussing our product standards and our goals.

All of us worked in harmony at setting and achieving those standards and goals, and that's why we were successful. We were all contributing, all sharing ideas and encouraging each other. We were all dedicated to what we were doing—each of the managers was working at least six days a week, and I was working seven. And we knew who our competition was—the other restaurants out there, not each other. Most important, though, we knew who our real boss was—the customer.

My biggest problem as proprietor—I didn't really think of myself as president then—was paying our bills. I had inherited a lot of bad bills from the partnership and had begun hearing from collection agencies. I devised a payment system that seemed to work pretty well: I'd go through all the bills and determine how much I wanted to pay each creditor. Then I'd check the cash flow from the stores to forecast how much money might be coming in during the week ahead. I'd start on Saturday with zero in the bank and write checks allowing for a week of float, time to get money into the account before the checks were processed. There was always a lot less coming in than I wanted to pay out, so I'd go through the whole column of creditors and shave each amount a bit. I'd keep repeating this procedure, shaving away until I had a total I could meet. In that way, every creditor got paid something every week. I felt this was a very important principle.

It was gratifying to see how the amount of our debts was reduced as I applied this system week after week. I was flying high now. I was generating ideas like sparks spewing from steel held against a spinning grindstone. To top it all off and make my happiness complete, Margie gave birth to our second baby girl, Susie, on May 7, 1965.

OMINO'S BUSINESS was fantastic during that yeasty summer of 1965. We'd established ourselves in the community now, so we didn't take a complete nose-dive when the students left at the end of the school year.

The most positive factor in sustaining our momentum, though, was the family-style communications among all of us who worked at Domino's. We had a flow of ideas and information that kept us constantly on top of things in all three stores. I'd get together with three or four people from the other stores every morning. We'd go to a restaurant for coffee and discuss what went right and what went wrong the previous night. Those sessions were better than most motivational seminars I've seen, and I sometimes wish I could revive them.

Margie left her teaching job when Mary was born. But she worked for me in the Cross Street store off and on. After Susie was born, I hired Margie to do our bookkeeping. She would

come into the office in back of the store and punch away at her
adding machine while the babies slept in cardboard boxes in the
corner. If we were shorthanded, Margie would pitch in and help
in the store.

I was working incredible hours, from 10:00 A.M. till 4:00 the
following morning, seven days a week. But it was fun, a real
labor of love. And seeing the profits mount every day made it
even more enjoyable. Soon we were current with all our bills and
I was able to break away for a working vacation.

My main reason for traveling east was to be best man at Steve
Litwhiler's wedding. He had been a driver for me since 1961,
while he was a student at Eastern, and we became close friends.
The wedding took place in his bride's hometown in Vermont. So
as long as I was up there, I decided to visit the World's Fair in
New York City, where they had a Pizza Pavilion that was supposed to be the greatest thing since the invention of mozzarella. I
was looking forward to the trip, though it would be my first time
away from Margie and I didn't like that.

I had read that a man named Frank Mastro was supposed to
be the top pizza man in the United States, and the Pizza Pavilion
was run by the Mastro organization. I wanted to meet Mr. Mastro, but it turned out he was dead. His son had taken over, and I
found the operation disappointing. It was supposed to be the
largest pizza enterprise in the world, but it wasn't even as big as
my Domino's on Cross Street in Ypsilanti! I really think that store
of ours was doing more volume at that time than any other pizza
place in the country.

While I was in New York, I took the opportunity to visit Times
Square, where all the legendary pizza places were. I found that
there weren't any more Italian pizza makers; by this time they
were all Filipinos. In one place I met an old Jewish man who had
been one of the pioneers of flipping pizzas in the store windows,

and we had a long conversation. I stayed there all day and into the evening while he showed me how he made his dough. I was pretty skeptical of the operation, because he used a poor-quality flour and cheap tomatoes.

He told me what a rough time he had keeping good pizza makers. He said that sometimes they just didn't show up for work, and as he was telling me that, in comes one of his managers with the news that their best pizza maker had not come in that evening.

"I'll take his place," I said.

The old man looked incredulous, and I assured him I meant it. I'd work for nothing, just for the experience of making pizzas on Times Square. He shrugged and gave me a big smile. I worked a whole eight-hour shift, and I literally stopped traffic. I flipped pizzas like crazy while people gathered around the window and gaped. What a night!

I returned to Ypsilanti feeling much more secure about my own business. My pizza was better than anything I saw in New York, and I certainly had better personnel controls. The way that old man had accepted unreliable employees who came in whenever they pleased astonished me, because people I hired knew they didn't dare show up late.

The work schedule was our bible. It was posted on the wall and remained the same, week in and week out, unless the employees and I changed it by mutual consent.

I made up a nightly game plan, in pencil, on the bottom of a pizza box. I'd draw a vertical line down the middle and list the people who would be working inside the store down the left side and those who would be delivering on the right.

I drew a horizontal line across the center to separate pre-rush staff from rush time. During pre-rush, from 4:30 until 9:00, there'd be just me and one other person inside and three people driving. Between 5:00 and 7:00, we would be making sure the cars were gassed up, the cheese broken up, and boxes folded in preparation for the rush. Around 9:00, when the rush hit, we would have five people inside and eight drivers.

I had only a few work rules, but I was strict about enforcing them: Nobody is late for work; everybody works at least one weekend night; nobody sits down in the store. I found that sitting down caused a letdown. In fact, if you sat down after a big rush, it was more like a collapse.

When I finished with the pizza box that had my schedule on it, I'd put a pizza in it. I wouldn't dream of letting it go to waste. But I sometimes wondered what the customers thought if they happened to look on the bottom of their box of Domino's pizza and saw my scribblings.

The idea of stressing thirty-minute delivery grew out of my insistence on giving customers a quality pizza: It didn't make sense to use only the best ingredients in our pizza if the product was cold and tasteless when the customer got it. So early in 1965, I set thirty-minute delivery as a goal and started talking it up among my employees in the three Domino's stores. At that time, though, it was still just an objective. I didn't make it a policy until after I started franchising in 1967. But in the same vein, early in 1965, I began reinforcing the emphasis on rapid delivery by giving a bonus to drivers who collected the most cash on deliveries. The contest was called Delivery Champion, and Steve Litwhiler was the first record holder, with one-night receipts of $245.14. This later led to a contest called Driver of the Week, which became a permanent fixture in Domino's operations.

Our backroom work was made a lot easier by the arrival of my dream machine for chopping cheese. I'd discovered it the previous year during a trip to the 1964 American Restaurant Association show.

We bought cheese in five-pound bricks, and we'd been preparing it by cutting the blocks by hand into chunks small enough to be fed into our meat grinder, which operated on a power take-off from our mixer. The stuff looked like spaghetti as it came worming out of the grinder. Then it had to be broken up into tiny pellets. It was quite a lengthy process, and it was made even more time-consuming by the fact that we were now using two different kinds of cheese, blended in precise proportions.

Walking through the trade-show exhibits at the Chicago convention, I had happened upon a German machine called a VCM, which looked like a giant kitchen blender. The Hobart company was planning to import it if the prototype at the show attracted any interest. I was all eyes. The more I looked, the better I liked what I was seeing. The Germans had designed the VCM to emulsify meat for making bratwurst and weiswurst, so it was extremely powerful. I arranged to give it a try, and it worked beautifully. We'd take whole bricks of cheese, toss them into the VCM, and in about fifteen seconds it would all be ground up and mixed in the right proportions. That was a first in the pizza industry, and the VCM was widely used by us and others for years after that.

We also used the VCM to mix dough. Bakers considered this ridiculous. They felt good dough could only be made by the old, slow conventional mixers. But we'd mix a batch of dough in the VCM in about forty-five seconds, as compared to the eight or ten minutes it normally took, and nobody, not even a master baker, could tell the difference in the final product.

Another innovation I came up with was using fiberglass boxes for keeping dough. Up till then, like just about everyone else in the industry, we kept our dough balls on bun pans, eighteen- by twenty-six-inch aluminum pans. The pans were comparatively expensive, and dough kept on them would form a crust that made it difficult to slap it out without tearing. We tried to prevent crusting by painting the dough balls with vegetable oil and cover-ing them with oily towels to prevent contact with the air. This was pretty messy and wasn't very effective. One day, while look-ing through a supplier's catalogue, I found some intriguing-look-ing fiberglass boxes. I think they were intended to hold machine parts to keep them from rusting. The wheels really started spin-ning in my head when I read the word *airtight*. I envisioned these boxes full of plump gray mounds of pizza dough. I bought several boxes to experiment with, and they were great. They stacked up neatly and kept the dough almost crust-free. These boxes also became a standard in the industry. By the mid-seventies, there were very few pizza places in the country still using bun pans.

Each of these advances was small and, in itself, fairly insignifi-cant. But every one of them gave us a little boost toward my goals of consistent product quality and thirty-minute delivery. I kept harping on these things at every meeting we had. My employees might moan and groan at hearing me repeat them, but I didn't let that bother me. It isn't enough to know what you want: You have to make sure that the people who can get it for you know you want it. You'll know they know when they start saying it back to you. If you show them you want it enough, they'll want it, too—and when they do, they'll get it for you.

This principle works with suppliers as well as with employees. I've driven a few suppliers crazy with my constant questions and explanations. Many suppliers try to sell you what they've got in-stead of what you want, and it can take a long time to get them going your way. A good example is my campaign to get the right kind of box to put pizzas in for delivery.

A pizza comes out of the oven at about 200 degrees; that's the internal temperature of the crust. To meet standard board-of-health regulations, it must have a surface temperature of at least 140 degrees when it is delivered to the customer. We've done a lot of laboratory tests on this over the years, so we have a pretty good fix on what the average pizza eater wants. What he wants is a *hot* pizza, which means one with a surface temperature of 150 degrees. Of course, it's true that some people like to have pizza so hot it cooks the roof of their mouths, while others would rather have it cool.

Domino's standard is to get the pizza to the customer at 150 degrees. There are a lot of devices we've used to help accomplish this, including various heaters in delivery cars and insulating pouches. But the critical item in heat retention is the box we pack it in. In the early sixties, nearly all suppliers of pizza boxes were using chipboard, which is used to make a regular cake box. I hated those boxes because the heat and steam of the pizza inside would weaken them and make them soggy. Another problem was that they were too flimsy to stack up effectively when you folded them in advance, in preparation for the rush.

My box supplier was a man named Barney Barnes, a cheerful sales pro. He worked for Indiana Carton, a chipboard pizza box manufacturer, and several other companies as a commission rep. Every time I'd see Barney, I'd say, "When are you going to get me a corrugated box?"

"Don't worry, Tom," he'd say. "We're working on it. Something will turn up."

"I'm sure it will, Barney. I just hope my toes don't do it first."

I finally located a manufacturer myself—Triad Container, a corrugated-container house in Detroit. They needed business, so unlike others in the industry, they were willing to work on designing a special box for us. Barney went to work on it with them, and it was no easy task. The first boxes they made were too shallow. The machinery wasn't designed to make a deeper box. Barney talked them into changing the machinery.

Then they had difficulty perforating the corrugated material so it could be folded and still retain its strength.

Barney kept coming in with samples and showing me why they weren't working. We needed to have vent holes in the top of our boxes to allow the steam to get out. But their holes weren't being cut clean, so the prototype boxes would drop little round pieces of cardboard onto the top of the pizza.

"Look, Barney," I said in exasperation, "American technology is putting space satellites in orbit these days, and you're telling me you can't punch a clean hole in a piece of cardboard?"

Well, Triad finally solved the problem by putting the holes in the side corners instead of in the lid, so we got the kind of boxes we needed. They were sturdy and tight, and I thought it was beautiful to see a pile of them stacked high in a store. It was a pleasure to hand one to a customer and feel confident that it wouldn't sag open and drop the pizza on his porch, which happened from time to time with the old chipboard box. Best of all, they were less expensive than the chipboard boxes, which was a surprise. The new boxes, it turned out, used less material, since they were rigid, and we no longer needed to put a circle of corrugated paper under the pizza as we had with the chipboard boxes.

After Labor Day 1965, when the colleges were back in session, I began to get pretty strung out from working such long hours. My temper was on a shorter fuse than ever. One night I fired an employee, and he called me a name as he was going out the door. I went after him.

I used to go berserk when I got in a fight. In the Marine Corps, that was an advantage. For example, the night we landed on Okinawa, we were herded into a darkened barracks and told to find an empty bed. The one I picked happened to be above the bunk of a big black guy named Pickett. I was told later that he was the baddest guy in the whole outfit.

When Pickett came back from liberty that night—it was pay

day, and he'd been drinking—he discovered me sleeping peace-
fully. He decided to have some fun with this rookie fresh from
Stateside, so he hauled me out of bed. I woke up swinging blind
furious punches. We slammed each other around in the dark until somebody separated us. I was wearing nothing but my skiv-
vies, so my feet and shins were all bruised from bumping into
beds and footlockers. I got in some good licks, though. I don't
know how much drinking had affected his reflexes, but I was
doing as much damage to him as he was to me. Anyhow, after
that, I was treated with considerable respect. That Tom Monaghan was a lot different than the one who had joined the Marines a few months earlier. For years I had backed down if I was
threatened by somebody bigger and stronger, but the Marines
taught me to stand firm regardless.

That carried over into the pizza business. I didn't take abuse
from anyone. If someone refused to pay a driver for an order, I
didn't call the police. I just went and demanded the money. Usually, the culprits were a bunch of college guys who'd decided to
have a party at my expense, and I didn't hesitate to swing a
punch to persuade them to pay up. From time to time, we'd have
a rash of pizza thefts from parked vehicles while drivers were
busy with customers. I'd hide in the back of the car the next time
it went to that neighborhood and wait for them to try it again. I'd
carry a meat-tenderizing mallet or a pop bottle as a persuader,
and that approach always solved the problem.

When I tackled the guy I'd fired, I tore into him in a fury. I had
him down and was slugging him when a driver who'd just come
back from a delivery pulled me off. Then I started beating up the
driver. I wound up in the police station over that, and came close
to going to jail. The guy I'd fired sued me for assault and battery.
The charge was dropped, though, and the driver, who was a decent guy, just laughed the incident off and forgave me. I took the

episode to heart, however, as a good lesson in personnel relations: Fire a guy if you have to, but don't beat him up, too.

I also decided I was getting too tense; I was feeling the pressure of working so furiously seven nights a week. I had to have a breather. So I started closing the stores on Monday nights.

Those nights off were the opportunity I'd been looking for to visit other pizza places in the Midwest. Margie and I would get in the car with the babies early on a Monday morning and take off in whatever direction struck our fancy. We'd drive until we came to a town that looked interesting and check the Yellow Pages for pizzerias. Then we'd visit the places and I'd talk to the owners about their business. Once they found out I was a pizza man, too, and from out of town so I was not in competition with them, they were cordial and helpful. It was a two-way street, though; I was often able to give them tips, too. And one owner I visited, Jerry Liss in Bowling Green, Ohio, was so intrigued with my methods that he came to visit me in Ypsilanti to see them in operation. We later became competitors as Domino's grew, and our friendship created some interesting complications for me.

Perhaps the most important thing I learned on these research trips was that everyone is convinced that his pizza is the best in town. It didn't matter what kind he was making—thin or deep-dish—and it didn't matter how appealing or awful his pizza was. He thought it was great. "Why is this?" I asked myself. Then I figured it out. These pizza people were getting their feedback from their own customers. If you only listen to people who like your product, of course you're going to hear good things about it.

That was an important turning point for me, because it taught me that I'd better examine my own product pretty carefully, using unbiased subjects. That's what led me to taste tests. At one time, we had a panel of blind people as tasters. I'd read somewhere that a blind person's senses of taste and smell are sharper than those of a sighted person. Our taste tests were fascinating and led to a major improvement in the blend of spices we use in our secret sauce.

My concern with customer reactions also led me to devise my own man-in-the-street public opinion survey. I used it for years whenever I was in the vicinity of a Domino's store. I'd ask people where I could get a good pizza, and if they said Domino's, I'd ask them why it was so good. They'd describe it in their own words, which frequently was very revealing. If they mentioned some other pizza place, I'd ask if they'd heard of Domino's. They'd often say "Oh yeah, it's good," or "It's not so good." I'd ask them what was wrong with it or what they liked about it. I interviewed thousands of people this way. Often, I would have the franchisee who owned the store in the area along with me when I'd do my little survey, and he'd really squirm and sweat out the answers. If the person I was interviewing didn't like the product, I'd hand him a business card, tell him I was embarrassed about his response, and explain what Domino's was trying to do. I'd encourage him to give us another try.

One terrific idea I picked up in our Monday travels came from a place called Dino's in Detroit. It was a well-run operation that later grew into a chain of about 170 stores. I introduced myself to one of the owners, Benny Laquinta, and he gave me a tour of his place. Everything looked familiar enough until I saw them sliding pizzas into the ovens on round screens. That stopped me in my tracks. Benny explained that the screens allowed the heat to get to the pizzas fast enough, and made the pies easier to handle, both going into and coming out of the oven. To put an uncooked pizza in the oven, a pizza maker used to set the pie directly on a wooden paddle or "peel" that looks like a short-handled oar. He shoved the paddle into the oven and yanked it out from under the pizza like a magician whipping a tablecloth out from under a table setting. This motion required delicate timing and took a lot of practice to master. Some pizza makers used cornmeal on the paddle to keep the pizza from sticking to it; I never liked corn-meal because it made a mess of the oven deck. My method was to use a little flour. Screens eliminated the sticking problem. They also made shoving pizzas into the oven a breeze, which cut train-ing time for pizza makers nearly in half. What a pleasure it was to see every pie come out round! In the old days, before screens, half our pies came out oval shaped, and many of them were "crew pies" our term for a pizza so bad it can't be sent to a customer and is eaten by the employees. I wish I had a penny for every second of time screens have saved us in the years since we adopted them.

Over three years, Margie and I must have visited three hun-dred pizzerias. Somewhere in a box in our basement I have re-cords of each one and mementos from many of them. It didn't matter to me whether a place was fancy or just a dump; if it had a sign saying PIZZA, I wanted to investigate it. Margie would sit in the car with Mary and Susie while I went in and checked the place out.

We drove over to Chicago several times, primarily for the res-taurant show, which was about the closest thing we had to a vacation for years. Chicago, of course, is regarded as one of the capitals of pizza. Ike Sewell had founded two pizzerias there, Uno and Due, which became famous for deep-dish pizza. I found them interesting, though not as busy as I'd been led to believe they were.

There was another place in Chicago, the Home Run Inn, that was billed as the busiest pizza place in the world. It, too, was a disappointment. It made a lot of wholesale pizzas that were sold through grocery stores, but that's another type of business en-tirely.

The place I really wanted to see most, though, was called Father and Son, because it advertised that it had thirty-two delivery men. That was astounding to me, since nine or ten delivery men at a store was usually tops for us. I couldn't imagine one store doing that much business. And I was right to be skeptical. They may have had thirty-two delivery men, but they each must have made only one trip a night, because the place wasn't doing as much business as we were in Ypsilanti. That was a real letdown. The trip paid off, however, in a way I never expected. Father and Son introduced me to an exciting new concept: the mechanical oven. This was a monster of an oven that had a big Ferris wheel assembly of trays on the inside. Pizzas were placed on the trays to cook as the wheel revolved. I yearned to get my hands on one of those ovens. I bought one that fall. My second one was the world's largest pizza oven, a fabulous piece of machinery we called Big Red.

I wasn't going to these places to compare the size of their operations and see if Domino's was really the largest in the world. I was looking for methods I could use to handle more business. The tempo in our stores was increasing every night, and we were hard put to take care of it. I even told Sam Fine when he called me about placing some advertising: "Don't get us more business, Sam, get us more help. Advertise for some good managers." He came up with a newspaper ad that said: "Get your hands in our dough . . ." and it brought us some good help.

Late in the fall '65, I began looking for another location in Ann Arbor to replace the loss of Pizza King. I needed another location on the University of Michigan campus to bolster the Prop. Besides, as I told Margie, "Little Caesars is growing in Detroit, and we need to get Washtenaw County sewed up so tight that competition can't penetrate it."

I felt confident I could take on another store now, because Margie's handling of our books had made it possible to meet our payroll consistently and keep all our bills current.

In looking around Ann Arbor, I made a point of having lunch with Howard Miller, one of our equipment salesmen. He had terrific contacts, and he kept up with things that were going on around town. I told Howard what I was looking for, and he suggested I contact Jim Gilmore about buying the Pizza King store from him. That hadn't occurred to me. I hadn't seen Jim since we dissolved our partnership. But Howard thought Jim just might be ready to sell, and he would know, because his company, Serwer's Wholesalers, Inc., of Detroit, was one of Gilmore's major creditors. It sounded like an interesting possibility.

Coincidentally, Gilmore's name came to my attention again a few days later, this time in the form of a notice that he was behind on a note.

"Damn!" I thought. "I hope that old rascal isn't up to more of his tricks." I was too busy with Domino's to take on any problems caused by Gilmore, yet I had to think about his well-being and pray for his survival, because if he ever went under, he'd pull me under with him.

After considering all sides of the idea, I decided that if Jim really wanted to sell, it would be wise for me to buy Pizza King from him. It would solve two problems: first, it would give me a store with an ideal location on the U of M campus; second, if Gilmore could concentrate on running just one restaurant, it would enhance his chances of surviving.

I could see no serious down side to it, so I contacted Jim and offered to take Pizza King off his hands. As Howard Miller had suspected, he was glad to get rid of it. So we began negotiating. This was never an easy matter with Gilmore. He was a heads-I-win, tails-you-lose guy.

Finally, in February 1966, we completed the deal. I was to pay Gilmore six thousand dollars, a relatively small amount, but I agreed to assume ten thousand dollars' worth of debt on the place. This, I hoped, would take the heat off him so he could satisfy his other creditors. I borrowed two thousand dollars from the bank, using my house trailer as collateral, and gave the cash to Jim as a down payment.

My payments on the note were steep in comparison with what I was paying on my other stores, so I thought it would take some time to generate enough sales to give me a profit. But by sticking to our knitting and concentrating on pizza delivery, the store did more business right off the bat than it had been doing for Gilmore.

Since money was tight, I had to cut corners wherever possible, and my plans for remodeling the store proceeded more slowly than I would have liked. My first move was to change the sign to DOMINO's. Then, since I was using only a small part of the equipment Gilmore had in the place, I started looking around for buyers for all the non-pizza hardware.

The store soon eliminated the need to make long campus delivery runs from our shop in the old Pizza from the Prop location, so both stores improved. This, of course, was exactly what I'd hoped would happen. I could see that my forecast for the campus store was going to be met easily. It would soon be challenging the weekly sales volume of our Cross Street store.

We put a classified ad in the *Ann Arbor News* for drivers. It drew a good response, and among the student applicants hired was a guy named Robert Cotman. He was driving a 1963 Chevrolet Corvair, which I remember well, because one night I was stranded without a car when the store closed and he gave me a ride home. He'd seemed quiet, almost diffident, when I watched him at work, but on this drive we immediately got into a conversation. He said he was an architecture student at Michigan, which set him apart for me, of course, and it turned out that we had similar tastes in design. He was twenty-one years old and was completely at sea about his future.

"My problem is that there are so many things I like to do," he said. "I have more than a hundred credit hours, and you only need ninety to graduate, but I haven't majored in anything. I'm still a sophomore in terms of concentration. I have taken Beginning Everything."

Cotman turned out to be a good pizza maker, and he and I clicked. One night a couple of weeks after he started working inside, I found a bottle of wine in the Prop store and had to get rid of the manager. I told Cotman I wanted him to take over the store and assured him that I'd help him get started. After a few nights he asked me how to manage a store, and I said, "Well, you just watch every individual customer. You make each customer happy."

"Okay, how do I know I'm doing that?"

"You keep watching the orders. If you make each customer happy, they will reorder. They'll stay with you and they'll tell someone else. So each week your sales will go up a little bit. To manage the store, all you have to do is make the sales go up a little bit each week."

I didn't tell him that there might be weeks when sales wouldn't go up. So he went in there and made the sales go up each week for thirteen weeks—thirteen record weeks in a row—which was an astonishing accomplishment. It stood as the record until about 1982.

Cotman was always the star of our weekly management meetings. He prepared his reports thoroughly and illustrated them with charts and graphs. His approach complemented mine, which was analytical and pragmatic: I'd ask myself, What are we doing, based on sales and demographics, and what should we be doing to improve? Each morning I got all the sales slips from every store and went over them carefully, so I knew precisely when and where we were delivering pizzas, and I would try to discern patterns and principles in them that could be applied elsewhere.

Sometimes I would drive to a competitor's store and just sit there in the car for several hours watching what they were doing. I'd try to estimate how much business they had and think about what they might do to be more successful, which in turn would tell me things we might do to make Domino's more successful.

I'd do the same thing at our own stores. I'd sit there in the car, maybe with Cotman or another manager, and just watch the store, keeping track of how many drivers left it during a fifteen-minute period and how many pizzas each one was carrying. I'd estimate how many dollars' worth of business they were doing in an hour. Now that may seem a bit odd, because I could have simply gone in and asked the manager for those numbers. But the numbers weren't the important thing. What was important was the intellectual exercise, providing a medium for stimulating significant observations about our business. It was totally absorbing and extremely satisfying.

On a more practical plane, I was coming to grips with the idea of expanding the business beyond Washtenaw County. Franchising on the McDonald's model was an obvious approach, and I kicked around a lot of ideas for tiptoeing into that arena. Up to this point, my policy had been very conservative, a step-by-step pace, making sure that each operation was able to pay its own way before opening another one. But franchising clearly was the way for us to go.

It was an exciting time. Everything was really beginning to come together. I could visualize Domino's stores springing up in all kinds of college towns. I already had my sights set on East Lansing and Michigan State University. After we got our franchise act together, Lansing would be the next big plum on the tree for me.

But on November 8, 1966, I got a telephone call from a very sober sounding Larry Sperling. "I hate to tell you this, Tom," he said. "But I've just been talking to Jim Gilmore's attorney, and he is filing for bankruptcy!"

O N THE THURSDAY AFTER THANKSGIVING 1966, I sat
down with my wife in the living room of our house
trailer and gave her the news I had been struggling to
avoid.

"Honey," I said. "I don't really know how to tell you this after
all we've been through together with Domino's. But it looks like
this is it."

Margie knew the problem. The principal holder of notes
against the mortgage on Gilmore's Restaurant had me on the
hook for fifty-two thousand dollars. But that wasn't all. There
was an additional seven thousand dollars in secured debt against
the equipment in the restaurant, plus a large unsecured loan.
Then there were stacks of unpaid utility bills and city taxes, plus
sales and withholding taxes due. In total, I owed more than seventy-five thousand dollars. Larry Sperling and I had been scurry-
ing around negotiating with all the different creditors. Most were

willing to work out a deal. We had found a solid buyer for the place, an experienced restaurant-management professional named Panos. But the note holder was unreasonable, in my opinion. He had demanded his money in full—the whole fifty-two thousand. If he continued on that course and rejected the plan of selling to Panos, he would force me into bankruptcy.

"Sperling had a final meeting with him this morning," I told Margie, "and the answer is no. He says he wants the money. In cash. Now!"

That evening, there was a meeting of the Washtenaw Restaurant Association at the Heidelberg Restaurant in Ann Arbor. I attended, but I was in a state of shock. I felt numb all over. My eyes weren't focusing; I didn't hear what people were saying to me. I recall being steered up to a young man who was introduced as the owner of the Heidelberg, Fritz Kochendorer. He stuck his hand out to shake, and I just stood there looking at it thinking it was the biggest hand I'd ever seen in my life.

I couldn't make myself accept the fact that there would be no more Domino's Pizza. I couldn't imagine such an end to everything I'd worked to build. The sad part was that I'd built up a good volume by never taking anything out of Domino's; everything was sacrificed for the future of the business. Now, that future was going down the tubes.

Early the next morning, I got a telephone call from Sperling. He was so excited he was stuttering and babbling. After making his ultimatum the day before, the creditor had changed his mind and now said he would allow Panos to buy the restaurant and assume the debt. So all I had to do was pay up the six months' worth of installments that were in arrears.

In retrospect, I think the ultimatum had been a ploy to try and squeeze the cash out of me. The note holder probably thought I had plenty, since Domino's was doing so well. It's true that the company was bringing in a lot of money, but I wasn't keeping it. If it hadn't been for Margie's ability to scrimp and save, we wouldn't have had a penny, because all our income was committed. When it became evident that I couldn't pay, the note holder relented.

The sale of Gilmore's Restaurant went smoothly. No cash changed hands in the deal, except $3,500 that Panos paid to the landlord, the utility companies, and the property tax office. The note holder not only accepted Panos's assumption of the notes, he even lowered the monthly payments! I was delighted; I wanted Panos to succeed, because I was still liable; if he failed, I was back on the hook again.

It was nice to have the secured creditors off my back. That took care of $55,000 of the $75,000 in debts. Now I had to deal with the $20,000 in unsecured claims, including some back sales taxes that Gilmore had failed to pay. I contacted all but one of the remaining creditors and let them know I intended to pay them. It would take time, but they would get every cent of their money. The creditor I didn't contact was the state director of tax collection. A burly deputy from his office was after me, threatening to throw me in jail, so I let Sperling handle this one. He wrote a letter requesting that the amount of sales tax we owed be reduced and that Panos be granted a tax license without posting a $1,500 bond. In the letter, which by the way accomplished its purpose, he summarized the outcome of our involvement as follows:

". . . If Gilmore's Restaurant, Inc., had gone into bankruptcy, all the assets would have been repossessed by the secured creditors and sold for considerably less than the secured indebtedness. Many people would have suffered severe financial loss, there would have been not one penny for payment of past-due sales taxes, and the restaurant probably would have (remained) closed, unproductive, and paying no sales tax at all for many months while the bankruptcy proceedings went on. Because of the action we took, we were able to salvage some of the value of the business and put in a new, productive owner who is paying substantial sums of sales tax . . ."

As it turned out, I think I was the only one who *suffered severe financial loss,* although Sperling certainly wasn't a big winner on the deal. For all his hours of grueling effort, his bill to me was only $2,500. Sometimes it seemed that he was more personally involved than I was. For example, he had telephoned me at home that Thanksgiving Day, when we were in the midst of our negotiations with creditors, and said:

"Hi, Tom, what are you doing?"

"Well, if I weren't talking on the phone to you right now, I'd be sitting at the table with my family eating Thanksgiving dinner."

"What!" he shouted in mock anger. "You mean to tell me that I'm here in my office slaving away trying to save your skin and you're lazing around and gorging yourself on turkey?"

I explained that I took only three days off a year: Thanksgiving, Christmas, and Easter. I don't remember what else we discussed, but there was some suggestion that I should choke on the wishbone.

"I trust you'll visit me in the hospital," he said, "when they're treating me for nervous exhaustion and the ulcers you've no doubt given me!"

Although we're still good friends, time has moved on and the pressures of business prevent Sperling and me from seeing each other much these days. But when we do get together, I'm sure some of the newer hands around Domino's wonder how we can laugh so hard at recollections of "the bad old days." I guess the answer is that we managed to survive them.

In the early years, Sperling was on Domino's board of directors—Margie and I were the only other members at that time—so naturally, I had told him about my hopes for getting into franchising. He said he had an acquaintance named Chuck Gray who might be a good candidate as a franchisee. Gray had a lot of experience in state and local politics, and I was impressed with him at our first meeting. I was especially gratified by his enthusiasm for Domino's.

I took Gray over to Ecorse Road on the east side of Ypsilanti and showed him our operation there. We had moved it to a new location down the road from Marty's Diner, and it was beginning to make money. Gray liked it, so we worked out an arrangement for him to purchase it. I promised him I would train him personally, and I was glad I did. Gray had a natural talent for the pizza business. It was interesting to see how he took hold and how he made that store's sales blossom after he took it over.

Sperling drafted a franchise agreement, which we signed on April 1, 1967. It gave us 2½ percent of Gray's sales as a royalty, another 2 percent for advertising, and 1 percent for providing all his bookkeeping, from P&L statement to payroll, all of which was done by my wife. By today's standards, the royalties were far too favorable to the franchisee. But it served our purpose then, and I was not concerned about covering all possible future contingencies.

My impatience with legal technicalities kept getting me into arguments with Sperling. He nagged at me to slow down and pay more attention to managing the company. He was always telling me: "You've got to get your costs under control, Tom. You are great at generating business; sales are terrific. But your net is nowhere near commensurate with your gross." That was true, but I was concerned about building a base. "You don't understand," I told him. "You can always cut costs. Any idiot can cut costs. But you can't always build sales, and that's what I am doing."

Larry's gripe about what he called my "cavalier attitude" toward legal details was expressed in a letter that I pinned on my bulletin board as a reminder to myself. It said:

"Marjorie brought in the Security Agreement to Huff Refrigeration that you and she signed . . .

"I just wanted you to know that the way you handled and executed this agreement violated every principle of operation that I have suggested to you in the handling of your business affairs, and may cause us many problems in the future."

I wished I could be more careful about such matters, but in truth, I was much more concerned about sales and the people who were working for me. By this time I had about a hundred fifty employees, and I was determined to maintain our high morale and excellent communications.

One of the people I worried about was Bob Cotman. He kept saying he wanted to be in advertising. I made a decision that I wouldn't promote anyone who didn't have his heart in the pizza business, even if he was one of the best managers I'd seen. After thinking it over, I decided to bring Bob into the office and gave him all kinds of miscellaneous chores to justify paying him sixty dollars a week. That was a big cut in salary for him, but he didn't seem to mind. He took over *The Pepperoni Press*, a weekly company newsletter that I started in 1966 and often wrote myself. He also became a kind of administrative assistant to me. I told him he could live in the apartment on the second floor of the Cross Street house, and since his salary was so low, I made his rent only fifteen dollars a week.

Cotman's lowly position did have one perk: After he'd been on the job for a while and was doing well at it, I bought him a 1949 Bentley as a company car. I'd wanted to get him a used Rolls-Royce but couldn't find one I could afford. The Bentley, which I got for thirteen hundred dollars, was truly elegant. It had plush upholstery and carpeting, a sun roof, and a retractable radio antenna. Cotman loved that car. He kept it spotless, even though at times he had to use it for a van. He even hauled bricks and lumber in it when I assigned him to build a store on Packard Road in Ann Arbor.

The Packard Road unit would be the first Domino's store to be built from scratch, within a vacant structure. I picked up the lease on the building because I thought Dean Jenkins was ready to handle it as a franchisee. Dean had been so methodical when he first came to work for me that his fellow crew members called him Slow Motion. I'd forced him to become a fast pizza maker. His goal at first had been to own a doughnut shop someday; now he was doing a good job of managing our campus store. I wanted to make him our second franchisee, partly as a reward for his efforts and partly because I wanted to help him fulfill his dream of having his own business.

We had a lot of unforseen problems in getting that store completed, but we improvised in various ways. We had to scrounge up second-hand fixtures, and ended up using bricks for oven bases when legs failed to show up. Improvisation has grown into an operational style among our store-development people: *Think fast, solve problems on the spot, and don't worry about finding out what caused any screw-ups until after you've got the store open.* In this and many other ways during this period, we were setting the whole tone for the development of Domino's in years to come.

In the beginning years, there were also some early signs of future problems. Robbery, for example. Our first manager to have someone come in and demand money at gunpoint did exactly the wrong thing. He refused to give the guy the money. He just stood there and stared the gunman down. Luckily, there was no incident. In later years, we hired a sophisticated security force that developed policies for dealing with such intruders.

In July 1967, when Jenkins's franchise was running smoothly, I decided the time had arrived to grab the big plum: a location in East Lansing. The reason I saw this as such a ripe, juicy market was that Michigan State had twenty thousand students housed in dormitories, more than any other university. At that time I knew, within 5 or 10 percent, the dorm capacity of every college in the country. I also knew the comparative breakdown at each school between men's dorms and women's (a lot more pizzas are ordered from men's dorms) as well as their total enrollment.

Sperling, in his typically cautious way, wanted to be sure that if our venture into Lansing didn't work out, it wouldn't jeopardize our operations in Washtenaw County. So we set up a separate corporation, Domino's of Lansing, Inc., with me as sole stockholder. I went along with his plan, but I certainly wasn't planning to fail.

In fact, I had come up with a concept for Lansing that I was excited about. It was simplicity itself: First, build a company store and commissary on campus; that commissary could then serve other stores, which would be franchised in the surrounding residential area. Each new store added would make the existing ones stronger.

Another concept I was eager to try was selling twelve-inch pizzas only. In Ypsilanti, at least 80 percent of the orders from dorms were for twelve-inch pizzas. So why have any other size? If customers wanted more pizza, they could order two or three twelve-inchers. I was thinking of installing a computerized order-taking system, so I wanted to have as few variables as possible. With this in mind, I cut the choices of toppings down to six. The computerized system didn't get going, but limiting the menu was still a good idea.

The main argument for having only twelve-inch pizzas was faster service. But quality would be improved, too. A pizza maker has to learn how to make each size pie. The twelve-incher is easiest. Larger ones are much harder: Applying the cheese and toppings takes more skill, and they are more difficult to handle. If you're doing nothing but twelve-inchers, you can become proficient as a pizza maker twice as fast.

There would be fewer mistakes, too, both in taking orders and boxing them. With three sizes of pies and just two inches difference between them, it sometimes happened during a rush that a worker would ruin a large pie by trying to jam it into a medium-size box or mess up a medium by putting it in a small box.

Then there were the savings we would make in purchasing. Having one size would cut our box inventory requirements by two-thirds. It would also eliminate the time it took our dough makers in the commissary to switch sizes.

The only problem with my single-size plan was the negative reaction of the people who opened the Lansing store. They all thought I had lost my mind, and they complained about it so much that after about eight months I pulled back. I decided that maybe I was wrong. We compromised by eliminating the medium pizza and going with two sizes, small and large—twelve- and sixteen-inchers. I can see now that I should have stood firm. The effect would have been the same as when I eliminated subs or the little six-inch pizzas back in DomiNick's. When the manager of that Lansing store saw how much more he was making by selling twelve-inch pizzas only, he would have loved the idea.

Even though the plan was altered, it set the pattern for having two sizes instead of three, and within the next year we eliminated the fourteen-inch pizza from all Domino's stores.

One of the memorable events connected to that first Lansing store was the installation of Big Red, the world's largest pizza oven. It had ten Ferris-wheel trays, each twelve feet long. Theoretically, it would hold at least nine twelve-inch pizzas on each tray, baking 90 at a time. At first, it seemed oversized. It was like using a blast furnace to grill hamburgers. But the day would come when we managed to make Big Red strain to keep up with orders.

The Lansing store was a hotbed of innovation, thanks to a young manager named Terry Voice, who made Domino's history by inventing the strip stub for taking pizza orders. Instead of copying orders from a sales slip onto the side of the pizza box, which led to errors and blurred directions, the phone person writes the order only once on a self-carbon strip form. The strip indicates the time the order was placed, the customer's address and phone number and, sometimes, information helpful to delivery men, such as "watch out for neighbor's German shepherd!" The original is torn from the order book and handed to the pie maker. It then moves down the line with the pie, serving as a check for proper toppings before the pizza is put into the oven. Then the strip is taped to the box and awaits delivery. This simple form added immensely to our speed and accuracy.

One of the toughest things I've had to deal with in developing Domino's is loss of a talented person who has contributed a great deal and who leaves for what I think are the wrong reasons. Terry Voice was one of those people. He joined us in Ypsilanti as a driver and was promoted to manager in Lansing. He and I became good friends, and I was best man at his wedding. But I think his wife saw Domino's as competition. It's easy to see how a wife might feel that way, but it can make things difficult. I've been blessed in this respect personally, because Margie has always been at my side, helping me in Domino's. Our business can put a lot of stress on marital relationships, and we try to help through our company-sponsored Partners program. Members have their own newsletter and share ideas at regular meetings and outings. Whenever I talk to the group, I tell them they shouldn't hesitate to seek marriage counseling. Margie and I do, and it helps us, even though we have a strong marriage.

I wish we'd had something like Partners when Terry Voice was still with us, although I can't say that his wife was the only reason, or even the main reason, he left Domino's in August 1969. Some of his problems might have been my fault. But the upshot was that he went off to Wisconsin to start his own pizzerias. He also got divorced. Sometime later, when our paths happened to cross at a convention, Terry told me he wondered what his career would have been like if he'd stayed with us. Unfortunately, we'll never know.

Another highly talented guy who left a mark on Domino's and whose loss I regret—mostly because I think I contributed to his problems—was Dave Kilby. I first met Dave in 1963, when he was working for General Motors as a labor-relations analyst; he ran a free-lance advertising agency on the side. I hired him to do a little radio copywriting for Domino's. Then in 1967, the Ypsilanti Junior Chamber of Commerce put on a pizza sale. I was a very active Jaycee, and the sale may have been my idea—I don't recall. At any rate, Kilby and I worked together on it. He was past president of our chapter, and we hit it off well. He was a handsome guy, polished and articulate, and also extremely energetic.

Kilby seemed interested in what I was doing with Domino's, and we talked about his becoming a franchisee. He was tentative about it and couldn't seem to make up his mind. However, he had known Chuck Gray when Gray was secretary of the Ypsilanti Township Board of Commissioners, and when Gray bought his franchise, Kilby decided that he would come in, too.

Dave bought the store that had been Pizza from the Prop, on West Stadium Boulevard in Ann Arbor, for $10,000 with no money down. I helped him finance it. I trained him personally, spending almost as much time with him as I had with Gray, and sales in the store increased dramatically after he took over. I was really impressed. That performance added to my already high estimation of him. He had a degree in political science, which I think he got by going to night school at Eastern for twelve years. I was impressed by that, too, as well as his experience as an executive with General Motors.

As we worked side by side in his store during his training period, I told Dave about all the problems I'd had in organizing the business. He made some excellent suggestions. He said he'd like to work in our office part-time. So we worked out an arrangement for him to spend twenty hours a week consulting with us at headquarters, on Cross Street. The rest of his time, of course, would be spent tending his own store.

I wanted to put Kilby's office in the second-floor apartment, so Bob Cotman moved his bedroom and layout tables for the *Pepperoni Press* out onto a screened porch above the garage, where we kept the Bentley. Our building became a kind of entrepreneurial tenement, with the store, the commissary, our offices, and Cotman's living quarters packed into its aging confines. It was charged with an atmosphere of excitement that seemed to touch everyone who worked there.

I told Kilby that one of the first things I wanted him to do was to compile a store-operations manual. He and Cotman worked on it, using some instruction sheets that a manager named John Correll had put together for his store in Lansing. I was eager to get such a manual printed, as it would reduce the amount of time I was spending on training people. I felt my own effort would be more profitably directed to franchise expansion.

I knew I had a great deal to learn in order to fully exploit the potential of Domino's, so I attended every trade show, meeting, and seminar that seemed likely to help me. My schedule grew even more crazy than ever.

During these years, on a typical day I would get up at about ten o'clock in the morning and check in at the office. There were always problems to deal with there. Then I'd have a business lunch and meetings afterward until about 4:30 P.M., when I'd go to the commissary and check on the work there. After dinner at home, every night was spent checking on stores and brainstorming with managers and Kilby and Cotman. I rarely returned home until 4:30 A.M. It was a bizarre existence, but also very stimulating. Ideas were popping out of my head like mad. I was constantly doing store layouts, using graph paper and paper squares to represent ovens and other equipment. I turned Cross Street into an "automated" store. Howard Miller helped me design an elaborate system of roller conveyers that allowed pizza boxes, pulled from special gravity-feed bins, to move along automatically from order taker to pizza maker to oven tender to delivery rack. It worked like a charm. Unfortunately, it couldn't be easily duplicated in other stores.

Kilby made an immediate impact at headquarters, but it was not quite what I'd expected. Suddenly, the place was buried in a blizzard of paperwork. I've never seen such a fanatic for forms and office supplies. I admired his drive and enthusiasm, but I had the feeling that a lot of his effort was unnecessary. Our little business didn't need that much paperwork. I asked myself whether I should put the brakes on him, but I failed to do it. I should have. Both Dave and Domino's would have been a lot better off if I had.

My problem in dealing with Kilby was that I didn't want to dampen his enthusiasm. He could think big, and that was rare. I thought big, too. The difference was that I had to pay for the ideas and he didn't.

We ended the year 1967 with a net profit of about fifty thousand dollars. Larry Sperling thought it should have been a lot more, but I was pretty happy with that sum. At least I was able to get clear of the debt from Gilmore's Restaurant. In addition to that obligation, however, there were a lot of other debts to be paid: There were lease and equipment payments on the three new stores (with the addition of the Lansing shop, Domino's now had a total of six units), plus the payments on the dozen Checker cabs I'd purchased for use as delivery cars.

All in all, it had been a great year. Margie and I celebrated the holidays in our first real house, a brick ranch home in the countryside between Ann Arbor and Ypsilanti. We were both pleased with it, even though it had no basement. Margie was especially glad to get our two kids out of the trailer.

My joy in ringing in the new year was diluted a bit by two sour notes. One was Chuck Gray's attitude. He seemed to find something to complain about every time I saw him. I found this hard to comprehend, since his store had grown steadily more profitable. It had been grossing about fifteen hundred dollars a week when he took it over, and now was taking in at least twice that. But he was never satisfied with the commissary charges, and he argued with Margie about the bookkeeping. He was a fiercely independent person who didn't take to franchising. It was ironic that the first person I picked as a franchisee was one who seemed better suited to being his own boss.

The other sour note was Bob Cotman's draft notice. We were disappointed to be losing him, because he and Kilby and I were beginning to work very well together.

Dave Kilby had been spending more and more time at headquarters, and I decided he could do the job of supervising store managers that I'd been intending to give to Cotman. Dave agreed to hire someone to run his own store and to come to work for me full-time. I needed him, because I was determined to make 1968 a year of tremendous growth for Domino's. And so it might have been but for an event that took place early in the morning of February 8, 1968.

I was jarred out of a deep sleep by the telephone. The night before had been slow, a Wednesday, and I had gone to bed early because we had a busy weekend coming up. The glow of the alarm clock showed me it was 3:00 A.M., and I was disoriented. The phone buzzed again, bringing me out of bed in a bound as I realized that something must be wrong. The caller was a former employee of mine who was now driving a taxicab in Ypsilanti.

"Tom," he barked. "Your store is on fire!"

I careened out of our drive and sped down the icy roads to Cross Street in record time. I was praying, as I always do in stressful situations. There was a lot of smoke and several fire engines were parked around the building when I pulled up, but there seemed to be no blaze. As I was getting out of my car, however, a sheet of flame shot up the side of the house. I went running around looking for someone to tell me what was going on, and I spotted Bob Cotman in the backyard, jumping up and down, yelling at me.

Bob's teeth were chattering with cold, and he was so excited he could hardly blurt out what had happened. It seems he had come home from a party slightly tipsy the night before. He realized he was out of cigarettes and was trying to decide whether he should go out and get a pack or do some work. He went up to his office and shuffled some papers around, then stretched out on the floor behind his desk and fell asleep about midnight. He awakened sweating a few hours later. The floor was hot. The wall was hot. He could see red lights flashing against the ceiling. So he ran back to the balcony of the porch and saw a fireman on a ladder.

"I yell down at him, 'Where's the fire!'" Bob said. "He points right beneath me.

"'What are you doing up there?' he says.

"'I live here,' I say.

"'No you don't. The neighbor told us nobody lives here, it's just an office.'

"'Well, I live here anyhow.'

"So he says okay, he believes me, and I ask him how bad it is. Should I get my stuff out? He says yes. It's bad. He's getting the ladder up to me. So I run back to the office and start stuffing papers in my briefcase. Then I walk to the hall door to see how bad it is, and when I open it, the smoke just blasts out at me. I panic and run toward the balcony again, except I miss and end up in the closet. I shout, 'My God, I'm in the closet!' And I think, *Reader's Digest* says to get your clothes out, they won't be covered by insurance, so I grab a pile of laundry under my arm, get out of the closet, and run to the porch. I toss this pile of clothes down, and they all land in a huge puddle. I stand there watching my clothes sink into the muddy water. Then the fireman is in front of me saying, 'You'd better get down from here, son.' So I go down the ladder with him."

Bob then got the Bentley out of the garage and parked it down the street. Next, he ran into the commissary section on the ground floor of the building and tried to cover up the machinery with some canvas. All the while the firemen were yelling at him to get out of there. So he came out and grabbed a big propane tank at the rear of the building and rolled it over into the neighbor's yard so it wouldn't explode.

The flames had subsided again by this time, and I could see big holes in the building with water dripping through, and it made me sick to my stomach. An inventory of all the things we were losing in that place kept running through my mind, and I felt weak and helpless. Then the fire burst back out with an awful swoosh, and the firemen just stood there. They didn't seem concerned at all. That made me mad.

One fireman was squirting water from the top of a high ladder, but he wasn't shooting it where the flames were. He was missing them! So I ran over and clambered up the ladder beside him to point out where he should aim the hose. He was really amazed to find me there with him, but he followed my pointing and shifted the stream onto the fire.

It didn't do much good, though. When daylight came, Bob and I stood there wrapped in blankets, drinking coffee from tin mugs someone had given us, and it was obvious that the house was completely gutted.

"Listen, Bob," I said. "What we have to do right now is get busy and figure out a way to get food to the stores so they can open tonight. Don't worry about this mess. We'll come out all right. I'm insured."

It was a comforting thought, but I learned a few days later that I was whistling in the dark.

I T WAS A GRIM-FACED GROUP of Domino's employees that gathered in Dave Kilby's house while the ruins of our headquarters were still smoking. The store had only received smoke damage, but the commissary and our offices were completely destroyed. Our remaining stores wouldn't be able to open for business unless we found a way to supply them with food.

I outlined my plan. Each of the stores would handle a single part of the commissary operation: One would make dough; another would slice pepperoni and ham; another, cheese; and so on. A special detail of drivers would run a pony express-style circuit, picking up and delivering food items from store to store. The response of everyone at the meeting was so positive, so enthusiastic, that I had no doubt we would come through in good shape. We did. Everyone from headquarters, including me, went into the stores to work, and I doubt we missed a single order.

In the days that followed, we got busy cleaning up the mess left by the fire and counting our losses.

We had to post guards around the clock to protect the ruins from vandalism. The Ypsilanti Jaycees helped us get temporary office space in a building owned by the chamber of commerce. They also volunteered a lot of muscle power to help us move what was salvageable from our headquarters and dispose of the rest. It did my heart good to see my buddies doing this for me.

The health department ruled that all food that had been stored in the commissary must be discarded. A lot of it appeared to be undamaged and perfectly good, but it had to go. In all, about $40,000 worth of supplies were trucked to the dump. Another significant part of our loss was in leasehold improvements: plumbing, wiring, and equipment we had installed. Added up, our loss came to almost $150,000.

Our insurance paid only $13,000. I had increased my coverage some, but not nearly enough to keep pace with what we were putting into the place. I didn't like dealing with insurance matters. But the sucker punch the insurance company hit me with was its refusal to pay for business disruption. In order to get reimbursed for that, I had to show that our costs of doing business had increased. Robert Boduck, my first controller, and I worked hard to prove this—I think we spent about $10,000 in accounting fees on it—but the insurance company allowed only $4,600 on that part of our claim. When I got the check, I said to Boduck, "This is what I paid thousands of dollars for?"

Finding a new headquarters was another problem. Not a single building large enough to house both our office and commissary was available in our price range in Ypsilanti. I had to settle for a small office above a barbershop at the end of a long stairs and a storefront nearby for the commissary. I organized the office, and Kilby took on the job of setting up the commissary. He and

Boduck were always arguing about expenditures. Boduck was a good counterbalance to Dave, but their budget meetings drove Boduck nuts.

Bad as they were, though, the financial loss and business dislocation were secondary to the dilemma I had with our new franchise program. Five new leases had been signed at the time of the fire. I was committed to paying rent on them. So while I was cutting back on all corporate spending and trying to figure out ways to cover our fire losses, on the other hand I was in the midst of the biggest expansion in our history: nearly doubling the number of stores. I was retrenching and expanding at the same time!

In order to get these new stores going and paying royalties as soon as possible, I had to find trained people as franchisees. Gene Belknap, who was managing one of our Ann Arbor stores, was my first candidate. I knew that he and his girlfriend, Becky Blackburn, were pretty committed to one another. She was a student at Eastern and worked in his store part-time. I figured that when they got married, they'd make a great pair of Domino's operators. I told them I'd help them buy a store, and they jumped at the opportunity. I borrowed the money, $25,000, from Eldon Huff, an equipment supplier and good friend of mine, who had his own finance company. Gene agreed to pay me back at the rate of $844.19 a month. That was a lot of money for a guy who was just opening a new store, but I was confident he could make it. We had a franchising agreement, of course, but the loan was between us, done on a handshake.

Gene had started with us three years earlier—I'll never forget the day he came in and applied for a job, saying he had experience making pizzas at a place in Jackson. He was a skinny guy with a great big cast on his right arm, which he'd broken in a fall down some stairs. I felt sorry for him and couldn't turn him away. But hiring him didn't make much sense: I wasn't doing too well, yet I was taking on a pizza maker who couldn't make pizzas. I put him on the phones and found he couldn't write very well left-handed, either. But eventually, after his arm healed, he turned out to be a good all-around pizza man.

While I was working on putting together the Belknap franchise deal, I got a phone call from my friend in Vermont, Steve Litwhiler. He'd been teaching school up there and didn't care for it. "It's kind of boring and the pay is lousy," he said. "I was making more as a pizza driver. What I'd like to do is set up a Domino's store up here. How about helping me get started? I don't have any money."

I had no interest in having a franchise way out in Vermont. But I liked Steve. He was one of the most dedicated and reliable employees I'd had. I trusted him completely. So I said, "Sure, Steve, I'll put you in business."

We exchanged a couple of letters in which I tried to outline what he needed to do to get started. But he had a hard time putting it together. He seemed unable to find a suitable location where he wanted to be in Burlington, near the University of Vermont. Finally, I decided to fly out there and give him a hand. Burlington is a difficult place to get into, and my flight was canceled due to bad weather.

I'd been taking flying lessons because I wanted to be able to get up to Lansing frequently to help supervise our store there—I felt that driving the 120-mile round trip wasted too much time. I'd also invested in a company plane, a Cessna 172. Eldon Huff, who was an expert pilot, had helped me pick it out, and it was sitting right out at the Ann Arbor Airport.

So I made up my mind that the decision of a commercial airline was not going to prevent me from going to Burlington. I'd just hop into the Cessna and buzz out there. I brushed aside the fact that I had only a student-pilot's license and had just soloed.

Hiring a pilot was out of the question; the company couldn't afford it. Besides, I was confident of my ability. Of course, it would have been better if I had known how to read all the instruments and how to operate the radio. But since I didn't, I thought, "What the heck. It's a nice clear day, so I can follow the landmarks, and shouldn't have any problem."

I had a map of the United States on my office wall, and the route I would follow was apparent at a glance: I would hug the northern shore of Lake Erie to Buffalo, then fly along the southern shore of Lake Ontario until I got to the St. Lawrence River, from which I'd head due east over the mountains to Lake Champlain and cross it to Burlington.

I stopped at a gas station on the way to the airport and bought a good road map. I figured that if I had to get away from the lake for some reason, I would need to pick up highways and follow them. Thus armed, I took off into the morning sun. I didn't file a flight plan, because I simply didn't know it was required and had never done one before. Our field was unregulated and had no control tower, so there was no one to ask where I was going.

Once aloft, I got a bit nervous as the broad, silvery scroll of Lake Erie unrolled beneath me. But I was determined to get to Burlington. My discomfort increased as I neared Buffalo and clouds began to close in. Soon I could no longer see anything. I pushed the nose down and descended a bit, but the clouds seemed to go all the way to the ground. I was sweating bullets now. I turned the radio to the only frequency I knew, Unicom, without much hope of picking up anything, because it's for use at unregulated fields. I was elated when I got a response to my call. I explained my problem with the radio, and the voice told me what button to push to reach the tower frequency. When I established contact and described my situation, the operator gasped in disbelief. Then his voice grew very measured and calm. He told me to turn north and fly to Niagara Falls, where I would find a break in the clouds.

It seemed like a wild goose chase and I was the goose. But after churning along blindly for what felt like hours, I busted through a hole in the clouds, and there was good old Mother Earth spread out to welcome me. However, when my radio contact said there was a forty-seven-knot wind, I still had a problem. I only knew how to land with the engine power turned almost off. "You're right," he said. "That is a problem. If you cut your power, the wind will blow you out over the lake." He patiently talked me down, telling me how much throttle to apply and how to adjust the attitude of the plane. I made a kangaroo landing and rolled to a stop near an ambulance and fire truck that were waiting to pick up the pieces. I was a basket case as soon as I climbed out of that plane. I made it the rest of the way to Burlington that day all right—by bus.

The rest of the trip was more successful. Steve and I found a good storefront location, which wasn't easy because all the buildings we looked at were genuine antiques. The custom in the area was ten-year leases. This made me a little apprehensive. I thought that any location we got now would be only temporary, so I talked the landlord into giving us a lease for ten one-year periods with options to renew.

As it turned out, Steve did stay there. I ordered all the equipment for him from our supplier, Eldon Huff, and arranged it to be trucked out to him.

I returned home by commercial plane, and one of our drivers who was a pilot picked up our plane in Niagara Falls and flew it back. Not long after that, in late April 1969, I was involved in another hair-raising flight, this time with an experienced pilot at the controls.

Dave Kilby and I had been laying plans to open franchises on all the major college campuses in the Midwest. I knew all the details of their enrollments and dorm capacities, so we listed them in order of potential as Domino's markets and arranged a very thorough series of scouting trips.

Our first target was Purdue University in Lafayette, Indiana, a predominantly male campus. We needed to look for possible store locations, see if it would be possible to go into the dorms to deliver, check out the competition to see what their prices were, and find out if we could strike a deal with a landlord.

Eldon Huff had agreed to fly us on these expeditions, but he couldn't make this one, so my flying instructor, who was a United Airlines pilot, agreed to take us. Terry Voice was still with us then, and we had transferred him back down to Ypsilanti from East Lansing with the intention of giving him a major role in operations when we launched our big franchising drive in the fall. For the time being, as we prepared to enter our summer slump, we assigned him to run one of our Ann Arbor stores. But the Purdue trip would be valuable training for his future position, so we asked him to come along.

Anyone who has lived in Ann Arbor for any length of time knows that from late fall to late spring, the area is prone to occasional ice storms that topple trees and pull down power lines. A nasty one was building on the morning we were to leave for Purdue. It didn't seem too bad yet when we were cleared for take-off; we thought we could get into the air and climb above it. But no sooner were we aloft and headed west than the windshield started growing a skin of ice. Of course, ice was forming on the wings too, and the pilot had his hands full trying to keep us in the air. He got on the radio to ask permission to make an emergency landing.

"No, no!" I yelled. "We can make it." And I started beating on the windshield with my fists, trying to knock the ice off.

The pilot told me to cut it out, that he was in charge of the blankety-blank plane. I was afraid he might have a heart attack, so I sat down. We tried to land at Tecumseh airport but couldn't. We headed for Willow Run airport, and the storm worsened as we approached. The instruments quit working, and the wind tossed us around in the sleet until it felt like we were being mixed in a giant milkshake. The pilot couldn't see through the windshield, but there was some visibility out the side windows, so Kilby and I each took a side and peered out, keeping up a running commentary on what we saw. When the runway lights appeared, we would call out how close they were and whether the pilot needed to move left or right. He brought us to a landing that, under the circumstances, was incredibly smooth. We had to practically chop our way out of that plane; it was an absolute cake of ice.

That experience put a freeze on our campus exploration program until after the summer. We felt we had to visit campuses while the schools were in session, or we'd miss some important details. But shortly thereafter, I had one more airplane adventure that was just about my swan song as a pilot.

I flew over to Pontiac one day that summer to see Eldon Huff. The ceiling was very low when I started back, and once again clouds closed in on me. In trying to ease myself below them, I lost control of the plane. It stalled, and I found myself in a spin. I pulled back on the control yoke with all my might, but I couldn't budge it. Plowed fields were whirling up toward me, and I realized there was nothing left to do but pray. I released the controls, closed my eyes, and folded my hands under my chin:

"Father in Heaven, please help me . . . ." I began, and I felt a miraculous change take place. The spinning stopped and suddenly the plane was flying level again. Chastened and thankful, I took it down to a landing. I vowed then that I'd never again attempt to pilot a plane if there was any kind of weather problem.

My instructor listened to my story and nodded sagely. "You did exactly the right thing," he said. "One way to get out of a spin is to release the controls. The plane will drop its nose and allow the wings to regain lift, which will take you right out of it."

I'm told that experts in aeronautics disagree about whether a Cessna 172 will come out of a spin that way. I have to believe my prayer helped it along.

There is a rather grim footnote to my experience with that plane. I sold it shortly afterward, and it wound up at the bottom of Lake Erie, crashing through the ice and killing its passengers, a family of four.

Domino's headquarters was a beehive of activity that summer. Everybody in Ypsilanti who had any money at all wanted to buy stock in the company or get a franchise. It was a pretty heady feeling to have people waving money at me like that. I refused to sell any stock, but Kilby and I were busy setting up a franchising plan that would allow outside investors to own quarter-shares in stores.

Our growth was just a symptom of the franchise fever that was sweeping the nation at the time. McDonald's and Kentucky Fried Chicken were widely copied, and all kinds of celebrities from "Broadway Joe" Namath, the New York Jets' quarterback, to Minnie Pearl, the queen of Nashville's Grand Ole Opry, were lending their names to restaurant chains. TV's Johnny Carson promoted a string of eateries called "Here's Johnny's" and baseball star Mickey Mantle was behind a chain of "country cookin'" restaurants. Boxer Rocky Graziano championed stores he called his "Pizza Ring."

Business magazines were packed with ads for franchising opportunities that appealed to what *U.S. News & World Report* called "a long-cherished American dream, 'to have a little business of our own.'" The magazine went on to state that the dream was sparking a whole new industry—franchising—that was "changing the face of retailing in this country."

From my perspective, of course, the boom was a blessing. We had just recovered from the losses of the fire, and we were getting positioned to take advantage of this surge of interest in franchising.

However, we had a few problems to iron out before we could move ahead with our store expansion that fall. One of them was our accounting. We couldn't seem to get caught up and produce current statements. The worst mess, though, was the commissary. The stores were complaining about the quality of the food and service they were getting. There was good evidence that as much food was being stolen as was being shipped to the stores. The operation was running into debt. I hadn't intended it to be profitable, but it had to make enough money to grow and improve, or it would be a ball and chain to us.

One day in August, the man who would be the solution to our commissary problem appeared. His name was Mike Paul, and Margie introduced him to me. He had worked with her on our payroll account at the Ypsilanti bank, and she was impressed with his quiet competence. He'd majored in business administration at Eastern Michigan but became impatient with classroom work and dropped out. In our brief interview, I discovered he'd picked up a lot of insights into Domino's and several other small businesses through his work in the bank. I was impressed, too, and turned him over to Kilby, who hired him and put him into a training program in one of our stores. He was to learn our system from the ground up by doing one particular job each week for five weeks. At the end of about three weeks, Mike came back into my office looking bewildered. He said he wasn't sure he'd made the right move. When he left his position with the bank, he hadn't expected to spend his days slapping out pizza dough. He was making about 40 percent more money, but he'd anticipated more responsibility. I told him to be patient, we'd find a job that would be challenging to him. Kilby and I talked it over and decided to let him run the commissary as soon as his training period was over.

After that move was made, Mike Paul never again fretted about being overpaid for the work he was doing. First he had to have his employees show him how the operation worked, which was really a case of the blind leading the blind. But he soon got a grip on the situation, identified the problems, and moved quickly to straighten them out. He fired more than half the staff, required those who remained to get haircuts and wear caps and aprons, and held frequent spot checks on fingernail cleanliness. It was amazing to see how favorably the employees responded to his gentle discipline. Complaints about food quality evaporated, and the losses stopped. The commissary grew vigorous and healthy during the seven months that Mike Paul was running it.

Some of the credit for Mike's success has to go to Dave Kilby. I admired Kilby's method of operation. He was extremely well organized. He always carried a yellow legal pad with a list of things to be done. When he completed something on the list, he'd scratch it off and go on to the next thing. I noticed that a lot of our people started imitating that practice, including me. I'd always jotted down "to-do" lists and written out my goals, but not in an organized way. I had used paper napkins or the back of paper placemats, any scraps of paper that were free. Up till then, I'd always thought legal pads cost too much, but I followed Kilby's lead.

I didn't agree with all the paperwork he created. His penchant for forms and voluminous correspondence had concerned me when he was in the office only part-time, but now that he had turned his store over to a manager and was with us full-time, it got worse. He ordered all kinds of business forms and stationery. He used company letterhead; I didn't. Kilby would dictate letters and always file copies. I doubt I had a single file folder. He kept hiring typists, and gradually each new one would fall behind in her filing and be lost behind a mountain of documents. It was ridiculous.

I also disagreed with Kilby's ideas about adding levels of management between us and the people in the stores. His organization chart for our expansion program called for no less than a dozen people in headquarters. This meant we'd soon have to move to a larger office. However, his argument for this new structure was persuasive—Kilby could sell kazoos at a funeral. Besides, he was just responding to the kind of growth numbers I was talking. He got excited by my projections, and we were convinced that our plans would succeed. I had already celebrated my thirty-first birthday, and though I was not yet a millionaire, I was certain, the way things were going, that I would be in that bracket before the next year was out.

I was in awe of Kilby's diplomacy, and I wanted to pick up some of that polish from him. I was strictly a hands-on guy. If I walked into a store and saw something that wasn't right, I'd see red and lose my temper. Dave was more politic, and he'd tell me, "Don't chew a guy out in front of everybody in the store. Take him aside." But unfortunately, our store managers didn't get the advantage of Kilby's diplomacy—there were too many intermediaries between them.

That fall was a season of baseball madness in Michigan. The Tigers won the pennant and took on the St. Louis Cardinals in the World Series. I was glad I'd had the foresight earlier in the season to sign up some of the Tigers players to appear at future grand openings of Domino's stores.

And what a stomach churner of a series it was! Detroit immediately fell behind two games to one. Bob Gibson, the Cardinal pitcher, seemed unbeatable. Our ace pitcher, Denny McClain, who won thirty-one games that year, couldn't seem to do anything. Gibson whipped us 10−1 in the fourth game. Then Detroit managed to win the next two, and left-hander Mickey Lolich went against Gibson in the crucial seventh game on Thursday, October 10, 1968, in St. Louis. Both pitchers had won two games in the series, and Gibson, who had led the Cardinals to the world championship the previous year against Boston, was on a roll of seven consecutive World Series wins. It seemed like the entire world had stopped to watch that game. When the Tigers won it, I was struck by the idea that we had to give the players some hot Domino's pizzas in celebration when they arrived home at Detroit Metro Airport.

Everybody in headquarters got pumped up about that idea, and it was organized almost before I finished getting the words out of my mouth. We made a hundred pizzas with a variety of toppings and put them in hotboxes—portable sterno heaters. These hotboxes, by the way, were another thing I pioneered in the pizza industry. An inventor named Al Whit had come in to show me a prototype and I bought it on the spot for fifty dollars. I bought a lot more of them after that, and Whit wound up with a large company that made tens of thousands of them a year.

Anyway, we weren't worried about having cool pizzas when we got to the airport, but we soon began to wonder whether we'd get there at all. We were barely outside Ypsilanti when we found ourselves in bumper-to-bumper traffic. A trip that normally takes twenty minutes began to look more like forty. Then, in the last mile before the airport exit, we came to a complete standstill. Radio news bulletins told us there was no hope of reaching the exit, much less geting to the airline terminal. It seemed like every man, woman, and child in a three-county area had decided to drive to the airport to greet the Tigers.

"What a shame," Dave Kilby said. "All these pizzas will go to waste."

"Like heck they will," I declared. "Let's get out there and sell them!"

That's exactly what we did. We each took several pizzas in our arms and ran hawking them among the cars stalled in that traffic jam. We sold every last pizza, and we had so much fun doing it that we didn't regret missing the players.

When the colleges were back in session, sales in all twelve of our stores were up dramatically—even Cross Street, which was cleaned up, sealed off from the burned-out house behind it, and reopened soon after the fire—and there was a tremendous amount of enthusiasm in the company. By the end of October all our bills were caught up, and we were ready to launch phase one of our expansion program.

The method of franchising we'd come up with was designed to appeal to small investors. We would sell quarter-shares of ownership in a store for $1,500 down. We would finance the remaining $15,000 with my wife, me, and an equipment supplier named Bernie Morin cosigning on a note with Westinghouse Credit Corporation. Two quarters of each franchise would be purchased by nonoperating investors and one quarter by Domino's. The remaining fourth would go to an owner-manager. The owner-manager didn't have to pay cash, but he would not receive his quarter until after the store had earned $6,000 in profits. Domino's would provide a complete turnkey setup, including training of the owner-manager, and we'd bill the franchise 5½ percent of receipts for our services. That may sound like a lot, but with all the services we were providing, we would just break even on the deal.

The first location to be opened under this new arrangement was at Ohio University in Athens. Terry Voice and Lester Heddle remodeled the store in what had been an old gas station, and

Kilby assigned Heddle to stay and train the manager. I liked Heddle. He grew up in the neighborhood of my DomiNick's store and drove for me while he was still in high school. Later, he put in stints as a pizza maker and manager.

We already had investors for the store and Heddle came up with a manager in short order. Within a few weeks, the store was booming. It took over three-fourths of the pizza business at Ohio University, and Heddle got ready to move on to Columbus and find a location near the Ohio State University campus.

I was elated. Things were working out precisely as planned. We moved quickly to build more stores—too quickly, as it turned out. Our growth looked like the path of a kite that shoots straight up, then flips and dives to earth. Our fall, which we came to call the Crash, was the result of two executive decisions. Both were carefully considered and had the endorsement of all our advisers. But both were dead wrong.

Our first mistake was to change our policy of concentrating on college campuses. A crew went to eighteen different campuses that fall and came up with only the Athens, Ohio, site. Campuses are generally a lot tougher places on which to find locations than other areas. Campuses are narrow targets, and they are usually overretailed. I've always felt, though, that if you work at it, you can ferret out a campus location. You have to spend the time, you have to talk to the people in the neighborhoods, you have to study the area's traffic patterns.

My theory was that we wanted to be on the back of a campus, where the dorms usually were, not on the front, where most of the retail shops were. Oftentimes there were no retail stores on the back side, just cornfields. That was the kind of location I would look for, hoping to find a business that wasn't doing much, something I could convert.

I don't know if the people we had looking for sites really un-

derstood my approach. In any event, they didn't come up with
any locations, and we decided to go after the residential market
without campus stores as anchors.

Our second executive error was the decision to force rapid
growth so we could impress the financial community and take
Domino's public.

The idea of going public had been shimmering in the back of
my mind ever since McDonald's had done it with such a rash of
national publicity in April 1965. I'd heard Ray Kroc tell banquet
audiences the story of how he and his secretary, June Martino,
and his right-hand man, Harry Sonneborn, had celebrated when
they realized that they'd become multimillionaires the instant
McDonald's stock went onto the Big Board.

The possibilities for us looked juicy. But I had no idea what
sharp fishhooks were concealed in them until I bit.

NEW YEAR'S 1969 was one of the happiest of my life. I was being hailed as the boy wonder of Ypsilanti's business community. Domino's had risen from its ashes. I was being sought as a luncheon speaker to tell area service clubs about the franchising dynamo we had harnessed.

The wonderful part was that it was all so true. We seemed to have gained strength from the hardships of the fire. Our goal was to open a new store each week, and we were attaining it, week after week. We now had a dozen stores operating, and a dozen more were in various stages of development.

Our projections showed Domino's locations all across the country. We visualized the company then as becoming even larger than it actually was in 1985. We had one future organization chart that showed positions for twenty-one vice-presidents. There was no doubt in my mind that we would grow that large.

We were steadily becoming more professional. The *Pepperoni*

Press had been transformed into a slick publication in magazine format, and we had a five-week training program for new owner-managers that spelled out all the details of our operations. I also appointed an advisory council that met once a month.

The brokerage firm I was talking to about taking the company public was excited about the prospect, but they emphasized that we had to lay a solid business groundwork first. Basically, this meant establishment of a strong record of growth and profits. But there were some other moves that were deemed advisable, such as shifting our accounting to a CPA firm, computerizing our bookkeeping, and getting more "management depth," which translated to hiring more people with degrees.

We developed a presentation to the Ann Arbor Bank for a $400,000 line of credit, which would accelerate our expansion program, including my plan to open forty stores in Detroit, all of them black-owned, black-operated, and staffed by black employees.

Victor Oleson, a member of my advisory council, was an advertising executive with Wells, Rich, Greene, Inc., the hottest agency in the country at the time. He told me that if I was going to be successful in dealing with all these brokers and bankers, I was going to have to upgrade my personal image. So I bought three Hickey-Freeman suits and a trenchcoat, on credit. Margie did a double-take at that. She didn't think we could afford my new splendor, and she was right.

Actually, I was less concerned about my own appearance than I was about the way our delivery cars looked. We had a total of seventy-five company cars, mostly old Volkswagens and Ford Falcons, and half of them needed to be phased out. We worked out a deal with American Motors to get a fleet of eighty-five brand new Javelins painted red, white, and blue. I was really proud of those new Javelins. It was inspiring to see one of them pull up in front of a store.

Our broker also said we should retain a big Detroit law firm to represent us instead of Larry Sperling's one-man office, and Larry agreed. He was uncomfortable about the fact that I was not being uniform in all the franchising deals I was making, and he didn't have time to research all the possible legal consequences. I was sorry to cut Larry out of Domino's growth, because he was not only a friend, he was also a good sounding board for me. I would often stop by his office while I was doing store visits late at night, and he was always in there working. We had some great discussions, and they weren't all about work. Sperling was one of the few people I enjoyed talking with about subjects like religion and politics. I didn't agree with him. My Roman Catholicism was a sharp contrast to his Jewish background, and my conservative Republican opinions would make him gnash his teeth. I'd kid him about being a bleeding-heart liberal, but I don't think our views about the basic worth of other people and the important values of life were very dissimilar. We both believed in the Golden Rule, even though we might approach it from opposite ends.

Another of our broker's suggestions for improving our level of professionalism was that we computerize our accounting. So we hired a service bureau recommended by our CPA firm. It started doing the monthly statements for our stores, and we ran them parallel with our manual statements for several months. They could never seem to get caught up. Then, when we tried switching everything over to them, the computer lost our records—everything was wiped out.

After that, our accounting was a shambles. Robert Boduck was a good controller, but he left for a better, less chaotic job, and I went through a succession of other guys. No one could get us current statements, which were critical in talking to the investment bankers, who were wining and dining me. It was frustrating. All the while I was going to Detroit and telling these bankers about our great plans, our accounting was falling further and further behind. Then we began having serious cash-flow problems, partly because of the trouble we were having in getting stores opened.

We had set up six city areas for store development and supervision: Ann Arbor-Ypsilanti, Flint, Kalamazoo, Detroit, Toledo, and Columbus, and each was to be directed by a general manager. Mike Glance was in charge of the Kalamazoo area, and his experience with a location near Western Michigan University was fairly typical of the troubles everyone was having. After we signed the lease, the store sat empty month after month despite Glance's best efforts to put together a group of investors. When he finally came up with an owner-manager candidate, it was not an individual but a husband and wife team, Al and Mary Morrison. By this time, though, the other investors had backed out. It got so I would explode in anger every time I'd see an operations report with the Kalamazoo store marked "unopen." Margie and I were expecting our third baby in mid-August, and I was determined that Domino's would be open in Kalamazoo before that child was born. I told Mike Glance that I would buy a quarter-share in the store if he would; then we'd form a corporation with the Morrisons. He agreed, and we set up TAMM, Inc., an acronym for our first names: Tom, Al, Mike, and Mary. It was a close race. But Margie won. She had our third daughter, Maggie, on August 15. The Morrisons opened their store one week later, on August 22. I'm not sure which birth was more difficult.

Bernie Morin, who was setting up the equipment in most of these stores, thought he had everything ready to go when the Morrisons moved to Kalamazoo. But the water hadn't been turned on yet. The Morrisons solved that problem by running a garden hose to their neighbor's building for their opening night. The kid they'd hired as a driver didn't show up, so Mike Glance spent that first night delivering pizzas.

I was a little disappointed with that store. I thought it would do at least $8,000 a week. As I recall, after school started at Western Michigan, it was doing about $6,000 a week. I would have been happy, however, if our residential stores had done half as well.

An example of the problems we had with the residential locations was in Columbus, where Les Heddle was general manager. His two campus stores were doing fine, but his first residential location was a loser. Les phoned me one night and told me he couldn't make that store go.

"Tom, as you know, there are two hundred eighty-four pizza shops here in Columbus. They all sell subs and spaghetti and everything else," he said. "When our phone people tell callers we have nothing but pizza, they just laugh and hang up."

"What are your sales running, Les?" I asked.

"You don't want to know."

"Yes I do."

"Well, last week we did four hundred dollars."

I don't want to quote my response.

Sales that low were absolutely unheard of for a Domino's store. But the story was much the same at the other residential locations. And in addition to their lower sales, it was costing us more to advertise in these areas. On a college campus we had what amounted to a captive audience. The students read the campus publications, so it was easy and relatively inexpensive to reach them with our advertising. Our best advertising on campus, though, and the fastest, was word of mouth.

Appealing to the general public was a completely different ball game. We had to put our ads in larger papers that charged higher rates and weren't as well targeted to our potential customers.

During the first ten months of 1969, we opened thirty-two stores, most of them in residential neighborhoods. Few of them did more than six hundred dollars a week. I just couldn't believe it. We kept pumping more and more money into them, trying to get them on their feet. But they were too weak. We were paying their bills, doing their payroll and sending them food they couldn't pay for, and the result was that we began falling behind on our bills, too.

As late as the end of August, I still felt we might be able to turn the situation around. But I wasn't bursting with confidence. Neither was anyone else. In fact, some of my executives were advocating that we add non-pizza items to the menu and put table service in the residential stores. Terry Voice was a particularly strong advocate of this. I, of course, would not even consider doing such a thing.

Terry came into my office one day and told me he was going to form his own pizza company with a couple of partners and some backing from his father. I said, "Well, Terry, I'm sorry to see you go. I wish you the best. I can understand your frustration with the way things are going here. But we will get through this somehow, and it will all come out in the wash."

I really believed that, and it happened. But it's probably just as well that I couldn't see into the future, because the *wash* would be no ordinary laundry; it would be more like a long bath in battery acid.

We had pulled Mike Paul out of the commissary and made him general manager in the Toledo area. In October, he gave me a memo summarizing his first six months on the job. It was depressing.

"Our stores in Toledo have been disasters," he wrote. "I have worked for 185 straight days, and I still can't get on top of the situation. There is no evidence that it will improve. Domino's is not known in this area as it is in Ann Arbor and Ypsilanti, so our assumption that we could walk in here and set the place on fire was wrong.

"I hire managers and give them three or four hours of training each night for a week in our Ypsilanti store. To do this, I have to drive them up and back every day. When they finish their training, they are all charged up about the pizza business. But after a week or so on the job here, doing almost no business, they quit. So most of the time, I have to manage two stores myself."

Several years earlier, through my friendship with Jerry Liss of Bowling Green, Ohio, I had unwittingly planted the seeds for what would become a major problem for Mike. Liss had been trying to build a business to serve the campus of Bowling Green State University. I gave him a lot of pointers from my experience with Domino's. He came to Ypsilanti and I showed him how we operated. I wanted to help him because of the more than three hundred pizza operators I met on my research trips, he was the first one to ask me any questions. Jerry had seen the potential in concentrating on delivery, and his sales skyrocketed.

So when Mike Paul opened his store in Bowling Green, which was supposed to be his high-volume operation with sales of at least five thousand dollars the first week, he found Jerry Liss firmly established there, selling ten-inch pizzas by the carload.

The minute I got Mike's sales reports from Bowling Green showing a weekly gross of fifteen hundred dollars—the worst we'd ever had for a major campus—I got on the phone to find out what was wrong. He said, "It's your friend Jerry Liss," and he went on to detail the competitve situation. It was tough. Liss had a lock on the market that could only be broken, Mike believed, by doing something extraordinary to get the attention of the entire campus.

"I've been thinking about having a grand opening and giving away free pizza," he said. "What do you think?"

I told him it sounded like a good idea.

But the pizza business is a lot like baseball or football in the way the breaks can go against you when you're floundering. Mike put a lot of planning into his grand opening. He had extra ovens trucked down from Ypsilanti, and he brought in a crew of our top pizza makers. I went down to make pizzas, too. As the big day approached, he did additional advertising and had a huge new sign installed on the roof of his store. Unfortunately, the sign job wasn't properly done, and it caused a leak in the roof. There was a torrential rain on the night before the grand opening, and Mike's crew opened the store the next day to find the place awash in a foot of water. They were still mopping up when orders began pouring in for the grand-opening giveaway. They fell behind immediately and never caught up. The promotion made Domino's name familiar all over campus all right, but not in the way we had hoped. That was the last time we ever gave away pizzas.

The failure of one promotion was not going to break us, though. We had more serious problems to contend with, not the least of which was investors who were beginning to ask when they were going to start seeing some return on their money. Many of these men were Jaycees from the Ypsilanti area who had been mesmerized by Dave Kilby's sales pitch. Dave and a former real-estate salesman he'd hired, Doug Nadeau, were an effective team. Nadeau was a good closer. The investors expected to become instant millionaires with their quarter-shares of a Domino's franchise. Some had invested in more than one store; Gordon Wallace, who was independently wealthy, had quarter-shares of ten stores. When I heard rumors of unrest among the investors, I called them all to a meeting and laid the situation on the line for them. The fact was that we were paying all bills for their stores, which owed us a lot of money. The average store owed us about thirty thousand dollars. So the problem was not going to evaporate. As I spoke, I could see the hope dying in the eyes of these men.

Our general managers, most of them at any rate, were towers of strength in this pinch. I had been through the kind of torture they faced, with bills piling up and no money coming in to pay them, so I could appreciate their fortitude.

I didn't blame them for putting Domino's bills last on their list for payment. There were certain bills they had to pay, such as taxes and utilities, or they wouldn't be able to keep their doors open. But since they weren't sending us money, our corporate debts were multiplying. Our bills grew beards, and then the lawsuits started coming in.

Part of our problem was due to our nightmare in accounting. We kept a checkbook for each one of our forty stores. But when the computer lost all our records, we no longer knew what the balances were or who had been paid and who had not. We attempted to catch up by adding to staff until, by November 1969, we had twenty-nine people working in our little office. It was a madhouse. We were tripping over each other all day long, and I felt I had no choice but to move to larger quarters. The building I found was an old factory on a gravel road in Ypsilanti. It was really an assemblage of corrugated-iron Quonset huts of World War II vintage. It wasn't pretty, but it would have to do.

The move, however, did nothing to stem the tide of bad news. It got so we couldn't pay our insurance premiums anymore, and we were falling behind in payments of sales tax, which we had never let happen in the past. Our checks were bouncing left and right; banks wouldn't cash a Domino's check. All this trouble—and this was infuriating to me—came from those residential stores that just wouldn't do any business.

I had been in financial trouble before, but never like this. I couldn't correct this situation by working harder myself. I had nowhere to cut back: Margie and I were living modestly. I was drawing only $200 a week, and many of my paychecks were still going uncashed.

Another example of how bad things tend to proliferate when you're floundering was the mistake our controller made in the amount of withholding taxes we sent in one quarter. He was off by one digit—he sent in $4,000 when the amount owed was $40,000—and we didn't discover it until three months later. By that time, the next quarterly payment was due, and we just couldn't pay it, let alone what we owed from the previous quarter. We started getting socked with penalties and interest on the penalties, and we fell further and further behind.

Things were so bleak that I didn't even feel like having a company Christmas party that year. I reflected that in other years at Christmas we had always seemed to be on the threshold of something big. We'd be finishing a big burst of fall business and be moving on toward bigger and better things. Not this year. I felt like Scrooge. I found myself resenting the fact that all the college students had gone home for the Christmas holidays, making it a completely down period for our business.

Dave Kilby finally had the company party in the house he had recently purchased. I didn't enjoy Dave's Christmas party at all. I felt numb, just as I had years earlier, when I thought I would lose Domino's because of Gilmore's bankruptcy.

After the holidays, the pressure from the IRS increased. So I decided to go against my better judgment and, for the first time, sell some of my stock in Domino's. The person who had pressed me the most to sell him stock was Dan "Punk" Quirk, whose family owned the Peninsula Paper Company, the largest business in Ypsilanti at that time. He had earlier offered $10 a share, and I said I was willing to sell at $7 now because we were in a pinch with the IRS and needed the money right away. The Quirk family bought about $30,000 worth of stock, part of which went to George Elliot, the vice-president of the Ypsilanti bank. Punk Quirk was on the bank board. Gordon Wallace bought about $20,000 worth. The $50,000 in cash took care of our immediate problem with the IRS; even though it did not cover our entire bill, it was enough to keep them from shutting us down.

I thought that solving our IRS problems would put us in pretty good shape. But we had so many stores losing money, it was like being in quicksand. There was simply no way to stay above it. Actually, the writing had been on the wall since late summer, and now I could ignore it no longer. We were going to have to close some stores. We would have to lay off some of our people. I detested these moves, but there was no alternative.

Every franchisee who was with us in those days has war stories about the Crash. I'll always be grateful to them, people like Harold Mitchell, Steve Litwhiler, and Bob Watson, who stayed with me through it. There also were people like Mike Paul who showed tremendous loyalty. It got to the point where the banks in Ohio would no longer cash Mike's paychecks, so he'd mail them to his mother and she'd cash them at her bank and send him the money.

Dave Kilby proposed that he go to Florida and start building Domino's down there as an area franchisee. At the time, it seemed like a good idea. I couldn't afford his salary anyhow.

I sat at my desk for several days trying to figure out exactly how much I was in debt. It was difficult to determine because our CPA firm had quit us since we couldn't pay them anymore. But the figure I came up with was $1.5 million. I was a reverse millionaire! It was humiliating.

But I was soon to learn that I was just beginning to learn the meaning of the word *humiliation*. It started with a call from the president of the Ypsilanti bank, which had extended about eighty thousand dollars in credit to us, mostly for delivery cars. I told him I was in the middle of a meeting and would have to get back to him. He swore at me on the phone and told me to get my worthless carcass down to his office immediately.

In one short year, the boy wonder of Ypsilanti had become the village idiot.

I LOST CONTROL OF DOMINO'S on May 1, 1970.

My hope had been to find a company to merge with. I spent a lot of time talking to the owners of a Detroit-based submarine-sandwich chain called Mr. Tony's, who seemed very interested in acquiring Domino's. Since my employees were already nervous about the future of the company and I didn't want to alarm them unnecessarily, I had the Mr. Tony's people come in at night, after the office had closed, to go over our books. Their enthusiasm made me pretty certain we'd be able to work out an agreement. When they finally got around to making an offer, however, their attorney began by giving me a sermon on the evils of bankruptcy and proceeded to offer me a mere ten thousand dollars for the company. I was astonished. I guess they thought they had me over a barrel and could take advantage of me. Whatever their plan, it didn't work. I thanked them for their interest but said I thought I'd be better off going it alone. That decision proved to be the right one, because in 1982, Mr. Tony's itself declared bankruptcy.

I might have gone on searching for merger partners, but while I'd been dickering with the Mr. Tony's people, my bank in Ypsilanti apparently was hatching a plan to protect its interest in Domino's. I first heard about it when Punk Quirk suggested that I talk to Ken Heavlin, a local businessman he said had made a lot of money by turning troubled companies around. "He's very astute and I think he'll be able to help you," Quirk said. I said I was willing to talk to anyone who might be able to help me.

Within days after our initial discussion, Heavlin proposed that we enter an agreement in which I would assign all my remaining stock in Domino's to him, to be placed in a trust. He would run the company without salary, and he would make loans to cover our IRS debts, if necessary, taking some of the assets as security. At the end of two years, I would get 49 percent of my stock back and he would control the company. Meanwhile, I would continue to have the title of president, but I would have no authority. I didn't like the idea much, but I figured that part of something is better than all of nothing. The bank board's trust in Heavlin was persuasive to me, so I agreed.

When I told Margie about the arrangement, she nodded sympathetically and indicated that she would do her best to help me live with it. When I told her I would continue to draw the same salary, two hundred dollars a week, she laughed and said ironically, "Oh good!" She had about twenty of those salary checks in a drawer, uncashed. At the moment, they were worthless.

In some ways the arrangement with Heavlin was a relief. It avoided bankruptcy, which everybody but me seemed to think was inevitable, and it took some of the pressure from creditors off me. A few weeks earlier, three of our biggest suppliers—N. Leone & Sons, our main food product supplier, and two box manufacturers, Bay Corrugated and Triad Container—had gotten together and called me into a creditors' meeting. They had an attorney who raked me over the coals. I couldn't blame them. I owed them a total of about a hundred fifty thousand dollars, and they had a right to know what I intended to do about it. That hundred fifty thousand was only a fraction of what I owed, of course. The IRS, state tax agencies, and secured creditors were all lined up ahead of these guys. So their chances of collecting looked pretty remote.

All I could tell them was that I'd closed the unprofitable stores to stop the outflow of money and that I was cutting back on staff and reorganizing. I promised they would get every penny we owed them, that Domino's would redeem itself somehow.

I credit their agreement to go along with me to Jerry Kolassa, Sr., who was doing my accounting at that time. Before the meeting, Jerry got into a conversation about me with Arm Leone, president of N. Leone & Sons, and he told Arm, "You know, that guy doesn't have any furniture in his house." It was true. Margie and I had a kitchen table and a couple of chairs, our beds, and that was about it. I was driving a beat-up old Checker delivery car. Apparently, Arm and the others had come to the meeting suspecting that I was using the money I owed them to maintain a fancy lifestyle. They left with the impression that I was doing everything that could be done in their interest. They realized that no one else would work at Domino's as cheap or as hard as I would, and I told them I would stay with it for as long as it took to get it turned around.

I was hopeful that the arrangement with Heavlin would be a major step toward putting us back on an even keel and paying off those debts. But it didn't work out that way. I was put in charge of supervising the twelve corporate stores. I welcomed this responsibility because it allowed me to take refuge in work I loved. It also afforded me the occasional therapy of slapping out dough,

helping to handle the rush. I drove down to Ohio regularly and
checked out the stores there. On these trips, I cut expenses by
sleeping in my car.

Les Heddle had been struggling diligently to keep his two remaining stores in Ohio going, but he came to me toward the end
of May and said he couldn't continue.

"I'm burned out, Tom," he said. "I've been working hundred-
hour weeks for too many months. I found a note from my wife on
the hall table this morning. It begged me to take her and the kids
back to Ypsilanti. I'm going to do it. I have to quit. I'm sorry."

What could I say? We had already lost many of our best people, and my nerves were numb to the pain of it by now. So I just
nodded and mumbled something about wishing him well.

The man Heavlin hired as his operating representative spent a
lot of time reorganizing our commissary. He seemed to understand that part of the business better than anything else. However, instead of treating it as a service, he began handling it
strictly as a profit center, which created problems with our franchisees. Heavlin's man did improve the commissary, but he had a
manufacturing background and didn't understand the human-
relations aspect of franchising, which makes up a large part of the
business. As a result, he failed to communicate properly with the
franchisees, and this, combined with raises in prices in the commissary, led to complaints.

I'd never had any real problems with franchisees before, but
their loss of communication with Domino's and their belief that
they were being gouged by the new commissary policies led them
to form a protective association. They held a series of meetings to
prepare a class-action antitrust suit against the corporation. Most
of them quit paying royalties. They stopped using our commissaries, too.

Meanwhile, the corporate stores I had been nursing along

were gaining strength, and I had talked Mike Paul into becoming a traveling supervisor to help get these operations going again. I felt we had to work at increasing cash flow one step at a time.

Not long after we opened in Columbus again with a corporate store, Heavlin came to me and said he wanted to terminate our agreement. I told him, "Fine," thinking to myself that nothing could please me more. We parted company on March 22, 1971. He proposed that he would give me back my stock and take over our Cross Street store, both the property and the business, under a franchise agreement and a mortgage for about sixty thousand dollars. The profits from the store would go toward paying off the mortgage, and when it was satisfied, I would own the store again.

Heavlin wanted to get his hands on that Cross Street store to protect the bank, of course, because he assumed that I was going to go bankrupt. Unfortunately, most of the creditors felt the same way. They panicked when he left, and I had my hands full trying to calm them down. I told them the truth. I planned to pay everybody back a hundred cents on the dollar, and I would do it in an evenhanded way. I was not going to be pressured by the one who made the most noise. But there was no way I could pay anybody back yet. First I had to take care of the things that kept our doors open—the rent, taxes, and cheese to make the next day's pizzas.

Most of the creditors responded positively to this approach. I was elated to be back in control, and I thought the franchisees would be happy about it, too. I had often heard them say, "Domino's isn't like it used to be when Monaghan was running it." I believed they understood that I'd always treated them fairly and that our old friendly relationships would be reinstated.

How wrong I was! They persisted in pressing their lawsuit. When I was served with notice that they'd filed against me, I sat at my desk and cried.

The rumors about the suit were incredible. There was talk of treble damages, with each franchisee receiving a huge sum. One figure I heard bandied about was ninety thousand dollars for each franchisee. This was absurd, because even if such a judgment were rendered, there was no way the company could pay it. Even liquidation would render far less than was owed to the creditors—never mind the franchisees—because our assets were a bunch of delivery cars that had seen hard use, and things like ovens, coolers, and countertops, none of which would bring half of what we'd paid for them. Some of the franchisees told me they were suing the company, not me personally, but I found the distinction unrealistic.

To make matters worse, our law firm, Cross, Wrock, had sued us, and they garnisheed all our royalty income. This really got me at the jugular because several of the franchisees were looking for any excuse to avoid paying their royalties. I finally talked the lawyers out of pursuing the garnishment, using the same approach I took with the other creditors: I told them the truth.

I cut our headquarters staff back drastically, leaving only Esther Long, Margie, and myself. The office often seemed crowded, however, because of the swarms of creditors who descended on us. Lawsuits were coming in wholesale, and a lot of writs of execution were waved under my nose. A whole series of inspectors came marching in, too: sales tax was behind again. The IRS was after us, too, and we got socked with back payments and penalties of about eighteen thousand dollars. I managed to pay part of the fine by borrowing from Steve Litwhiler. I just called him up and said I needed some money. He asked how much, and I told him ten thousand dollars. He said, "I'll send you a check." That was it—no IOU or anything. We just agreed that payment would be applied against future royalties. It was one of the greatest acts of friendship I've ever experienced. I raised the rest of the money I owed the state by borrowing from one of our suppliers and by selling the 51 percent interest we had in one of our stores in Illinois to the operator, Tom Ahlers.

It wasn't unusual for a bonded agent to come into our office with a writ and appropriate anything of value he could get his hands on: typewriters, adding machines, cash registers. One day, just as Esther Long handed me a check to sign, one of these guys appeared with a pistol stuck in the waistband of his pants. He put his hand on the gun and said, "I'll take that check!"

"No you won't!" I said, and tore it up.

"Okay, then," he said. "I'll take that truck out front."

He did, and there was nothing I could do to stop him. But I called the creditor's lawyer and worked out an arrangement to get the truck back.

Such confrontations made me furious, but I could deal with them. The franchisees' antitrust suit was another matter. I hate to fight friends. In this case, of course, I had no choice. I hired Dykema and Gossett, a fine law firm in Detroit, and they assigned a young attorney, Robert Seymour, to the case.

While Seymour was handling the legal maneuvers, I went to the franchisees personally and explained my position. I was able to persuade them that Domino's would survive this financial crisis and that eventually they would be better off trying to help me than fighting me. It was a tortuous process, but one by one, over the course of nearly three years, they all dropped out of the suit. Some of them also dropped out of Domino's under mutual termination agreements. I bought back these units as corporate stores, and I paid through the nose for them. But it was worth it.

Ultimately, I think, the Domino's franchise system was strengthened by this healing process. Among the last of those who dropped out of Domino's was Chuck Gray, and he left the company to start his own pizza-delivery stores. Our parting wasn't pleasant.

I felt like I was living a double life. During the day I was bob-
bing and weaving like Muhammad Ali doing his rope-a-dope to
escape the onslaught of creditors. My hands were numb from
clenching my fists so hard during these endless explanations. But
at night I was out visiting stores all over Michigan and Ohio, and I
mean seven nights a week. One of my favorite stopping points
was Dick Mueller's store in Ann Arbor. I had a special appreciation for Dick because when Domino's was at the bottom of its
slump in the middle of 1970, with Heavlin and his man running
the show, he came to see me all dressed up in his Sunday suit and
asked if he could buy a franchise. I could hardly believe it. Domino's was a laughingstock; a lot of our stores were closed, with
legal notices in the windows saying their contents were "Property
of the U.S. Government." Yet here was this young guy with a
check for $4,400, most of which he had borrowed from his par-
ents, asking if he could buy a franchise. I called Gene Belknap,
who assured me that Mueller would make a good operator, and
we signed the franchise agreement. Mueller now says jokingly
that he was too stupid to check out what kind of company he was
getting into. He just knew from his work as a driver for me and
then as a manager for the Belknaps that he loved the pizza business. And, of course, that last was probably the critical ingredient
in his eventual success.

I let Mueller take over the equipment from a store we had
closed, including a couple of beat-up Javelins. He had a rough
time getting his store going, because it was in a residential neighborhood in Ann Arbor and he had been accustomed to the fast
pace of business in a campus location. I went in there three or
four times a week and helped him, giving him tips on how to
build business and showing him how to hold down costs and
handle his crew more efficiently. But most of our discussion centered on what we were going to do when we were making more

than a hundred thousand dollars a year. I found his attitude refreshing because, like me, he never questioned whether we would be successful. Success was merely a matter of time and effort. We talked about how we were going to spend all the money we'd be making, what kind of houses we would buy, what kind of cars we'd drive, all the interesting places we'd go. It was mutual dreaming, and for me it was a stimulating contrast to the grueling daytime drag of fending off creditors.

Another thing I liked about Mueller was his dedication to serving the customer. The Belknaps had taught him well. One time I was in his store when a man who was obviously hard up came in and asked the price of a large pizza. He had a family to feed in his car, and when Dick told him the price, he shook his head and walked out. Dick asked me to watch the store, and I nodded. He ran out after the guy with his order pad and pencil in his hand. He stood by the car talking to the man and his wife for about five minutes. When he came back, I asked, "Did you get the order?"

"You're damn right I did!" he said. "They have a couple of real small kids. All they need is a small pizza with extra thick crust. The kids just want pepperoni, so I told them to order half pepperoni, half sausage and mushrooms, and split it among them."

After about a year, Mueller had his store built up from $1,200 a week to $2,200 and he was getting restless. He had dropped out of U of M in his senior year and he wanted to complete his education, so he enrolled in the restaurant school at Michigan State in East Lansing and commuted to class, trying to run his store part-time. That didn't work at all. Business went downhill, and he couldn't afford to pay tuition for his second quarter of school. He had been waiting to be drafted into the Army, but they turned him down because he was overweight. So now, he confided to me, he was getting depressed. He complained that his Ann Arbor location was surrounded by other Domino's stores and there was no way for him to grow.

Meanwhile, I had a store in Columbus that was shaky. Mike Paul had opened it, but he and his wife wanted to settle down in Ypsilanti and start a family. Mike was hoping to buy into a store on the north side of Eastern's campus, and I wanted him to have it. So I had to do something about Columbus. Bob Cotman was out of the Army now and had moved to Columbus to study design. I had him working part-time, supervising the store there as well as the ones in Lancaster, Zanesville, and Bowling Green, but that was just a stopgap measure. Bob wanted to put his energies into his schoolwork.

It occurred to me that Mueller was from Ohio. His family lived in Cleveland, and I figured he might like to move down there. So I proposed that he exchange his 49 percent ownership in the Ann Arbor store for the same share in the Columbus store. I knew he could make that place hum. It was shabby at the moment, but it was in a good campus location and its potential was terrific. Dick was very interested, but I told him I thought we ought to finalize the deal before he went down to Columbus.

"If you saw the store first, you wouldn't buy it," I said, tongue in cheek.

"No Domino's store could look that bad," he said.

"Dick," I told him, "it doesn't look that good."

"How many ovens has this place got?"

"It has four ovens."

"Does it have a cooler?"

"It has a walk-in cooler just like yours."

"How much business does it do?"

"It's doing six hundred dollars a week."

"Holy cow," he gasped. "You want me to trade a store that's

doing twenty-two hundred dollars a week for one that's doing six hundred dollars?''

"That's right, but that six hundred dollars is in the summer," I said. "After you get that store going, you can use the profits from it to build others. You'll have the whole city of Columbus to develop." I could see he was eager to grab my offer, but I had one other proviso I had to put on the deal. "What you're buying here, Dick, is potential, and I'll let you have it for ten thousand dollars."

He drew a deep breath at that, but he quickly agreed to give me his first ten thousand dollars in profits from Columbus.

A few days after we shook hands on the deal, I got a telephone call from Dick. He told me he should have believed me when I said the place was bad. Business was so slow, he said, that the manager sat out front and played his guitar all evening. The landlord had started eviction proceedings because the rent was in arrears, the sign company had repossessed the sign, and the auto dealership had taken back the two company cars.

"You have to make the commissary deliver food to me," he said. "They cut us off because we were behind on their bill, too." I promised to take care of it and was about to hang up when he said, "Oh, one other thing, Tom. You know, you told me there were four ovens in this store. You were right. But you forgot to tell me there is no ventilation hood. It gets so hot in here we can hardly stand it. Oh, and by the way, the cooler doesn't work."

I sympathized with Mueller's problems, but I knew he would handle them, and he did. Within three months, that store was doing seven thousand dollars a week and he had paid off all the debts. He then leased an old garage and built a second store, and on the profits from the first two, he built a third and a fourth. It wasn't long before he had ten stores and had incorporated as Ohio Pizza Enterprises, Inc.

Energy like Dick's was beginning to run through the whole

Domino's system, revitalizing the company. We were on the move, building stores again. New England was beginning to cook. Litwhiler had opened five stores from his base in Vermont, and Dave Kilby was going great guns down in Florida. We ended 1971 with thirty-four stores in six different states. I was beginning to regain my idea-generating powers and catch fire again.

John Correll, who had worked in our store in East Lansing back in 1967 while getting his MBA in hotel and restaurant management from Michigan State University, dropped into my Quonset hut office one day in May 1970 and asked for a job. He'd been out of contact with the company for two years, teaching school in Texas.

He asked me if I'd been ill. I guess I looked sick—I'd lost thirty pounds since I'd last seen him. I said no, I'd just been having a few problems, and I filled him in on what had been going on: the fire, our recovery and growth, the Crash, how I had lost control of the company. I told him I needed a manager in our Trowbridge store in East Lansing. It had been a phenomenal success when he was there working under Terry Voice. The second week it was open, the store was doing $6,000 in sales—which by 1986 pricing would be the equivalent of $30,000. In fact, that store had earned back our investment within the first year. So I knew it was a good location. But it had gone downhill, and I couldn't keep a manager in place. John agreed to take it on, but he said he didn't have any money to put down on an apartment, could I lend him some money? All I had was my payroll check, so I asked him if $220 would do.

"Sure, fine," he said.

So I endorsed my check and handed it to him. "I sure hope you show up in East Lansing on Sunday," I said, "because I'm gonna catch it for this from my wife tonight."

Correll recently reminded me of that incident and how I sent him a note saying Margie wanted to thank him and his wife after he paid me back in twelve monthly installments. Margie thought she'd never see that money again.

It didn't take Correll long to turn the Trowbridge store around, and when he did, I appointed him supervisor of the whole Lansing area. He got results, and he pulled off one promotion I really admired. It showed how creative a company can be when it has employees who are highly individualistic, entrepreneurial types.

One Sunday in January 1971, I phoned Correll around midnight and asked him how business had been that day.

"Not that good," he said.

"Why?"

"Well, I ran a promotion and really got bombed. I had to take the phones off the hook."

I was indignant. I detest the idea of turning people away. It isn't the way Domino's treats customers. Also, the need to turn off phones indicates inadequate scheduling by a manager, and I'm a stickler on that. I told Correll what I thought in no uncertain terms. He apologized profusely. Then he told me he'd taken in thirty-five hundred dollars that day.

I did a double-take. Thirty-five hundred dollars in a single day? That was astronomical! What kind of promotion was this?

He explained that he'd taken big newspaper ads and a lot of radio time promoting twelve-inch pizzas for a dollar on what he called Super Sunday. He was confident he could handle a rush of any size in his store because he had Big Red, the monster rotating oven. But just in case, he had an auxiliary oven set up out in the parking lot. He ordered extra food from the commissary and brought in all his drivers and extra help to handle an avalanche of business.

"For the whole first hour we were open, we didn't get a single call," he said. "I was scared. I thought the thing was going to flop. Then, at about five-forty, all hell broke loose. I've never seen such a rush. Somehow I didn't realize that I'd scheduled this thing on the Sunday of the Super Bowl Game!"

"John," I said, "I'm proud of you. Super Sunday was a terrific idea. We'll do it again next year."

Domino's was back to its normal Christmas upsurge in 1971, and we enjoyed it.

In January 1972, I did some serious reflection on what had happened to the company during the two terrible years we'd just experienced. I analyzed our mistakes and did some goal-setting aimed at insuring that they wouldn't happen again.

The first and most serious mistake we made was to send untrained managers into stores. We thought we could get by with a quick training program and heavy supervision, but there's no substitute for experience. Making pizza in itself requires great skill, and a manager also must handle complex problems of delivery and shop management. Therefore, I noted, Domino's number one priority, now and in the future, is the recruitment, training, and motivation of shop managers.

Our second mistake was overexpansion. I vowed that there would be no more expansion for expansion's sake. I wanted to grow, and we would grow. But there must be a better reason for expansion than simply addition of another store and more income. Stores need to complement each other. For example: If we have one store in a town, we do fine. But if we add a second store two or three miles from the first one, business at the first store *always improves*. This is the kind of expansion we should foster. But we should never add a second store in an area until the first store is solidly established, with steady sales of at least $2,000 a week, in those days the mark of a profitable store. In keeping with carefully planned expansion, I made my goal for 1972 a modest twenty new stores, which would bring our total to fifty-four.

Yet another mistake was overstaffing in the home office. I was determined that never again would we get as top-heavy as we had been. Eliminating all that bureaucracy hadn't been easy. But I found that most of the paperwork that had been maintained by twenty-nine people was useless. I kept only the accounting records, the papers Uncle Sam required us to keep, and one little file that I had in my office with the leases and legal documents for each store. The reaction to this from the field was terrific. They were delighted with the way things were getting done at the home office. We were acting on problems immediately instead of wrapping them up in red tape and sending them through channels.

A final and, in my mind, potentially fatal mistake was the lack of good financial statements available on a timely basis.

From where I sat at the start of that new year, I could see that Domino's had barely scratched the surface of its potential. I knew we already had the best-run pizzerias in the country—any of our competitors would have to admit that. We weren't too well thought of in financial circles, but that would change.

My main resolution, which I intended to make every executive and supervisor in the company make with me, was to visit the stores. You don't get what you *expect* unless you *inspect*. When you ask questions on the telephone, you get the answers you prefer to hear. If you visit the store in person, though, you get thousands of impressions, a lot of them pointing to things that need improvement. When a store is running smoothly, visiting it seems like a waste of time. But just stop visiting that store for a few months, and it will deteriorate dramatically. I learned that lesson the hard way, through experience.

More than once, I have walked into a store and found the

situation so bad that the manager had to be fired on the spot. Tom
Ciccarelli, the president of the North American Pizza Association
and publisher of its magazine, was traveling with me on one of
these occasions. He was waiting in the car because my intention
had been to simply walk into the store, say hello, look things
over, and leave. Imagine his surprise when I came out and told
him, "Come on in. You're answering phones, and I'm making
pizzas and tending the ovens. I just fired my manager." We put in
a hard night's work, and as we were closing, Ciccarelli said to me,
"I think I learned more about the pizza business tonight than I
did in a year of running the North American Pizza Association."

A note I put at the end of my list of goals for 1972 stated my
underlying philosophy and my new determination: "I believe we
should concentrate on the only business we know, the operating
of pizza shops, and not get sidetracked into areas we know nothing about."

I WAS CONFIDENT ABOUT ACHIEVING the goals I had outlined to Domino's managers in 1972. I knew our system worked. If we persisted, it would make us successful. But this was only one battle in my campaign. Far more difficult, and every bit as important to me, was regaining the trust and respect of the bankers and the business community in general.

However, we couldn't begin to improve our image until all our debts were settled, and there hadn't been enough progress on this front. I was still pinned down by the demands of our creditors. The pressure was easing with every passing month, though, partially because creditors were giving up and writing us off as a bad debt. They figured they'd never get their money. I was determined to show them they were wrong.

Meanwhile, out in our stores, spirits were improving. Morale was bolstered by the smashing success of our second Super Sunday promotion in East Lansing. This time, Correll did an even better job of advance promotion, and we invited some of our franchisees like Bob Watson and the Belknaps and the Morrisons to come up for the day and help handle the rush. Get a bunch of people with sauce in their veins working together in a situation like that, and you have a pizza man's dream of heaven.

We had thirty-seven drivers on duty that day, and I'd never seen such huge quantities of toppings on the make-line of a Domino's shop. Mushrooms alone filled two big plastic-lined garbage cans. Correll had rented a dry cleaning shop next door for the weekend and used it to store boxes and other supplies. Once again, we set up an oven in the parking lot as a backup for Big Red, and we used it all night long.

One of the guests I invited was Tom Ciccarelli of the North American Pizza Association. He was astonished by the blitz of business that took place—we turned out a thousand pizzas an hour for five hours straight. We loaded Big Red's ten trays full for the first time ever and sent the overflow to the oven in the parking lot. We just cranked 'em out. Ciccarelli was so excited about what he was seeing that he wrote a press release for the newspaper wire services, the Associated Press and United Press International. They picked it up, and several papers around the country printed stories on the tidal wave of pizza we produced that day.

Ciccarelli's enthusiasm on Super Sunday led to a rather unusual consulting arrangement. I really couldn't afford a consultant, so the relationship remained informal—I paid him $150 a week and gave him something of value, such as a used car, from time to time. Since he was already publishing the pizza association magazine (now defunct), it was easy for him to put out the *Pepperoni Press* for us too. He collaborated on it with his wife, who was a cartoonist. Ciccarelli also organized our first conference for franchisees, which was held in July 1972 at Howard Johnson's motel in Ypsilanti.

That first conference was small in comparison with the extravaganzas Domino's regional organizations hold these days, but it bubbled with company spirit and the desire to improve the business.

One of the featured speakers was Dick Mueller, who described, step by step, how he'd set up the coupon campaign that worked so well for him in his Ohio stores. We had some other business sessions, too. But I made sure we also had fun, and I came up with some hoopla—a contest to determine who was the fastest pizza maker among our franchisees. Gene Belknap won by slapping out a pie in thirty-eight seconds flat.

I gave the keynote address for the conference, and as I still do frequently on such occasions, I took the opportunity to stress the thirty-minute delivery. I was determined to make thirty-minute service standard throughout the company. "Whenever you franchisees think about me in the future," I said, "I want you to remember me by my initials, TSM, but in this order: TMS, which stands for *thirty-minute service*." This brought a burst of knowing laughter from my audience; all of them had heard my harping about thirty-minute service. But some franchisees had been lax about demanding thirty-minute service in their stores, and I wanted to put them on notice that I meant business. The reaction to my tough talk was positive. In fact, the sessions succeeded in bringing out a spirit of shared values and objectives, which went a long way toward healing the breach caused by the antitrust suit. I decided we would make the conference an annual event.

Two months after the conference, I gave company spirit another shot in the arm by putting the word *pizza* back into our name. I realized that dropping it had been a mistake. I had agreed to change our name to Domino's, Inc., in 1969 because our brokers thought that the designation *pizza* in our title was undignified, not suitable for a corporation that intended to go public.

But I'd lost all sympathy for the neutered name. I now considered it pompous. So on September 14, 1972, we filed to amend our articles of incorporation. Never again would I apologize for being what I am, a pizza man. I'm proud of my calling, and I'm proud that Domino's is a *pizza* company.

When the name change was approved, we filed a request with the U.S. Patent Office to make Domino's Pizza, Inc., our trademark. Nothing happened on this for nearly two years, and in the press of other business, I forgot all about it. When our notice of application was finally published in the patent office's *Official Gazette*, it brought on a legal dispute with Amstar Corporation that made me wish I'd never heard the word *trademark*. Amstar took us to court for allegedly infringing on its trademark for Domino Sugar, and the costly courtroom battle that followed dragged on for five years. It was one of the most difficult periods for me in the whole history of Domino's.

There was another name change within the company in 1972—calling our commissary Domino's Pizza Commissary, Inc., instead of ComCap—and I viewed this switch as something of a personal setback.

ComCap was part of a strategy I had devised to improve the image of the commissary with franchisees. I intended to wipe the slate clean by doing something new and different with the commissary, and I came up with the idea of staffing its units with handicapped people. Some of the work, such as lifting bags of flour and other heavy supplies, required physical strength but no degree of mental effort. Other jobs required mental skills but no physical dexterity. I got very excited about the possibility of hiring teams of handicapped people who could combine their skills to perform these tasks. We could have physically handicapped people supervising mentally handicapped people. I put a lot of time into designing such an operation, and I came up with the name ComCap. Cap stood for *handicap*.

This concept made sense in my corporate strategy, because I didn't want the commissary business to take attention away from the main task of making and delivering pizza. Therefore, I planned to separate ComCap from Domino's eventually by letting the handicapped employees take it over. I would sell them stock in ComCap, and their investment would be motivation for them to make the operation as efficient and productive as possible. Their management control would also provide them independence and job security.

It was a great idea whose time, as I discovered, had not yet come. The person who was in charge of the commissary didn't follow through on the plan. We hired a few handicapped people, five or six at most, and they did good work. But my ideal of making the commissary a business of, by, and for the handicapped was never realized. I'd still like to see more handicapped people employed by the commissary.

Although I was reluctant to give up the concept of ComCap, the switch to Domino's Pizza Commissary, Inc., accomplished another of my objectives: The commissary became a separate entity with its own checkbook so it could pay its own bills—giving us better financial controls. And we set it up with its own board of directors.

There were many indications of the growing momentum of Domino's. Getting back title to our Cross Street store from Ken Heavlin was important to me, because having our name on a store we had no control over was intolerable. But what pleased me even more were the strides we were making in store openings and the quality of the people being trained by our franchisees. For example, among the drivers hired from late 1971 through 1972 were Don Schindler, Rick Flory, Joseph Seagle, Dan Shefte, Mike Wyse, Ron Rzewnicki, Todd Kane, Dick Midlick, and Eric Marcus. All of them went on to become area franchisees, along with

Paul Callihan, Larry George, and George Hazzis, who joined us as managers in this same period. Dave Kilby was going great guns down in Florida, and he hired several people who were to become key Dominoids. Among them was Dave Black, a former delicatessen manager who would eventually work his way into what is perhaps the most important job in our company: vice-president of operations, responsible for all stores in the United States.

Our expansion now was on a different footing than our hell-for-leather growth of 1969, because it was being carried out mainly by franchisees. But I was still concerned about providing adequate training and store inspections.

John Correll had resigned in 1971 to become food and beverage director of the Ann Arbor Hilton. Late in 1972, I persuaded him to write a new operations manual for us since our first one had been based on his instruction sheets. I told him, "You ought to form your own consulting firm. Consultants make a lot of money and don't do much." So he went into consulting part-time, and after completing our operations manual, he developed course outlines for a training program that we established in June 1973 as Domino's College of Pizzerology. Mike Paul taught the first class. The college had a four-day curriculum that gave students a thorough introduction to our system.

Our basic pizza-skills training is now done by Domino's regional organizations, but the College of Pizzerology has continued and its classes are administered from corporate headquarters. The college offers a number of advanced degrees. About twenty individuals in the company hold a master's degree from the college, and in 1986 Dick Mueller and Jim Tilly joined me as holders of the degree of Doctor of Pizzerology.

I knew back in 1973, however, that no matter how good our training became, service and quality in our stores would continue to be erratic unless we carried out regular inspections. So that spring I appointed two inspectors: Jim Walters, who had done a terrific job as manager of our store in Bowling Green, Ohio, and Gordon Wallace, a stockholder and sometime franchisee who had a good overall knowledge of Domino's. I gave them the title field representative. They worked hard, but after several months it was evident that they couldn't begin to cover effectively all the new stores that were springing up.

I was really scratching my head and scribbling away on my legal pads in search of an idea that would allow us to do a better job of inspection. I wanted to make more personal visits, too. One day I saw a classified ad for a bus that had been converted into a motor home, and it hit me: of course! We could put an inspection team aboard this bus and take it all over the country. It would be economical because we'd save on restaurant and motel costs.

I thought this would solve my problem, but the converted bus, which I rented with an option to purchase, turned out to be less than an ideal vehicle for the purpose. It was too big and hard to drive. My plan called for the inspection team to sleep on the road so they'd be fresh for a whole night of store visits, but some of the guys complained that this contraption bounced us around so much that they got no rest.

Nevertheless, we drove all the way to New England in November 1973 and had some extremely effective communication with stores on the way out and back. We also had fun. John Correll did the cooking, and he put on some fantastic meals. Our fiftieth Domino's store had opened in Portsmouth, New Hampshire, the previous month, and as our touring team of inspectors approached the town, someone came up with the calculation that Domino's would soon be selling its twenty-millionth pizza somewhere in the country.

Why not that very night, in Portsmouth? And why not make it a big public relations event, with me delivering this historic pizza in person?

In no time at all we had set the scheme in motion and notified the store manager and the local media. The lucky couple to order that pizza were Al and May Brown of Portsmouth, and they were flabbergasted when our big old bus pulled up in front of their house to make the delivery. The ceremony took place on the Browns' front porch, with newspaper and television cameras recording it for posterity. I managed to carry off my role fairly gracefully, despite the insolence of the Browns' dog, which decided to use Jim Walters's trouser leg for a fireplug just as I was presenting his master and mistress with Domino's Pizza No. 20 million.

Our next inspection tour a month later was aboard a GM motor home, which I purchased for the company. It was vastly more comfortable, easy to drive, and we used it with what I considered to be terrific results. I think that motor home probably was the most effective communications tool we have ever had in the company. Our arrival in it was an event the store manager or franchisee could use to motivate his crews. The visits gave us personal contact with people in the field, and not only could we discover the problems they were facing, we could help them find solutions on the spot.

Our financial position had improved by early 1973 to the point that I felt we could start paying off our creditors. This was a day I'd eagerly awaited, because I'd been promising to pay these people for so long. Many Domino's creditors were friends of mine, yet I knew that few of them expected we'd ever be able to pay them back. So I decided to have some fun and let them help celebrate our solvency by proclaiming Operation Surprise.

I set up a schedule dividing all the creditors into two classes: those we owed more than $1,000 and those under that amount. We would send the first group monthly checks for 2 percent of the amount we owed them. Those we owed less than $1,000 would get 4 percent monthly. We'd continue paying at those levels until all the debts were erased.

Rather than describe all the gory details of our troubles in my letter announcing the program, I had Tom Ciccarelli's wife draw a five-panel cartoon showing a man in an airplane. The sequence traced Domino's rise and crash, another rise and crash, and then our slow but steady recovery. I also had special checks made up, imprinted with the legend *Domino's Pizza, Operation Surprise* and a little cartoon character wearing nothing but a barrel. We continued to send those checks out for the next four years.

Operation Surprise had an unexpected payoff for me in the uplift it gave to our employees and franchisees. They were proud of it, and this gave me an idea for my address at our second annual franchisee convention, Super Seminar II, held at Cedar Point, Ohio, a popular amusement park located between Toledo and Cleveland.

On a business trip to New York a few months earlier, I had picked up a book called *Try Giving Yourself Away*, by David Dunn. I read it on my flight back to Detroit and found it captivating because it got right to the heart of what I thought Domino's service to customers was all about. I bought a hundred copies of the book to give to everyone at Super Seminar II, and I tried to arrange for Dunn to be a speaker on the program, but his schedule was full. I decided to address his theme myself.

What Dunn had learned, I explained, was that although he was brought up to look upon life as a process of *getting*, as most people are, he was much happier when he was *giving*. He started what he called "giving myself away" in the 1930s, when he sent a suggestion for an advertisement to the New York Central Railroad. The idea came to him aboard the Twentieth Century Limited, now only a nostalgic memory, but then the queen of passenger trains. He began wondering where the Chicago-bound and New York-bound Centuries passed each other in the night. He visualized the copy line "Where the Centuries Pass," and he offered it to the railroad with "no strings attached."

The idea was used on a calendar that Dunn took great pleasure in seeing the following year in nearly every railroad station and hotel lobby he entered in the United States and Europe. He wrote: "I made the important discovery that anything which makes one glow with pleasure is beyond money calculation in this humdrum world where there is too much grubbing and too little glowing." He developed "giving himself away" into "an exciting and thoroughly satisfying hobby."

Dunn's secret was that his *giving* was done without thought of reward. "Almost anything in the world can be bought for money—except the warm impulses of the human heart. They have to be *given*," he wrote. "And they are priceless in their power to purchase happiness for two people, the recipient and the giver." Another point that fascinated me was when he said that giving to become known as generous or self-sacrificing is not giving at all. It is merely selfishness in disguise, and is a slow poison to the spirit. In my speech, I used my wife as a fine example of the giving spirit. Margie had put up with my long hours, and went year after year without a vacation, giving her time and effort freely and cheerfully. I would never have gotten back on my feet if it hadn't been for her.

Dunn's idea appealed to me so mightily because it showed how to apply Christian philosophy, in a nondenominational way, to the day-to-day business of Domino's. It underscored my own belief that we enrich ourselves most in life when we *give* ourselves most fully and freely. I told the franchisees that we can do this in Domino's by seeking ways to give more service than the customer expects, by noticing things that will help the customer or coworkers, or by showing appreciation to suppliers for a job well done.

That speech was a turning point for me. Up till then, I had

labored over numerous drafts of every talk I made, writing them out in longhand and then having them typed. This message came from my heart, and I spoke without reference to notes except for occasional quotes from Dunn's book. The result must have been pretty good, because people mentioned it to me for years afterward. This casual approach to speaking felt natural and comfortable, and I've used it ever since.

Our principal guest speaker at Super Seminar II was one of my heroes, Bob Feller, the great Cleveland Indians pitcher. He gave a talk about handling pressure situations, and we had him autograph baseballs afterward.

But there was another impression from that conference that dismayed me. Someone took a snapshot of me sitting by the pool in my swim trunks. I couldn't believe it when I saw how much weight I'd put on. My shoulder had been bothering me for about a year, and I'd stopped working out. That photograph showed a spare tire around my middle that sent me back to my Royal Air Force exercises immediately, and I've been working out regularly ever since. I run six days a week now and work out with weights at least twice a week. I weigh myself every day and also count the calories I consume each day. Although some people think I am too fanatic about exercise and diet, they're habits I don't want to break because when I'm in shape, I feel better and work better.

By the end of 1973, Domino's had seventy-six stores in thirteen states. We showed a profit of $130,000 for the year, which, though comparatively small, was very gratifying after our long immersion in red ink. I knew we must be doing something right when I got a telephone call from Frank Carney, the chairman of Pizza Hut, who said he wanted to come to Ypsilanti and chat with me about buying Domino's. I told him I didn't think anyone could make me an offer that would persuade me to sell, but I agreed to listen. I told him I felt like I would if Raquel Welch had asked me for a date; I'd be tempted and flattered, but my marriage vows would make me turn her down. I was glad I talked to Carney, because some of the things he said served to confirm my already strong faith in the Domino's concept.

The success that prompted Pizza Hut's acquisition attempt was sweet, but it was not without problems. The main one grew out of the terrific job our franchisees were doing in recruiting and training. There was nowhere in our system for outstanding young recruits to go after they'd managed a store for a time and began looking for new challenges. As a result, we were in danger of losing valuable employees. A few had already left us to start their own operations in competition with us.

I talked this problem over with Mike Paul on several occasions. At this point, Mike was my best sounding board, because he knew store operations and our management approach so thoroughly. I trusted his judgment.

Mike and I were meeting quite often because he was in the process of looking for another area in which to start franchising Domino's. He'd spend his days off from his store in Ypsilanti traveling all over the country looking for locations. One day he flew to Raleigh-Durham, North Carolina, in the morning, returned to Detroit, and drove to State College, Pennsylvania, and back that same afternoon. At one point he was interested in some locations in Texas, and in retrospect, that would have been a terrific choice because he could have franchised the entire state. But he finally decided to locate in Minneapolis, and he moved up there in the summer of 1973.

In a way, Mike's restlessness was symptomatic of the very problem I'd been discussing with him. Our good people were eager to grow and were looking around at all kinds of possibilities. I believe there is an intelligent solution to any problem, and I was certain I'd find a way to turn this one into an opportunity.

The requisites were clear: We had to design a program that would encourage franchisees to let go of their best managers and help them become Domino's franchisees. Somehow, of course, the franchisees had to have a stake in the program. They had to get something in return for all the time and effort they put into training the individual. In fact, if the program were set up right, they should be rewarded according to how good a job they had done in recruiting and training.

One day I met one of the top executives of the Kirby Vacuum Cleaner Company, who told me about a program they'd set up to promote growth of distributorships. As he talked, the solution to our problem of retaining ambitious employees came into my mind. I'd create a sponsorship program whereby franchisees would encourage their best managers to open their own Domino's stores. The company would share its royalties from the new franchise with the sponsor for a period of time. I got excited about this plan because it was good for all concerned. It contained a double benefit for franchisees because it not only gave them added income, it also provided them with a powerful new tool for their recruiting efforts. The kind of young person the sponsorship program would attract—the individual with strong entrepreneurial interests—is precisely the type who tends to learn our system quickly and is most likely to have the makings of a store manager. As for benefit to the employee, how many part-time jobs hold out the possibility of eventually helping you go into business for yourself with both the blessing and the financial backing of your employer?

I had to be very careful about how I set up my program because new legislation regulating franchising was rampant at the time and we didn't want to run afoul of any of these laws. So the only condition we put on participation was that the sponsoree had to have at least one year of experience as a store manager.

There would be no legal obligation on the part of the spon-
sors—we wanted to avoid any possibility that they could be
construed as agents of the corporation or salesmen of franchises, which would have involved a lot of red tape and hin-
dered operation of their own stores, a situation I devoutly
wished to avoid.

We decided to begin by giving the sponsor half of the 5½ percent royalties paid to us by the sponsoree for five years. This percentage was reduced over the years as the program grew and
conditions changed. The sponsor's assistance, though, continues
to terminate with the opening of the sponsoree's store, when our
corporate supervision takes over. But the sponsor always gets
credit for his sponsorship. For example, every time a franchisee
who had a sponsor is mentioned in a company communication,
the sponsor's name is also given. We also developed incentive
awards for individuals who sponsor the most new franchisees in a
given period.

We even extended the sponsorship program to corporate
stores. During the early seventies, managers of corporate stores
had 49 percent ownership. The company's area organization
owned the other 51 percent. This approach allowed us to apply
the same regulations, standards, and types of inspection to a corporate store that we used for a franchise store. The only difference
was that with a corporate store, we had control and corporate
policies would always prevail. This was the concept I wanted to
grow with; more so than franchising to outsiders. It was the best
of both worlds. It had the benefits of franchising, since the operator had some ownership, but it avoided the legal complications
that can arise from a franchising contract with someone from outside the company.

The subject of legal problems with franchisees was much on
my mind while I was setting up the sponsorship program because

Chuck Gray and I were about to part company. Our relationship had gone from bad to worse, which irritated me because he had been my first franchisee. I was also having problems with franchisee number two, Dean Jenkins. To me, Jenkins just didn't believe in Domino's enough.

He told me, "I don't think it's really important to give thirty-minute service."

"Dean, if that's really how you feel," I said, "I think we should part company."

We worked out a mutual termination in December 1973, and Dean changed his sign and expanded his menu, and I think he's still happily plugging away in the same location.

I thought the sponsorship program would screen out problem operators before either they or Domino's were fully committed to each other. But most important, I saw it as a potential springboard to tremendous growth. Happily, it worked out in both ways. It has been a major factor in Domino's development.

At the same time I was creating our sponsorship program, I was working with a consultant named Jim Graham, who ran a motivational school in Detroit called the Personal Achievement Institute. Graham introduced me to Multiple Management, a system designed for McCormick & Company, the tea and spice firm, as a way to get people within the company involved in management decisions. Charles P. McCormick describes the theory in his book *The Power of People*, written in 1949. Multiple Management is actually a big suggestion system, and I think it's excellent because it fosters company policies that are easily enforced since they are developed by the franchisees themselves. Top management has veto power over the decisions made under the system, but I am confident that our franchisees make good decisions.

While studying Multiple Management, I also attended

Graham's classes in the PMA (Positive Mental Attitude) approach to employee motivation, a system based on the work of the late Napoleon Hill and insurance tycoon W. Clement Stone, who collaborated to write *Success Through a Positive Mental Attitude.* I like Graham's method because it makes employees aware of the need to develop personal goals—which usually turn out to reinforce company goals—and it shows individuals how to develop self-esteem, enthusiasm for their work, and a spirit of cooperation. But best of all, the PMA program stresses the importance of applying the Golden Rule in personal conduct.

Five Multiple-Management groups were formed within Domino's and each held a series of meetings in which a lot of good ideas bubbled up. Graham planned to set up a board of directors for each group, but before that could happen, the whole Multiple Management concept was sidetracked by administrative changes in the company.

Fortunately, franchisees liked Multiple Management and were able to keep it functioning. Their group grew and evolved into what is now our board of franchisees, a vital part of our management communications.

While working with Graham in the fall of 1974, I was spending considerable time thinking about the problem of how to reorganize the administration of Domino's. Our management structure, so simple on the store level, had grown extremely complex on the national level. The lines of authority were tangled in overlapping areas of responsibility, and it was getting to be too much for me to continue running single-handed. Besides, I knew my own weakness as an administrator. I felt that someone with solid executive experience could come in as my right-hand man and straighten out the situation without much difficulty.

I had just about decided to contact an executive-search firm about filling the position of executive vice-president of Domino's when I happened to be looking through the business section of the *Ann Arbor News* and came upon this advertisement:

AN IMPORTANT MESSAGE TO ALL BUSINESS PEOPLE

Here is a brief accurate story about a real outstanding man who has just completed his latest project and who wants to go to work for a good group of people in the general area of this city. This man is the most youthful person you will ever meet with such a great abundance of useful business experiences. Most of the experiences were in manufacturing companies large and small, but some were in nationally known food products companies. In each and every case he brought about the very finest of results to the investors. His fine record was always with the enthusiastic respect and trust and willing "drive" of all employees at all levels. Every effort, as a result of its healthy growth, resulted most often in the company being sold and then another challenging situation would be started. He is now available to start work immediately with an interested group and what position is offered and what kind of compensation are not important to him at this point. The kind of people he would be with and how he could help in the building of a sound future for the company are of number 1 importance. This man has been in the capacity of General Manager and President of most every entity he's been involved with directly and he is used to starting over again and again. He has an outstanding youthful open attitude realistic but full of confidence which he helps others build in themselves. He has these 25 years of multi company experiences to bring to some group in this area. He is really capable of doing a valuable job in most any kind of business. You should get to know this fellow. He is in real trim shape, excellent health (reflections of his attitude), is happily married and wants to do a job.

This was not written by or connected with any agency. This is a private individual ad. Some very fine local references can be supplied.

For immediate and confidential response write to **Box MB 934 of The Ann Arbor News.**

12

I NEARLY LOST CONTROL of Domino's for a second time in 1976.

There were no formalities, no signing away of rights this time. I simply handed over so much power to one executive that control was almost out of my hands. The situation developed so gradually I was hardly aware of it.

It all started in December 1974, when I interviewed the man who had placed that advertisement for himself in the *Ann Arbor News*. He marched into my office precisely at the hour we'd agreed on, stiffly put out his hand, and said: "Good morning. My name is Leroy A. Russell Hughes. My friends call me Russ."

I was impressed by his appearance. His dark blue business suit was obviously custom-tailored. I noted that the initials monogrammed on the cuff of his crisp white shirt were R.A.H., but it didn't occur to me to ask about the extra name he'd used to introduce himself. He wore glasses tinted so dark that I couldn't make

eye contact with him, and this bothered me a bit. But his credentials were so impressive that I pushed my discomfort aside.

Hughes showed me a list of the companies he'd served as vice-
president and president, with his salaries indicated beside each
position. His description of what he'd done for these firms was
fascinating. He kept repeating that he understood how to achieve
excellence in corporate management, that the company that followed his approach would achieve excellence. He was hypnotic.

Hughes's main reference was Bill Brittain, an outstanding executive in the Ann Arbor area. He had reported to Brittain in
several of the jobs listed on his résumé, including the presidency
of Franklin Dry Roasted Peanut Corp. "You should talk to Bill
Brittain," he said. "But unfortunately, he's on a business trip in
Japan right now, so I'm afraid you won't be able to reach him." I
later discovered that Brittain was not in Japan at that time.
Hughes may have made an honest mistake. But it resulted in a
major error on my part. I hired Hughes as executive vice-president of Domino's without checking his references.

I was excited by the prospect of working with someone who
had run a large corporation. Domino's was going to be a large
corporation, I felt that in my bones, and I wanted to know how to
run one.

I suppose there were all kinds of retired businessmen who
could have given me the type of knowledge I needed. But at the
time, I felt such knowledge was a rare commodity, and I was
willing to put up with just about any amount of discomfort in
working with Hughes in order to learn from his experience.

He came surprisingly cheap. Hughes explained that he had to
go to Japan for three or four months very soon, so he was willing
to start at Domino's for only eighteen thousand dollars a year; we
agreed that we would reopen the salary question after he got back
and began demonstrating results.

Hughes didn't seem put off by the problems I outlined for him: the costly inefficiencies in our commissary operations and our administrative foulups. He said he had perfected systems that would make those difficulties disappear. He assured me he could make Domino's run like a well-oiled machine.

I felt we finally were going to be able to get our entire operation moving in the right direction, and Hughes gave me no reason to alter that conviction when he returned from his trip to Japan that spring. He began cleaning up our administrative mess in an admirable fashion. He had been an expert cost accountant at Hoover Ball Bearing earlier in his career, and he applied that experience to our commissary with excellent results. After he'd been on the job six months, I boosted his salary to twenty-five thousand a year.

Much as I appreciated Russ's work, though, I found it difficult to communicate with him. He and I had little in common except for a deep interest in cars. He drove a 1960 Cadillac, which he talked about constantly. He also owned a Rolls-Royce Silver Cloud, which he kept under a cloth cover, and he said the Rolls-Royce was his standard of excellence. So to show my appreciation for the outstanding performance he turned in during his first six months on the job, I bought him a used Rolls as a company car.

I have to hand it to Russ for getting me to think about quality and service at levels higher than I'd ever considered. His standards of performance seemed even higher than mine, and this impressed me. He was brilliant, too. I wasn't used to people who could come up with ideas I hadn't thought of or top my ideas, as he did.

But Russ's brilliance was offset for me by an uncommunicative approach that was in contradiction to the openness I tried to foster in the company. This trait came out in unfortunate ways. For example, Russ cut back on trips to the franchisees by field consultants. He said he wanted the field consultants in the office, where they'd be available for meetings. In the same vein, he disliked the Multiple Management meetings. He seemed to want to stop them, too, but he didn't know how. The franchisees found the sessions useful and continued them.

What the difference between Russ Hughes and Tom Monaghan boiled down to, I believe, was his belief that "systems" are the important thing: If you have a strong system in which everything runs like clockwork, results will follow automatically. Russ believed that a manager should be judged according to how well he is able to apply and enforce the rules of the system.

I focused on goals. He focused on ways of achieving the goals. My approach was informal, his was strictly formal.

The problem with Russ's approach, in my view, was that its success depended entirely on the vision and judgment of the man at the top. He alone was the engineer who knew the design of the system. His employees had to believe in the system and look to him for interpretation of it. It reminded me of the description of the Navy given by a character in Herman Wouk's *The Caine Mutiny:* "A master plan created by genius for execution by idiots."

Russ deliberately created a mystique about his role. And I have to admit that I was mesmerized by it. He wanted more and more control, and I handed it over to him.

Finally, I made him president of the company and stepped aside so he would have free rein to work the miracles of leadership he was promising.

There's no doubt he did some good things for Domino's. One of them was bringing George Papineau into the company. George is a master salesman, a shrewd businessman, and also one of the most unselfish, giving persons I've ever met. He had worked for Russ at Franklin Peanut, and apparently his marketing skill was largely responsible for making the product a national brand.

Long before pizza delivery, I brought home the chocolate milk.

My brother, Jim *(left),* and me

Me at age three with my dad

I was proud to be a Marine.

St. Joseph's Orphanage in Jackson, Michigan.
I loved its architecture but hated
my confinement there.

Sister Berarda and me in August 1983.
She was a great inspiration to me.

Various views of my new office
at Domino's Farms

A model of the Golden Beacon
and the long, low headquarters
building at Domino's Farms

The design for McCormick House

Me in Tiger Stadium with my 1934 Duesenberg

It was a great moment when Jim Campbell, Mr. Fetzer, and I were drenched in champagne after the Tigers won the 1984 World Series.

Whenever I'm with Eugene Power, my mentor and a valued member of Domino's board, I always learn something.

That's me in the center of some of my young Honduran friends. I support Father Enrique's mission because I want to give kids like these a better chance at life.

Margie and me on our wedding day

The Monaghan family in May 1980 at Barbara's First Holy Communion

Another person I met through Russ Hughes, and I'll always be grateful for it, was Townsend Beaman, a patent and trademark lawyer from Jackson. Russ recommended I talk to Beaman about Amstar Corporation's claim that our use of the name Domino's infringed on its trademark for Domino Sugar.

What happened was that notice of my application for trademark, which I had submitted in 1972, finally appeared in the October 15, 1974, issue of the patent office's *Official Gazette*. On November 27, 1974, Amstar's attorney sent me a letter stating that Amstar would oppose my application. He strongly suggested that we would be in trouble if we didn't discontinue using the name Domino's.

My first reaction to Amstar's letter, which I received shortly before I hired Russ Hughes, was to contact Covington and Burling, the most prestigious law firm I knew about. An attorney named Harry Schniderman was assigned to the case, and I was astonished when he told me that his research revealed that the patent office had issued a default judgment against Domino's in 1970.

I recalled that I had applied for registration of Domino's as a trademark sometime in 1969, but I didn't know what became of it. As it turned out, the notice of application was published in the *Official Gazette* on June 24, 1970, and Amstar had immediately filed notice of opposition. Because Domino's did not respond, a default judgment had been entered against us. I did not know about any of this, including a January 1971 letter from Amstar suggesting that we discontinue use of the name Domino's, because I wasn't in control of the company at the time. Now, nearly four years later, it seemed that these little oversights had put me behind the eight ball.

Because of the default judgment, Schniderman believed we would never be able to register Domino's Pizza as a trademark. On the other hand, he said, we had been using the name so long that Amstar couldn't make us abandon it. He believed the patent office's acceptance of the name for publication in its *Official Gazette* indicated an opinion that there was no problem of confusion between our pizza and Amstar's sugar.

We discussed the possibility of registering another name, Red Domino. But I didn't like the idea of changing names, and when Russ suggested we talk to Townsend Beaman about it, I said I was always ready to listen to anyone who could help me. We made an appointment and drove over to Beaman's office in Hughes's Rolls-Royce.

I don't remember much about that first meeting except the big, cheerful smile on Beaman's face as we were introduced. I outlined as best I could the background of our problem with Amstar, and he said he'd look it over and get back to us.

At our next meeting, Beaman said, "I want to set your mind at ease about this situation. You've got nothing to worry about. I've done some research, and that default judgment in 1970 was not final. Your reasons for withdrawing after Amstar's objection were perfectly legitimate, given your company's financial situation at the time. You have every right to refile. Amstar will object, of course. But they won't sue you. They have never done so in similar circumstances in the past, and they know there is really no problem of confusion in the mind of the public between their product and yours."

I was glad to hear him say that. The expense involved in changing our name would be prohibitive, not to mention the other obvious negatives: the loss of the value we had built up in the name, the problems of changing telephone-book listings, and the uproar the change would create among our franchisees.

But some of the other attorneys I consulted about Beaman's opinion advised me to follow the counsel of Covington and Burling and change our name to Red Domino.

To change or not to change? I wrestled with that question through most of the month of June 1974. One advantage in switching to Red Domino would be its uniqueness. We searched the Yellow Pages of phone books from all over the country and found no pizza shops named Red Domino. Our current name had no such exclusivity. At least a dozen operations scattered around the country were called Domino's or something very similar.

Besides, the cost of changing our name might not be nearly as high as it would be to fight a suit by Amstar, which my various lawyers estimated could range from $1 million to $2 million. They said the case would involve at least a year of shuffling in and out of court, time I could ill afford to take from the business of running Domino's.

We were already spending more time on legal problems than I liked to think about: We had worked out a termination agreement with Chuck Gray, and he'd started a pizza business in the same location his Domino's store had occupied. Its name, when spoken on the telephone, sounded like Domino's. I believed this was a violation of our agreement, so we were getting ready to file suit against him. We also were preparing to sue Tom Ahlers, our partner in Champaign, Illinois, for what I felt was a breach of contract. We had an agreement with Ahlers under which we owned 51 percent of his stock and he received all profits for a certain period of time. I believed that our contract obligated him to open all subsequent stores under that arrangement. But he'd begun developing new stores under a different name, and we were suing for misappropriation of corporate opportunity.

We eventually dropped both of these suits before they got to court, but I couldn't foresee that at the time I was scratching away at my legal pads on the question of changing our name.

To change or not to change? I wrote page after page of notes weighing all the pros and cons and exploring the ramifications that developed. Finally, after a few more conversations with Townsend Beaman—who by this time was Towny to me—I came to a decision: We *would not* switch to Red Domino. We would fight to register Domino's Pizza, and if we lost and Amstar sued us, as some of my counselors believed they would, we would battle them for all we were worth.

Making that decision took a load off my shoulders, one that had kept me from spending time dealing with my organizational problems, which in some ways were more serious than any lawsuit.

I had expected there would be things Russ Hughes would do that I wouldn't understand, and I held back and just watched him operate because, as I noted in one of my automatic-writing explorations of the situation: "If I question everything he does, I may inhibit him. My main job is to learn from him." In an aside to that same entry, I noted: "Philosophical difference—he doesn't think it's important that a manager be a fast pizza maker."

I was trying to counterbalance that philosophical difference between us without getting into a ruckus with Hughes by constantly harping to managers on the need for speed and quality in pizza making. I made this the theme of my speech to franchisees at our Super Seminar IV that August.

Tom Ciccarelli and John Correll did some research on pizza making for me. They traced the origins of the pizza to sixteenth-century Italy, where Neopolitans made a pie by adding oregano and garlic to tomato sauce, spread thinly over a delicate crust. In the seventeenth and eighteenth centuries, pizzerias were to Naples what cafés were to Paris. Customers sat around for hours socializing and watching the pizza makers flamboyantly toss pizza dough in the air. According to their research, when Teddy Roosevelt visited Italy as the guest of King Victor Emmanuel III in 1906, he became the first American President to taste pizza. Tom and John uncovered a lot of other lore, including the fact that the first pizzeria in the United States was opened in 1895 on Spring Street in the heart of New York City's Little Italy, and that Enrico Caruso, the famous tenor, owed his voice to pizza, which he supposedly consumed in great quantities.

I used a few of these facts to set the stage for the message I wanted to get across: that Domino's pizza makers should become known as the fastest in the world. Our contest winners that year proved that a pizza could be made in sixteen seconds. I challenged all the operators to go back to their stores and start building for themselves the reputation of the world's fastest. My goal was to have every store turning out a pizza every thirty seconds during an entire rush.

The response to my challenge was heartwarming, almost like old times. Everyone seemed eager to start shooting at that thirty-second-pizza mark. So I returned to Ypsilanti in high spirits and began making notes like crazy on how we could get geared up for a year of fast franchise expansion.

Our traveling field consultants would have made that job a lot easier. Gordon Wallace alone had been aiming to open fourteen area distributorships with sixty-seven new stores in 1975. But since Hughes had cut down on the trips by our field consultants, we needed a different strategy. We no longer had a use for the motor home I'd purchased for the field consultants to travel in, so I sold it and loaned the money I got for it to Bob Cotman. This was to enable him and his second wife, Jan Muhleman, to move their new design studio, Group 243, from Columbus to Ann Arbor. I had been pushing them to do this because I wanted them to be Domino's advertising agency. They had designed a Red Domino logo for us, and we used it to have some business cards, stationery, and shipping labels printed up, just in case.

But after they moved Group 243 to Ann Arbor, it turned out

that for various reasons they got little business from Domino's except for production of the *Pepperoni Press*. I felt bad about this, but I explained the situation to Bob and Jan, and they seemed to accept it.

I began spending just about every Saturday kicking ideas around with Bob Cotman. He was a good listener. He had been one of my best sounding boards in the company in the days before the fire at Cross Street, and we were able to reestablish some of that brainstorming excitement now. My main interest was in capitalizing on having Russ Hughes aboard by spending my time on creative ideas. I was proud of the way we'd celebrated the opening of the one-hundreth Domino's store in May 1975. I'd remembered a speech by Ray Kroc in which he told how he'd located his one-thousandth McDonald's store in the same community where he'd built his first one—Des Plaines, Illinois. That appealed to me. So I made sure we built Domino's store number 100 in Ypsilanti, at 1643 Homes Road.

But probably the best idea I came up with at this time was our Mystery Customer Program. It was designed to help us improve delivery times and monitor product quality. The plan was to get a customer in each store's area to agree to order pizzas from that store at least once a month. Our headquarters would give the customers a healthy rebate on the pizzas in return for a report on how long the delivery took, the driver's appearance and manner, and whether the pizza they received was hot and tasty. We launched the program in the summer of 1975, and it has been working well ever since. The identity of the mystery customers is a closely guarded secret, so a store's crew never knows which order is one on which they'll be graded. The program is expensive—in the mid-eighties it was costing upward of a million dollars annually—but it's an excellent tool for paring down delivery times.

Consistent, fast delivery times have been a constant goal in Domino's. At the outset, the challenge was to establish that it was possible to maintain thirty-minute service. That was tough, like breaking the four-minute mile. But once we had some of our stores providing thirty-minute service consistently, their example helped us achieve the goal. By 1985 we had a system-wide average delivery time of twenty-four minutes, and quite a few of our stores were turning in average times of around eighteen minutes. Thirty-minute delivery is normal for us now. Our figures for 1985 show we were doing it 91 percent of the time. I don't know how much of that improvement in performance can be attributed to the Mystery Customer Program, but there's no doubt it was a big help.

As 1975 wore on, the year of rapid franchise growth I'd envisioned failed to materialize. In fact, we stopped growing at all. One reason might have been that Hughes felt he had to understand every action thoroughly before he'd make a move. He belabored even the smallest decision. But I was even more concerned about his policies that restricted opening of new stores. Franchisees couldn't move ahead with an opening until a proposed store was approved by a board meeting. And to get it approved, they had to submit a lengthy proposal. So everyone stopped trying to open new stores except Dick Mueller.

Mueller just played the game. He came in with books an inch thick on each store, and he'd submit fifteen or twenty at a time. His proposals had all the information Hughes asked for: demographics of the area, résumés of the people who were going to run the store, statements of where the financing was going to come from, photographs of the site from all kinds of angles. Mueller had the procedure down to a science: He had photocopied forms and would fill in the blanks for each new location and turn them out in batches. He was the only guy whose organization did any growing during this period.

Hughes had made George Papineau his assistant, and George later confided to me that Russ had proposed that the two of them use his Rolls-Royce to go on store visits in the Ann Arbor and Ypsilanti area.

"I talked him out of that," George said. "We went in my car. But then, when we'd get to the stores in the midst of a rush, Russ wanted to call the drivers in—make them stop delivering—so he could hold a meeting with them."

Our franchisees felt headquarters was not communicating with them. They held some meetings and came up with a collective strategy to jump ship. Their action was perfectly legal under our franchise contract, which said either party could terminate. But if the franchisee did so, the company would have the option of buying his stores with a 10 percent down payment of a formula price. The franchisees thought Domino's was so weak financially that it couldn't buy them all out at once; so they were all going to leave together.

Mike Paul was one of the two franchisees who actually left the company. He gave us his notice on April 15, 1976. I was upset, of course, especially when I discovered that other franchisees, representing a total of fifty stores, more than half the stores in the company, were planning to do the same thing. But I could understand Mike's point of view. He told me he hadn't seen anyone from the home office for more than a year. Then the guy who was supposed to be his contact went up to Minneapolis for a Brown Jug game between Michigan and Minnesota and didn't even stop to visit Mike's store.

I got so wrapped up in this dispute with franchisees that I virtually forgot about our legal problem with Amstar. But on September 30, Amstar dropped a bomb on us. They filed suit for infringement of trademark, in the United States District Court in the Northern District of Georgia.

I got on the telephone to Towny Beaman immediately, and he was astonished. He'd been certain they would never sue. But he was even more incredulous when I told him they had filed in Atlanta.

"You don't even have any stores in Georgia, do you?" he asked.

"No we don't," I said. "It's in Dave Kilby's distribution area, and he did have three shops there, in Atlanta, Thomasville, and Athens, but they're all closed now."

That made Towny mad. "We'll get a change of venue," he said. "They're just trying to make it too difficult and costly for you to defend." Then he added, "Of course it's up to you. I'm sure we can settle it out of court. It would cost you an arm and a leg to fight them, Tom. They can afford it. I don't know whether you can."

It didn't take me long to give him an answer. In the process of reaching my decision against changing our name, I had already considered the situation we now faced as a possible scenario. My only hesitation now was asking Towny to get into a fight this big. He was sixty-nine years old, and though he appeared to be in perfect health, I could understand that he might not want to take on this giant corporation with its unlimited resources and batteries of New York lawyers. I told him so, and I made it clear that I didn't want him to feel at all guilty about advising us that Amstar wouldn't sue. He assured me he was fit and would enjoy playing David to Amstar's Goliath. So I said, "Okay, Towny, let's fight 'em!"

Towny's first move was to hire an attorney in Atlanta. He needed someone who was licensed in the Fifth District to go through the formalities of introducing him to the court before he could file a motion to move the proceedings to Michigan. Towny knew Col. Edward Newton, senior partner of the Atlanta firm of

Newton, Hopkins & Ormsby, and believed he would be a good man for the job. When he called, however, he learned that Newton was on an extended vacation and couldn't be reached. So he talked to a young staff lawyer named William Needle. As it happened, Needle had recently appeared before Judge Richard C. Freeman, who would be hearing the Amstar case. He'd succeeded with a motion similar to the change of venue Beaman was seeking. Towny got Needle to send him copies of that motion and he told me he was pleased with it. Needle was only twenty-nine years old, but Towny thought he'd be up to handling our case. They had several long telephone conversations in which they composed a motion to transfer the trial.

To me, the arguments for holding the trial in Michigan seemed very reasonable. But the law moves in mysterious ways, and Judge Freeman denied our motion.

So we began the long, tedious process of giving depositions and planning legal strategy, which was complicated, of course, by the necessity of traveling between Ypsilanti and Atlanta.

Towny was a very practical guy. He covered all bases, and he had no illusions about his mortality. He wanted Needle to be well versed on our case just in case something should happen to him before the trial. Towny and Needle seemed to see eye to eye on things and got along well, which was good because they traveled all over the country together taking depositions of operators of pizza places with Domino or some variation of it in their names. I went along on many of these trips, and they were exhausting. On one, we crossed the country, from sea to shining sea, twice in five days. The trip wouldn't have been so bad if Towny hadn't insisted on staying in the cheapest hotels and eating in the least expensive restaurants. I couldn't complain, of course, since it was Domino's money we were spending. But I thought it interesting and uplifting to see his genuine concern about saving his client's money. I managed to talk him into having dinner in a nice place in San Francisco on his birthday, but otherwise it was strictly greasy spoons.

Needle compiled a long history of uses of the word *Domino* in trademarks. The first use he found was in 1885, on a brand of tobacco and cigarettes. Then came Del Monte Company's Domino canned fruits and vegetables in 1896. Amstar brought out Domino Sugar at the turn of the century, but it was followed through the years by a succession of other companies' products using the name, from matches to men's toiletries.

Needle put his findings into a colorful graph and pointed out, "If you drop a vertical line down through a year at any time after 1900, you will hit Domino Sugar, but you'll also run into many other commercial uses of the name long before you come to Domino's Pizza in 1965."

This sort of preparation was making me feel a lot more confident about the impending court battle against Amstar. But my attitude toward Russ Hughes was running in exactly the opposite direction. I was dismayed at the growing gap in communication between us.

One Friday morning toward the end of June 1976, he came into my office and said he had something important to discuss with me. It might take all day, he said. I canceled all my appointments, and he spent the entire day and part of the night outlining his plan for a leveraged buy-out of the company by himself and his friends.

He said he was giving me a unique opportunity. The transaction would involve no cash, but if I sold to him, I'd never have to work again the rest of my life. I was completely baffled by this approach. He knew I wasn't interested in retiring, and he knew I wasn't interested in money alone—I'd already made that clear by turning down a number of proposals he'd offered for going into other investments with him.

I asked a few questions about how he planned to structure the company, and I found it interesting that he planned to get rid of the franchisees and have corporate stores only. He hoped to bring Dick Mueller in as director of operations. The more he talked, the more startling I found his plan. It was extremely detailed. He'd obviously spent a lot of time on it. I began to get mad. I had given this man everything he'd asked for to help him do his job. I had increased his salary to $50,000 a year, plus bonuses, a chunk of stock worth about $150,000, and a car. But he hasn't been working for me at all, I thought. He's been working strictly for himself!

I don't remember how we concluded that evening. I was non-committal. My anger had been replaced by a sense of relief. I couldn't wait to start analyzing the situation and laying plans. I spent the entire weekend with my legal pads, outlining the various options I had and how I might deal with them. When I finished late Sunday night, I had my whole plan worked out. The first step in it would be to call Russ Hughes into my office the next morning and ask him to resign.

DOMINO'S CAME OF AGE as a company in the two years following Russ Hughes's departure. It was a maturation that would have been difficult in the best of times. But during this period—when we were being whipsawed by legal preparations for the Amstar trial, which made constant demands for more time, energy, and money—our growing pains were doubled.

My first priority after Hughes's departure was to replace his management philosophy with mine and concentrate on stimulating store development. We had dropped from 115 stores to 69. At the same time, I wanted to rebuild relationships with franchisees. I wanted to get Multiple Management going again, restore communications, and put our field consultants back into the field.

The fact that we were able to regain our momentum testifies to the basic strength of the Domino's concept.

When I asked for Hughes's resignation, I told him I wanted to make his departure as easy and graceful for him as possible. But he managed to undermine my efforts in his behalf. I wrote a letter to everyone in the company announcing that he was leaving to go into business for himself. He also wrote them a letter; his stated that he'd resigned "because of T. S. Monaghan's sudden announcement to me on the morning of 7–13–76 that he wanted to be in full charge again."

Al and Mary Morrison, our franchisees in Kalamazoo, were particularly upset when they received these two letters. They sent me a two-page complaint regarding "the sudden and confusing resignation of Russ Hughes as president." They said that after initially questioning my wisdom in appointing Russ, they had come to realize that he had a great deal to contribute to Domino's.

"His previous experience gave him insight as to what the company lacked and what needed to be done to further expansion . . ." they wrote. "Although not always popular, he persisted in making the company a business, trying to eliminate the 'hand holding' and 'family squabbling' which some in our organization wanted to maintain. He realized that to be big leaves no room for pettiness. He laid the groundwork for the company to have the ability to operate on a national basis." They went on in that vein, extolling Hughes's achievements, and concluded by asking me to hire him back.

In essence, my response was: "I have always tried to act in the best interests of DPI. That's why I hired Russ in the first place. Ironically, that's also why I had to terminate him. The decision wasn't easy, nor was it soon in coming." I noted that Russ had developed some good management procedures and corporate programs that were needed. "His service to the company will be remembered as exemplary and his departure, though necessary, will be remembered as a loss."

As I wrote that letter, I realized what is meant by the phrase "It's lonely at the top."

There were others who sided with Hughes. For example, Gordon Wallace, one of our field consultants, thought Hughes walked on water. He followed Russ out the door and went to work for him in another pizza restaurant venture after selling his Domino's stock back to me.

The thorniest legacy of Hughes's dealings with franchisees, however, was the mutinous movement among them. This dispute was aggravated by the Amstar suit, which gave the dissidents a convenient rationale for pulling out of the company: They claimed they were being asked to pay royalties for a name we no longer owned. Dave Kilby, our Florida-based area franchisee, was one of those who joined the mutiny. Dave's company had gotten into financial trouble early in 1976; first he stopped paying his royalties, then he had to begin closing stores. It was a bitter irony that he had already closed his three stores in Georgia when Amstar named his Georgia corporation as a codefendant in order to justify holding the trial in Atlanta.

I visited each of the dissident franchisees individually and told them we were returning to our old way of operating, that we valued them and wanted to work with them. I also made it clear that we intended to fight the Amstar suit all the way to the Supreme Court. One by one, I managed to convince them to stay with the company—except for Mike Paul, Dave Kilby, and Todd Kane.

In Kilby's case, we agreed to a mutual termination. He simply changed the signs on his remaining shops and went his own way. I didn't hear from him again for nearly two years. Then, sometime in late 1978, Dave called me up and asked if I would agree to a "merger" with his operation. Actually, he had very few stores left, but I thought his locations did have potential and I wanted to help him, so I agreed to buy him out. Then I hired him to come to work at corporate headquarters as director of franchising. By this time I believed I knew Dave's strengths and weaknesses and was convinced I'd be able to give him better direction.

Todd Kane had been brought up in the business by Mike Paul and was sponsored by Mike as a franchisee in Denver, Colorado. He joined Mike in the pizza rebellion and took down his Domino's signs. Todd held out until 1978, when he agreed to merge his stores back into Domino's.

Getting Mike Paul back onto the Domino's team was tougher. Mike can be almost as bullheaded as I am, and in this dispute we both believed truth and justice was on our side. I felt Mike had a legitimate gripe, but I wouldn't say he went about leaving the company in the proper way. I believed he'd probably ignored our legal notices that we wanted to buy his stores, but I was willing to give him the benefit of the doubt. I went up to Minneapolis in October 1976 with Jerry Kolassa, Sr., our new vice-president of finance, to have a talk with Mike. Kolassa had been around Domino's, off and on, since 1965, when he was my first tax consultant and auditor. So he had known Mike Paul a long time, too, and we hoped we'd be able to talk Mike into coming back into Domino's.

But Mike was stubborn. He pointed out that he had now changed all his signs to Pizza Park, he'd painted all his delivery cars green, and he'd done a lot of advertising of the new name.

He gave me no choice but to sue him for breach of contract. Even so, Mike and I felt no animosity. We had a lot of respect for each other. He hired an attorney who took the position that our franchise agreement was invalid in the state of Minnesota, and we argued that up one side and down the other for a few months. Finally, Mike called a halt to it. He was eager to leave Minnesota. His marriage was breaking up, and he wanted to get away from the cold weather. So he sold us his stores for three hundred thousand dollars and came to work for me as vice-president in charge of developing Domino's out west. He wound up in San Diego, where he is now one of our finest operators.

My efforts to rebuild good relations with franchisees were greatly aided by George Papineau, which was gratifying because he'd been brought into the company by Hughes. I walked into his office after I had taken over again and said, "George, I assume you don't want to work here now that Russ is gone."

"You're wrong," he said. "Now I want to work here more than ever."

"Well, I'm not so sure I want you. You've never made a pizza in your life. But I'll try you out for a while."

In the next six months, George put the whole company back together again. As I told our franchisees' convention the following year, George was our communications machine. He had an incredible rapport with the franchisees, and people would scream when he was reassigned away from their areas. I made him a field consultant and named him director of franchise relations.

I was enjoying being back in control of the company—in a way I was living a distant replay of the scenario six years earlier, after Heavlin pulled out—and I wanted to be the best president I could possibly be. So I was all eyes when I spotted an article in the Ann Arbor newspaper about an organization of small-company presidents that was being formed by Philip Alexander, of Ann Arbor Consulting Associates, Inc.

Six of us put up three thousand dollars each to pay for ten monthly meetings, and it turned out to be a terrific investment for me. Although the members' companies were quite different, after we got acquainted and were able to talk frankly about our individual problems, we discovered that we could give each other practical suggestions and new insights into the way we were running our organizations. In fact, this support group was so valuable that we reorganized it after the first year and have continued our monthly meetings ever since.

Part of the deal with Alexander was that he would consult

individually with members for a time, and from my sessions with him I developed Domino's Job Planning and Review (JP&R) system, which has been a mainstay of our management since 1977. It lets people know where they stand in their job, it encourages mutual goal setting by employees and supervisors, and it lets good ideas percolate up from the bottom. Everyone in the company goes through a JP&R regularly. It's not optional; it's part of every job except mine, and I've thought from time to time that it would be good for me, too. But I've never quite figured out who should conduct it with me.

I hold individual JP&R's with my top executives once a month. Others in the company may do them less frequently, depending on the type of job involved, but at the minimum, these reviews must be performed once every three months.

Here's how it works: Each employee gets a three-page form to fill out before sitting down with his manager. On the first sheet, he has to describe in his own language his job functions or tasks. This is the best way I know to find out if a guy understands what he's supposed to be doing. If he can't explain it, he doesn't understand it. If he doesn't understand or if he's wrong about his functions, the manager can straighten it out with him, face to face, in the JP&R session. On the first sheet there is also space to write down what the manager or the company is supposed to provide to help the employee do his job—things like working conditions, materials, or training. Lapses in training and support often get cleared up as a result of these responses. On the second sheet, the employee is to write down his personal achievements during the period and list things he needs to improve in his performance.

You'd be amazed how businesslike discussions about these sheets can clear up petty grievances and help both parties zero in on getting the job done in the future.

But the JP&R goes further. Two additional categories are filled out in the session by the manager. In one of these the employee is asked to list his goals for the coming period, with a description of how he intends to achieve them and a date by which they are to be accomplished. This list is reviewed in conjunction with the achievements sheet at the person's next JP&R session. It allows the employee to take credit for achievements without seeming to pat himself on the back, and this helps build pride and self-esteem. Establishing goals, agreeing on how they will be achieved, and then checking on how well the assignments were carried out so that performance can be improved—those are the elements of teamwork, and the JP&R process puts them together.

The final category of the JP&R is filled out by the manager and shared with the employee. The manager rates the employee by grades on such qualities as *knowledge of job and company policies, quality of work, attitude,* and *initiative.* If the employee supervises one or more other employees, there's also a space for *managerial effectiveness.* There is space on this page for comments by the employee, too, so if there's disagreement on how a person is doing, we know about it.

One of the rules I enforce about JP&R's is that they be informal. Doing one properly takes at least two to five hours, sometimes longer, and I don't want their format to be rigid or politicized. I enjoy conducting JP&R's, and I hope everyone else in Domino's does, too.

The JP&R sheets go into each employee's personnel file and form a work history and record of growth. One of the best things about them though is the ideas that bubble up from the "needs for improvement" section. Sometimes these improvements are things the company needs to do; in other cases, they represent the employee's self-criticism; either way, they can contain valuable insights. I've always said that our best ideas come from drivers— they're out making contact with customers, and they're usually young and have a fresh vision of how things can be made to work better. We want to share those visions, and any others we can get, all the way up the line.

One of the major indicators of Domino's coming of age was the repayment, at long last, of all our old debts, many of them dating from the Crash of 1969. For more than four years—since we started Operation Surprise in 1973—we'd been sending out those bundles of small checks, whittling away month after month at the principal, plus interest in most cases, on each account. Finally, on September 10, 1977, the naked little cartoon character in the barrel made his last appearance. I sent a letter along with the final checks to all the creditors, telling them how much I appreciated their patience. It felt good to make good on my promise and pay off those debts.

The end of Operation Surprise meant we could now concentrate on building, and another sign of our awakening maturity was our headquarters relocation to Ann Arbor. Our new address was 2875 Boardwalk, and it was the first presentable office we'd had since I'd been in business.

Our collection of lean-to buildings and Quonset huts in Ypsilanti had become a drawback for us. This was brought home to me late in 1973, when I decided I needed a good secretary to get me organized. I was determined to get the best money could buy, so I called Sally Hamilton, head of a local employment agency, and asked how much a good executive secretary would cost. She said about $150 a week, and I bit my lip and said, "I'll pay it."

A succession of talented women came out, and it seemed as though I wasn't interviewing them, but they were interviewing me and Domino's. After the eighth interview, I called Sally Hamilton, thanked her for sending me such fine candidates, and said, "I just don't know which one to pick."

"Well frankly, Tom," she said, "none of them wants to work for you."

I was really insulted. I got on my high horse and said, "Wait a minute, we're a great company. We're exciting. We've got about seventy-five stores and we're growing like crazy. We're the second largest firm headquartered in Ypsilanti. Why wouldn't they want to work for me?"

"Do you want to know the truth?" she asked.

"Yeah."

"Well in the first place, your building is in the worst part of town, and it doesn't present a very good image, especially with all those junk delivery cars parked out in front. One girl stumbled over the doorstep when she walked into the building. Another girl tore her nylons on a sliver from the plywood on the wall. Then she went into your office and saw it's got a cement floor. Tom, you have to put some carpeting on that floor. You have to fix the place up."

It took me three years to get around to looking for an executive secretary again. Fortunately, this candidate was not put off by our surroundings. Her name was Helen McNulty. Phil Alexander put her in touch with me because he knew she had outgrown her previous job and was looking for the kind of challenge I had to offer. I sensed immediately that she was right for the job, but neither of us had an inkling at that point of what a key player she would become on my executive team.

We didn't move to our new office until Helen had been with me for some months, and until we did, she and I sat facing each other across desks jammed together. I used to tell her she was learning to drink from a fire hose because I didn't have time to slow down and explain every step of what we were doing. She and I would just hand papers back and forth across the desks. I remember those days every time I walk into her spacious suite in our new headquarters—the difference is mind-boggling. But then, the difference between Helen's job now and what she was doing then is just as great.

One of my proudest achievements in that turnaround year, 1977, was the significant new financing we obtained for the company, thanks to a brilliant young financial consultant named John McDivitt. The infusion of four hundred fifty thousand dollars McDivitt arranged with Citizen's Trust of Ann Arbor helped us achieve our goal of 50 percent annual growth that year with a few extra points. We had started 1977 with 102 stores, and by the end of December we had 159. This wasn't easy work—we were still pioneering. Each opening was an ordeal.

Our system was full of bugs, too. For example, we hadn't yet figured out a formula for dividing profits from corporate stores that would be fair to managers and supervisors and still bring us an adequate return. So although we were growing, the company was not as profitable as it should have been. I needed a top financial person to help me solve such problems. Jerry Kolossa was stretched pretty thin and he was thinking about retirement now, so McDivitt and I began casting about to see what kind of talent was out there.

I was also looking for someone to sell franchises. A map of the country with black pins marking our current locations showed mostly wide open spaces. We had toeholds on both coasts, with Steve Litwhiler settled up in Vermont and Mike Paul getting started in San Diego. But we were actually represented in only eighteen states. The vast majority of the country was there waiting to be developed. We had decided we could fill in the map fastest by selling franchises to outsiders, and we set up a department to handle this. But we didn't have a major talent to run it. Dave Kilby's name kept coming to mind, but I'd lost touch with him and I wasn't positive he'd be the right choice. More than a

year after the franchise department was set up, Kilby contacted
me and I rehired him.

Once again, as always seemed to happen when attention was
diverted from our commissary, that operation had fallen into another major administrative mess, and my first step toward cleaning it up, late in 1976, was to reorganize it into a holding
company, Domino's National Commissaries, Inc. The following
year we added new commissary units in Michigan, Kentucky,
and North Carolina, to make a total of six across the country. We
also added an equipment and supply division, headed by a lady
with the wonderful name of Judy Silence. But I had trouble finding a president who could take on the commissary operation for
the long pull, and I began putting out feelers among our suppliers
for candidates for that job, too.

On the store operations front, I appointed Dave Smith and
Dave Black to join George Papineau as field consultants. I told
them I didn't want them sitting around the office. I wanted them
out in the field, visiting stores. This time, though, I thought they
should have a company airplane instead of a motor home. On the
day before Thanksgiving 1976, I made up my mind to buy an
airplane. I was at home that day giving a JP&R to Dave Smith.
He'd been having trouble with a store down in Florida, and while
we were talking about it, I made a phone call to see if the store
was open. No answer. I called several more times, and still no
answer.

"What we need is a company plane," I told Dave. "You could
jump on it right now, get down there and take care of that store
tonight, and be back in time for Thanksgiving dinner tomorrow."

I sat down with my legal pad that night and soon came up
with a plan that would easily justify the cost of a plane; it would
allow us to visit every store in the system at least once a month,
using only the three men we had.

The plane would take off on a Monday morning and fly to the East Coast, dropping George Papineau off in Courtland, New York; Dave Smith in Burlington, Vermont; and Dave Black in Rhode Island. They'd rent cars and drive from store to store through their areas. Then, later in the week, the plane would swing back out to pick them up and bring them back to Ann Arbor. The following week, they'd hit the South, then the Midwest, then the West.

My plan worked like a charm. But since the three men were traveling all week, I didn't get to see them very often. So I set up a daily telephone reporting system. They'd keep a log of all their activities during each day and phone in at night to dictate what we called the 006 Report to a tape recorder on our office telephone. First thing next morning, I would have a transcript of their calls, with a phone number where I could reach them if necessary. That was a terrific way to communicate.

In a speech to franchisees early in 1978, I said, "Last year was the best year we ever had, and you deserve the credit. In fact, we made up for the year before, which was our worst in a long time." Most of the franchisees had come around since my return as head of the company, but there were still some who gave us problems and I felt it was time for some straight-from-the-shoulder talk to them. I didn't mention the troublemakers by name in my speech. I didn't have to; they knew who they were. I pointed out gratefully that we got our royalty payments on a more timely basis than any other franchise chain. "This is important to our relationship," I said, "because if you owe someone money and don't pay it, you tend to start resenting them. You start justifying why you aren't paying them, and you soon spread the word to your fellow franchisees. One bad apple spoils the barrel. The next thing we know, we not only have friction with franchisees, we have cash-flow problems. I've been there before, and I don't care to look back.

"Our standards of quality are tough, but we're going to get tougher. Only strong franchisees can survive in this company. If you want to be part of a mediocre company, get out of DPI!

"Some of you complain about changes in our contracts. Well, times change, situations change, and if you're unhappy here, there's no anchor tied to your tail. Sell out. We might even let you take your sign down. We can help ten other stores in the time we spend arguing with one disgruntled franchisee over legal technicalities. So if you're that kind of person, you're the kind of competition we want."

I drummed away, as always, on the Golden Rule as policy throughout Domino's. Only half in jest, I said DPI must be living by the Golden Rule because in 1977 for the first time in years, we had not gotten involved in any new lawsuits. Of course, we had plenty to contend with in the one suit that was hanging over our heads—Amstar.

The goals I outlined for franchisees during this speech dealt with training, increased quality, and thirty-minute service. Our corporate goals embraced the same objectives, but as I told my executive staff, I also wanted to double the size of the company.

"I want to open one hundred fifty-nine new stores in 1978," I said, and that made some eyes bulge around our conference table. It seemed impossible, I admit. But I believe in aiming high. If you do, you'll stretch yourself to do better than you would if your goal were something easily reached.

My aspirations got a quick setback that January. We opened only one new location during the entire month. "The way we're going, we'll never hit even fifty percent," I said. "We need between twenty and forty new leases in the works at all times. We *must* speed up store openings!"

However, as events unfolded during 1978, I had to concentrate a lot more time than I'd anticipated spending on my search for management talent. Given the problems we'd been through and were still having as a result of preparing for the Amstar case, we weren't exactly prime targets for résumés. So I had to keep in touch with contacts who knew our potential from personal experience and hope they would find candidates for me. Barney Barnes, my old friend and box supplier, was one of those who knew about my search for a president of the commissary. He introduced me to Don Vlcek and gave him a glowing recommendation. Vlcek had a strong background in the restaurant-supply end of the meat business—a very tough business—and I liked his style. He became another key player on my executive team.

In some ways my search for a top financial executive should have been easiest of all. There were a lot of accountants out there who no doubt could do a good job and get our reporting done accurately and on time. But I was looking for an accountant with vision, someone with a flair for finance, who could take us into the future. My best candidate was Doug Dawson, who had audited our books as an employee of Arthur Andersen & Co. John McDivitt had strongly recommended him, and I was impressed with Doug's views of Domino's and his forward thinking. A Michigan State graduate, he had majored in marketing as well as accounting, just the kind of combination I was seeking. So I hired Doug as chief financial officer, and he turned out to be the most creative member of our executive team.

Dick Mueller seemed like an obvious choice to be vice-president of operations. His ability to open stores fast and his promotions were legend in the company. I had a tough job selling him on the idea of giving up franchising and moving up to headquarters. But he finally agreed, and he added a lot of drama and excitement to our management meetings.

Dave Kilby seemed just as obvious as the executive to direct our franchising sales. Dave was eager, but unfortunately our association didn't work out. The whole concept of selling franchises to outsiders turned out to be a bad one in the long run, although a few who started as outsiders, like Ron Conkey, became real assets. A major difficulty was getting the outsiders to adapt to Domino's way of doing things. They rarely measured up to our standards. Most of them failed to understand our system. They simply couldn't see why it was necessary to keep it very simple and deliver nothing but pizza and a soft drink. They were always asking, "Have you ever thought of tortillas?" or "Why can't we throw in a salad; it would be easy to do." I admit those are great ideas—for somebody else. Eventually, we called a halt to external franchising, and by 1983 we had bought back nearly all those stores.

We opened our two-hundredth store in November 1978 in Dayton, Ohio, and we added twenty-eight more that year, including fifteen from the merger with Todd Kane's company in Colorado. Although we fell far short of the growth goal I'd set for 1978, I felt good about the strides we'd made in strengthening our management. In addition to filling the top positions, we had brought in a training director who was developing programs for the whole company, and we hired a quality-control expert to test our product on a continuing basis and help us improve it.

Our new management team was the most visible, and probably the most significant evidence that Domino's had matured and was ready to make big strides. These executives really took hold during 1979 and began to pull our various disjointed programs into one unified system. Doug Dawson was the ramrod on this, working with Dick Mueller and Don Vlcek on streamlining our paperwork and reporting and changing our corporate-store formulas to make them profitable as well as equitable.

I had told Don Vlcek that I wanted to work closely with him to help pull the commissary together. But with all the final preparations in the Amstar case, I had to keep postponing our meetings. When we finally got together, it quickly became obvious that he'd grabbed hold of the situation and needed little organizational input from me. All I had to do was stand back and admire what he'd done. This, of course, was exactly the way I'd hoped the executive team would work.

I had to ask myself, though, how others in the company would react to my new role. Would they interpret my allowing strong people to work on their own without a lot of direction from me as a lack of leadership on my part? Odds were good that they would, considering what had happened during the Russ Hughes period.

How to handle this? I decided I'd simply have to make myself more visible in the company, by visiting stores and attending meetings where I could rub elbows with area franchisees and other key people in the field. Much of my visibility would be for show, and I didn't like the idea of putting on appearances, but I knew I would always learn a lot from mingling with these folks.

I'd also have to make certain that my executive team managers were recognized as able leaders by everyone else in the company. The main result of my changing role in the company was that it was forcing me to be more organized. I needed to make better plans for meetings, read more reports and memos, and send out more memos. Yet I had to get out and visit stores, too. Somehow, I would have to find more quiet time for future planning, and I resolved to devote evenings and weekends to my legal pads.

This last activity was, in many ways, the most important of all. I had to create a vision of what Domino's would be like in three, five, and ten years in order to give us a star to steer by. I could foresee Domino's in every state in the Union. We'd also have foreign stores. Certainly, we'd have locations adjacent to every

major U.S. military base, and we'd have at least eight more commissaries to serve our expanding chain. I envisioned a complete
research-and-development facility with test kitchens, a garage to
design special delivery vehicles, and a building to house our College of Pizzerology.

Important as it was, that kind of thinking got flash-frozen in
January 1979 by the beginning of the Amstar trial.

I HAVE BEEN IN SOME TOUGH FIGHTS in my life, but our five-year legal battle against Amstar was the worst.

More than three years passed before we even went to court. Amstar filed the suit in September 1975; the trial started in January 1979—a wait of thirty-nine months—and every day of that time I could feel the presence of that suit hanging over my head. It was like Chinese water torture. One by one, new legal questions would come up. One by one, we would deal with them. There were always more documents requested by Amstar's attorneys, more people to contact, more records to search, more depositions to be given, more questions, more delays, more indecision.

My first taste of what the Amstar courtroom combat would be like came in January and April 1976, when I was called to give depositions on our motion to transfer the trial to Detroit.

I was cross-examined on both occasions by Gerald W. Griffin, a tall, distinguished-looking New Yorker with a mane of white hair. His firm, Cooper, Dunham, Clark, Griffin & Morany, was Amstar's outside counsel for patent and trademark cases. He and Towny Beaman engaged in what seemed like endless legal sparring as he grilled me about the history of Domino's, our use of the name in advertising, and the status of Kilby's operations in Georgia.

We had submitted a list of people we believed would be helpful in documenting the company's development, and the transcript of the deposition shows a series of exchanges like this one over Les Heddle's acquaintance with Domino's:

Q (by Griffin): Mr. Heddle, Jr., what particular information . . . would he supply that you feel you would be unable to supply?

A (by me): Well, he was an employee of ours . . . probably—very possibly—the first, one of the first employees [the company] ever had. Because when it was called DomiNick's, he used to always hang around the place before he started working for us . . .

Q: Just liked pizza pies?

A: He's extremely knowledgeable about the history of the company over a long period of time, more so than just about anybody else.

Q: But my question is a bit more specific: sitting here, I mean, is there some specific area of knowledge that he has that is important to your case that you can't supply?

A: I'm sure there are a lot of things that he can remember that I can't remember.

Q: But you don't know particularly, sitting here, what that might be?

A: I don't know. How could I?

Q: I don't know either, except that you have listed him as a person that's necessary to appear at trial in Atlanta and someone you will bring to Atlanta to testify. It occurred to me that you might have some specific reason for doing so.

A: Well, I assume we need witnesses, eyewitnesses, the people that were around when we changed the name.

Q: So it's . . .

A: And you don't want to take my word for it, evidently.

Q: Okay. Moving on to Mr. Sperling . . .

And so it went, through a long list of names. One of them was Esther Long, and Griffin kept demanding to know what her job involved. I told him she worked in a general office capacity, but that didn't satisfy him.

Q: Stenographer, clerk, that kind of thing?

A: She's not a stenographer.

Q: Maybe you could detail a little bit more what her responsibilities are.

A: Esther is—describing Esther is kind of hard to do. She doesn't type, she's not a bookkeeper, she is just a darn good employee.

Q: Girl Friday, so to speak?

A: She is a hell of a nice person.

Q: I'm sure that's true. I'm just trying to get a handle on what she does here.

A: I'm sorry, I—she's just been around a long time and she does—she's a jack-of-all-trades.

I occasionally lost patience with Griffin's questioning, but he was far more diplomatic about it than his associate, Norman Zivin, who squared off against me a year later, in April 1977, in a lengthy pretrial deposition after our motion for transfer was denied. Zivin was tough and abrasive, and he and I clashed like steel against stone.

Our people began referring to Zivin and Griffin as Mr. Inside and Mr. Outside. Griffin was Mr. Outside, a gentleman, good-natured and friendly. Zivin was Mr. Inside, the hatchet man who did all the dirty work.

One of Zivin's jobs was to try to talk me into settling out of court. Several times, after a day of depositions, Zivin sat down with Bill Needle and me and had long, off-the-record talks. He was much more friendly in these situations than he was in a hearing room, and he tried to convince me that it would be best for all concerned, especially for me and my company, if I would back down.

I listened carefully and thought seriously about the alternatives. I knew that nine times out of ten, these kinds of cases are settled out of court. Federal judges have ways of encouraging such results, and we might be better off to cave in sooner rather than later. Besides, it would be no dishonor for me to settle.

Zivin's arguments about the evidence in favor of Amstar were pretty persuasive, and the power of the two-billion-dollar corporation we were pitted against was kind of intimidating. But Towny Beaman and Bill Needle thought we would win, and each time we discussed settlement, I found my resolve to fight stiffening.

When the trial finally opened, on January 15, 1979, in Atlanta's old Federal Courthouse, I was hoping for the best. Towny kept assuring me we would win. But after Amstar's presentations, which Judge Richard Freeman heard with approving nods and smiles, I was beginning to expect the worst.

Griffin was poised and confident, and his arguments were eloquent. He took pains to point out that the underdog position of

Domino's was not relevant to the case, that this was not a question of a large corporation attempting to rid itself of a small but
potentially pesky competitor.

"There is no concern that Amstar may lose a certain number
of dollars because Mr. Monaghan sells a lot of pizza pies," he
said. "The concern is far more serious. It involves the validity, the
value and integrity of a famous and celebrated trademark, which
has been established through the investment of hundreds of mil-
lions of dollars over the years.

"So successful and so well known is the Domino trademark in
grocery sales, for example, that it is, in volume and units, the
leading branded product sold in supermarkets today. Its Domino
five-pound package outsells the most famous food marks like
Campbell, Charmin Tissue, Star-Kist Tuna. Whatever trademark
one would think of as famous and known and visible in one's
home, sales under the Domino mark exceed it . . .

"Plaintiff's sales of Domino Sugar have exceeded $300 million
in every year since 1953. It has spent about $54 million since
1947 in advertising and promoting its Domino Sugar products,
and it was one of the first consumer product companies in the
country to extensively promote its trademark . . ."

He repeatedly made the point that packets of Domino Sugar
and other Domino products, including individual portions of
mustard, ketchup, jams, and salad dressing, are widely used in
restaurants, pizza parlors, and fast-food outlets.

"Patrons of these establishments have come to recognize
Domino Sugar and condiments," he said. "And plaintiff is justifi-
ably concerned that customers will associate the defendant's food
products with Amstar."

Judge Freeman commented favorably on this point. He said it
reminded him of one of the first cases he had been involved in as
a young lawyer, in which Carling Brewing Company, makers of

Black Label beer, sued Philip Morris for infringing on its trademark with a brand of cigarettes called Black Label. He had assisted in arguing the case for Carling, and it was won, he said proudly, on a claim of confusion in the minds of customers parallel to the one Griffin was making for Amstar.

My spirits really sank at that.

Bill Needle interjected, "We will contend, Your Honor, that sugar and pizza never mix, that you don't sprinkle sugar on your pizza, that people don't consider pizza to be a pastry product or one that contains sugar."

"Well," Judge Freeman responded, "you never dump cigarette ashes in a glass of beer either."

The following morning, the judge made a statement that shocked me. Bill Needle had read from a consent order between Amstar and the Federal Trade Commission regarding advertising of Domino Sugar, and the judge upheld an objection that it was irrelevant. Then he added:

"I don't care what the FTC has done or hasn't done. In my judgment, the FTC is about the biggest—I have my private opinions about the FTC . . ." A few minutes later, he told the lawyers of both sides, "Let me clarify one thing. I have a bad habit of talking too much on occasions. And what I said about the FTC is not to be construed by anybody that I agree or disagree with this consent order or find any fault with it morally, legally, or whatever. On the contrary, my chief complaint about the FTC is that they have not done enough. You know, they are here today and gone tomorrow. They are a typical bunch of bureaucratic idiots in my opinion, and that's the reason I find fault with the FTC."

I hadn't realized that judges were allowed to be so opinionated on the bench, and I hoped that this outburst wouldn't set the tone for the rest of the trial.

On the second day, Griffin fired one of his big guns, a survey made by Dr. Russ Haley, professor of marketing at the University of New Hampshire. It was conducted in ten cities among housewives who made most of the food purchases for their families. It showed that "close to 100 percent of the public recognize Domino as a trademark for sugar, that 44.2 percent believed that a company which makes pizza also makes other products, and of those who had such a belief, 75 percent thought that other product was sugar." In addition to those statistics, Dr. Haley claimed to have found three instances of "actual confusion among consumers between Domino Sugar and Domino's Pizza."

Our team had a troubled meeting over dinner that evening. Things didn't seem to be going too well for us. We discussed the strategy Needle would use the next day, when an expert witness from Alterman Foods, a large Atlanta supermarket and wholesale grocery business, was to testify for Amstar. Our session ended with a shopping trip to Alterman's Food Giant supermarket.

The following morning, we arrived in court lugging several cartloads of grocery bags. Zivin opened the day's testimony by introducing Arthur Levitt of Alterman's as an expert on consumer reactions to brand names on food products.

After a series of preliminary questions, Zivin asked: "Would you think that if there was a Domino Pizza for sale in your supermarket, consumers in your supermarket would think it was made by the same company that makes Domino Sugar?"

"Your Honor, we would like to object," Needle said. He pointed out that the question was hypothetical, based on no evidence or fact. Judge Freeman made Zivin rephrase it. A series of angry restatements and rejections followed. Finally, the exasperated Zivin asked, "Do you think Domino Pizza sold in a separate food store, outside of the supermarket, is made by the same company as made Domino Sugar?"

"I would think so," Levitt said.

Needle then cross-examined Levitt. "Isn't it true that your stores sell Morton Salt?" he asked.

"They do."

"Isn't it also true that your stores sell Morton Frozen Foods?"

"Yes."

"And I hand you . . ." Bill pulled from one of our shopping bags a Morton Pastry Shop cream pie and a package of Morton beans-and-franks dinner and placed them in front of the witness. "Isn't it true that the company that produces Morton Frozen Foods is not the same company that produces Morton Salt?"

"Yes, I know that."

Bill hammered home his point, using Hollywood mayonnaise and Hollywood bread, Blue Plate mayonnaise and Blue Plate canned vegetables, Comet rice and Comet cleanser, Beech-Nut baby foods and Beech-Nut chewing tobacco, Chuck Wagon dog food and Chuck Wagon onion ring mix, Rich's processed meat and Rich's dessert topping, Sunshine crackers and Sunshine canned vegetables, and half a dozen other items, placing them one by one in front of Levitt until they formed a huge pile. The surprised and obviously uncomfortable witness said he might have been confused by some of the brands "a long time ago, when I first got into the grocery business, but I know better."

"You know better?"

"Yes."

Needle nodded and said, "We have no further questions, Your Honor."

When Amstar finished presenting its evidence and our turn to bat was coming up, I called Margie and asked her to come down to Atlanta. We decided that she should bring our four daughters (Barbie was born in August 1972) along, because this was a historic event in my life and I wanted to share it with them. Judge Freeman had allowed me to sit down front in the jury box, because I have poor hearing—a result of the infections I had while attending the University of Michigan. When my family came in and sat with me, I think he believed it was a ploy to appeal to his sympathy.

Bill Needle's youthful eagerness was a sharp contrast to Griffin's suave manner and Zivin's hard-nosed style. But I felt he scored some heavy points when he brought out the chart he and Towny Beaman had developed, showing seventy-two different uses of Domino by various companies over the years.

"Amstar would like to have the District Court believe that it has had exclusive use of Domino on food products since prior to 1965, when Domino's Pizza began using that name," Bill said. "We have made this chart to prove that such is far from being true."

I was glad to see that the judge seemed intrigued by the chart and the history of companies displayed on it. The labels for cans of fruit and vegetables of the Domino Packing Company, predecessor to the Del Monte Corporation, were works of art. Obviously, that user of the name Domino was very proud of it.

Just as I was beginning to feel pleased about our progress and Judge Freeman's more favorable manner, though, Bill called on Claibourne Darden, a well-known Atlanta pollster, who had conducted a survey for us to counter Dr. Haley's survey.

Judge Freeman seemed to take a dislike to Darden. He criticized the survey pretty harshly. It involved seven hundred interviews in seven of our principal market areas and concluded that there was almost no possibility of confusion between Domino's Pizza and Domino Sugar. The judge was visibly irritated by Darden's broad southern drawl and his manner of presentation. "The more I hear cases like this, I think I am not going to pay any more attention to an expert . . ." Judge Freeman said. "I am going to appoint my own expert and let both sides cross-examine . . . it is so discouraging to have people get up here and testify as experts who contend that their methodology is superior to the other side, and they are both full of flaws and both so obviously slanted to produce the results favorable to their clients . . .''

His statement was a body blow. But we were glad that the judge had criticized both surveys. And though he had lashed out at Darden, at one point saying, "You are insulting my intelligence," the incident passed and our case seemed to gain favor as the trial proceeded.

Margie didn't stay for the conclusion. The girls had to get back to school, and Towny told her it would be an anticlimax now, anyhow. "We're going to win," he said. The opposition apparently thought so, too. After the trial, Griffin tried again to get us to agree to a settlement. "We will allow you to keep the name Domino's in the states in which you now have stores if you will agree not to go into any new states," he said. We told him we weren't interested.

When I got back to our office in Ann Arbor, Margie and the staff were waiting with bottles of champagne. I was pleased, of course, but I told them a party would be premature. It would take the judge several weeks, perhaps even a couple of months, to give his decision.

Never in my most skeptical mood could I imagine the deliberation would drag out, as it did, for most of the year.

We were now in a legal limbo, little better off than before the trial. I don't know how we would have managed to conduct business in a normal way during this period without Towny Beaman and Eugene Power. Both of these men had joined our board of directors in 1978, and they gave us the benefit of great wisdom and many years of business experience. Mr. Power had retired after selling his company, University Microfilms, to Xerox Corporation and he was able to spend a lot of time counseling me on the management of Domino's. Towny, of course, had lived with the law's delay through most of his career, and he taught me patience.

Spring arrived and merged gradually into summer. July and August dragged slowly by. Finally, on September 11, 1979, Judge Freeman announced his decision—in favor of Amstar!

The decree was a permanent injunction against our use of the name Domino's Pizza. No new stores could be opened under it, and we had only three months in which to change the signs on existing stores and use up all supplies of paper goods and cartons imprinted with the Domino's logo. The sign changes alone would cost us about two million dollars. We never dreamed the directive would be so harsh and immediate. We thought we'd have a year or so to make changes, and this was a cruel blow.

Our office was like a morgue. People wore long faces and acted as if their best friend had died. In a way, that was true. No one felt lower than I did. Luckily, though, during the long months of waiting for the decision, I had filled many legal-pad pages with notes on what we should do if the worst happened. These thoughts helped me act now, even though I felt paralyzed. I was fortunate in having Dick Mueller in operations and Dave Kilby as director of franchising. If anyone could be counted on to see opportunity in adversity, it was these two. We were able to keep Domino's moving ahead despite the big chill the judge had put on us.

We would appeal. There was never any doubt about that. Towny Beaman was really fired up about it. He pointed out that Judge Freeman had simply adopted all of Amstar's findings of fact and conclusions of law as his own. His decree stated that he had done so because he "believed them to be factually and legally correct. The court could have rewritten," he added, "but that would have amounted to no more than a paraphrasing of the fact findings and conclusions submitted. Such an act of pretense would serve absolutely no purpose . . .''

It was highly unusual, Towny said, for a federal judge not to draft his own conclusions. He thought it showed a prejudice in favor of Amstar that the appeals court would take into consideration.

Towny and Bill Needle decided to bring in another Atlanta attorney, Miles Alexander, to handle our appeal. Needle and his boss, George Hopkins, had been impressed by Alexander's representation of Rolls-Royce in a suit they had defended for a small manufacturer of Rolls-Royce-style hood kits for Volkswagens. They asked him to serve as an expert witness for us during the Amstar trial, but Judge Freeman had not allowed him to testify.

Alexander's first move was to try and get Judge Freeman to stay the effect of his injunction until after the appeal. The judge granted part of the request, allowing us to keep our name on existing stores, but we had to use a different name on all new stores. I scribbled a note to myself that this made three strikes against us with Judge Freeman: 1) venue, 2) decision, 3) appeal. I was thankful for the partial stay, but the cost of getting new signs and making other alterations for new stores was going to be significant. By this time, we were opening about five new stores a week.

Alexander next went to the appeals court and requested a stay of Judge Freeman's judgment, and though he didn't get the stay, the court did agree to expedite its hearing of the case. We were notified early in November that briefs would be due by the end of the month and oral hearing would take place in February. ''That's incredibly fast for anything but a civil rights case or a murder trial,'' Alexander said.

I had mixed feelings about the appeal. If we lost it, we'd need to worry about much more than a few million dollars in sign changes and other direct costs. It would mean that we'd have no valid contracts with nearly half the franchisees in our system. All contracts signed prior to 1975 stated that we owned the name Domino's Pizza and that it was valuable. Not until after the Amstar suit was filed did we start putting in a provision that gave us the right to change the name. Those pre-1975 franchisees would be free to simply walk out without paying us a cent.

Rumors spread like hot grease in a situation like this, where everyone has a lot at stake, and I wanted to hold the rumors down by keeping everyone in the company informed about the appeal. I sent letters, and Dick Mueller telephoned all the stores with updates. We had Miles Alexander attend a franchisees' meeting and explain the details of the case. The picture he painted was not very encouraging. In this particular federal court circuit, only about 20 percent of the cases appealed have been reversed, he said. Even though we had a very strong case, appeals courts prefer to sustain the decision of the trial judge unless it could be proven that he'd made an error in fact-finding. Alexander pulled no punches in laying out our prospects, and I think the franchisees appreciated his honesty more than any optimistic pep talk he could have given them.

Part of Alexander's strategy was to appeal to the interests of the justices' law clerks, who would, he felt, have a better understanding of pizza.

"The law clerks read these briefs very carefully, and they brief the judges on what their view of the case is," he explained. "I think it will shock these young people to learn that Amstar might be able to stop Domino's Pizza from using its name. They will not identify with Domino Sugar as would the middle-aged, grocery-shopping housewife, who sees it advertised frequently as a loss-leader in supermarkets. One of my points to the court will be that they have to see beyond the generation gap and recognize that the universe of customers who order in pizza tend not to be brand conscious of sugar."

The point to establish was that there was no possibility of confusion between Domino Sugar and Domino's Pizza because of "their starkly different commerical impressions" and that the trial court had ignored "differences in customers, products, and channels of trade."

Another element of Alexander's strategy was to dramatize the closeness of the case by quoting Judge Freeman on it after the trial, when our appeal was being prepared. He said several times that it was close, that he found himself leaning first to one side and then the other, and that it had been "difficult to decide, very difficult."

Alexander neatly tied these statements to the implication that the judge was severely overworked and had simply picked up Amstar's findings and conclusions and used them in a desperate attempt to clear his desk. Alexander quoted Judge Freeman from the trial transcript, underlining the crucial phrase:

"I don't like to state that I will decide or resolve this issue or find for the defendant or the plaintiff and then . . . tell him to prepare special findings of fact and conclusions of law without having stated at least generally and fairly completely the basis of that finding. I think the court might . . . think or suggest I have allowed one of the parties to manufacture these findings, and I am simply rubber stamping these findings . . . *my problem is to find enough time* to take my notes, take your proposed special findings, and when I say 'your' I mean both sides, and conclusions and prepare some little skeletal outline so when I start dictating onto the record the basis or reasons for my conclusions it will make sense."

Our lawyers worked through the Thanksgiving holidays, struggling mightily to finish their brief before the deadline. Then came Amstar's brief in response, and our side replied. This set off another exchange. With each volley the language of the briefs became progressively sharper, pointing out "absurdities" in the opposition's arguments and decrying "outrageous" assertions and "distortions of fact."

When the day of oral hearing finally arrived, it seemed like an anticlimax. Towny told me he thought Alexander had done an outstanding job and we had an excellent chance of winning. I had to smile and nod. Towny's enthusiasm was infectious. But I had heard this all before, and deep down, I was prepared for disaster.

CERTAIN SCENES are etched forever in my mind. I've mentioned some: grabbing at the lapels of my dead father's suit and begging him to "wake up"; hearing Sister Berarda tell me I could be anything I wanted to be; discovering while shoveling manure on the Crouch farm that I wanted to become a priest; taking the order from my first customer in our DomiNick's Pizza shop in Ypsilanti. There are others. But none is more vivid than the memory of April 10, 1980, when I learned about the appellate court's decision in the Amstar case.

As I walked into our building that morning, the office staff, including my wife, was standing around the lobby laughing and talking. I was confused. I said jokingly to Margie and Helen, "What the heck's goin' on here? Let's get back to work!" I heard the words *lawsuit* and *we won*, but they didn't ring a bell. "Come on," I said. "We've got work to . . ."

Then it hit me. *We won the lawsuit?*

"Amstar?" I asked. Everyone was smiling, nodding, and shaking my hand. Yes, they said. Yes, we won!

I got a big smile on my face and then I burst into tears. I grabbed Margie, pulled her into my office, and shut the door. I just sat there on the couch with her for twenty minutes and cried like I'd never cried before in my life. I was lurching, as if I were hyperventilating or something. I was a complete basket case.

When I recovered, I announced that the office was closing for the day and asked Helen to order champagne. Then we called up all our friends and had a party that lasted until after dinner.

The U.S. Court of Appeals had reversed Judge Freeman, finding that our use of Domino's Pizza "did not create likelihood of confusion with plaintiff's use of the trademark 'Domino' for sugar. . ." Towny Beaman pointed out that the appellate justices had also slapped down Judge Freeman for copying his fifty-four-page memorandum of findings of fact and conclusions of law "almost verbatim" from those submitted by the Amstar attorneys.

"While the practice of allowing counsel for the prevailing party to write the trial judge's opinion has not been proscribed by this circuit," the justices wrote, "it should nevertheless be discouraged. Even though the court, in adopting plaintiff's findings and conclusions, stated that it had 'individually considered' them and adopted them because it 'believed them to be factually and legally correct,' a cursory reading of the district court's memorandum leaves one with the impression that it was indeed written by the prevailing party to a bitter dispute."

I'm told that *Amstar Corp.* v. *Domino's Pizza, Inc.*, has become quite a famous case. It's frequently cited in briefs and in other decisions, and apparently legal scholars will be debating it for years to come. I just hope that all the law students who study it in the future will order a Domino's pizza to help them digest the case. Amstar later tried to take the case to the Supreme Court, but the justices declined to hear it, which made our victory final.

After the warm flush of triumph and the feeling of vindication passed, I began to wonder whether it might not have been better if we'd lost. We would have had a real good "Little Company Stands Up to Big Company" story to tell. *David beaten by Goliath:* It would have gotten us a lot of free publicity. Bob Cotman and I had come up with the name Pizza Dispatch as an alternative to Domino's just in case we lost to Amstar. In the period between Judge Freeman's ruling against us and our victory on appeal, we had opened forty Pizza Dispatch stores, and they were doing quite well in comparison with the record for new Domino's stores. Had we lost, Pizza Dispatch would have become an instant winner, because the American public loves to root for the underdog. When we won, we lost that story.

Ironically enough, most of my executive team was still in favor of changing our name. Cotman's Group 243 had done a market research study that showed customers preferred the name Pizza Dispatch over Domino's five to one.

It was a tough question. I didn't feel right about a name change; we had a lot of history tied to the name Domino's. The older franchisees we talked to felt the same way. The main problem, though, was the expense. Our financial situation wasn't so great that we could pitch several million dollars into a name change even if it was a better name.

My feeling now is that my decision not to change the name was wrong. It was a short-term decision. And what I learned from the whole bloody Amstar battle is that your name isn't all that important, even in the franchise business. Gerald Griffin had tried to tell me that one day at lunch during a deposition, long before the trial started. He said, "I don't think your name matters so much. You could call it Tom's Pizza and be just as successful." I got angry about that. I was protective of our name. Now, I think he was right.

Winning the Amstar case was like reaching the end of a space-launch countdown. Suddenly, I felt free of an unseen weight that had been holding us back. The sky above was clear and Domino's was blasting off. But I knew I was going to have to get my crew organized and focused better or this company would never achieve orbit. I had a big management problem in the lack of teamwork among my executives. It was preventing us from moving ahead toward my vision of what I wanted the company to be.

I knew I was too close to the problem to be able to solve it from where I sat. I had to get some distance and a different perspective. A way of doing this presented itself at a Young President's Organization meeting that spring in a seminar given by a consulting group called the Adizes Institute. Ichak Adizes, the founder, had written a book he called *How to Solve the Mismanagement Crisis*, which sounded like exactly what I needed. So I contacted Adizes, and an associate named Gerald W. Faust paid us a visit. He was a Ph.D., but he also had started a successful business of his own prior to joining Adizes. I liked his view of our situation. "We analyze companies on the basis of life-cycle growth," he said. "They go through a courtship phase before the decision is made to take the risk and start the company. Then there is an infancy stage, in which everybody is working real hard, the company isn't making much money, and nothing is organized. After that comes an adolescent phase we call go-go, dominated by emphasis on productivity and entrepreneurial efforts. In the go-go phase, everybody is coming in early, going home late, and everything's a mess. Your company is rampant *go-go.*"

We called my executive team together, and Faust outlined his concepts of what good management is supposed to do: 1) produce results; 2) administer the system so it functions smoothly; 3) take advantage of business opportunities in entrepreneurial fashion; 4) integrate personnel, ensuring that no one in the organization is indispensable by creating a climate of cooperation.

Then he outlined mismanagement styles, defining the traits of managers he labeled the Lone Ranger, the person who concentrates exclusively on results; the Bureaucrat, whose only interest in life is administration; the Arsonist, who concentrates exclusively on entrepreneurial activity; and the Superfollower, who is dedicated exclusively to integration. Faust's talk had our people rolling in the aisles as they recognized themselves and each other in the mannerisms he was describing.

That was all I needed to make up my mind to hire Faust and the Adizes Institute. We worked with them monthly for the next three years, and their help probably cost us half a million dollars. I can't say that we bought their concepts 100 percent. We had some strong disagreement with the approaches they proposed, particularly in the financial area. But on balance, the program was helpful. It gave me a place to stand while establishing a structural framework and a management method that worked for us.

Before Adizes came on the scene, I had called a meeting of the whole executive team and reminded them that Domino's operates on the Golden Rule. If we didn't follow it with each other as well as with customers, we were going to be in big trouble. "Perhaps we need JP&Rs with each other," I said. "Maybe we should tell each other all the good things and bad things we see in each other."

As it turned out, that was, to some extent, what Faust did for us in the Adizes team meetings. Nothing was sacred in these sessions, and there was a lot of anger and frustration released. It wasn't pleasant. But it helped to get the hostilities out in the open. That allowed us to deal with them honestly as individuals.

Dick Mueller and I, in particular, were having serious difficulty in communicating with each other during the summer of 1980, and our misunderstandings might have gotten out of hand without the influence of the Adizes sessions and the one-on-one meetings we had in JP&Rs.

Part of our problem stemmed from the fact that Dick and I are both creative entrepreneurs. I say, Don't tell me how to do something, just tell me what the goal is, and I'll get there. Dick is the same way. So when we disagreed on how to do things, we were like two rams in rut on a frosty morning. We butted heads, and I had difficulty keeping the impact from affecting the whole organization.

I had persuaded Bob Cotman to join our board of directors and consult with me and the rest of the executive team on business strategy as if he were an employee. But just when he and Dick Mueller and I had begun working smoothly together, Dick decided he was going to resign and go back into franchising. I was disappointed. The chemistry I thought existed between us was what had led me to hire Dick in the first place. But after he moved into his position at headquarters, we failed to click. Dick had been boss of his own operation for so long that perhaps he found it difficult to adjust to being a member of the team. First we argued about whether he should have a contract. He wanted one; I resisted it. This led to some heavy negotiations that started us off on the wrong foot. Then a rift developed between his staff and the rest of DPI. We had worked out those problems, however, and were making progress. Dick had told me that his goal was to become president of Domino's, and that was fine with me. I encouraged him to shoot for my job.

Dick and I had discussed the possibility of regionalizing his operations department—setting up autonomous regional offices around the country—and I thought we were getting close to doing it when he decided to leave, which was another reason for my disappointment. But I could see he was excited about running his own show again, and I didn't want to stand in his way. It was easy to work out a mutually beneficial arrangement. He sold his stock back to the company and used the money to set up RPM Pizza, which became our largest franchisee. So it all worked out for the best.

I can't help thinking that Dick's training to run that marathon helped him make his decision, and seeing him find the spot that was right for him in Domino's was my biggest payoff from that $50,000 reward I gave him. Dick and I continue to disagree on some things, but it's always in a climate of mutual respect and admiration for each other's contributions to Domino's.

A big problem the Adizes sessions brought to the surface was the way Bob Cotman was working with us. Since his Group 243 was one of our suppliers, some members of the executive team believed that his position as a director and his participation in executive team meetings constituted a flagrant conflict of interest. Their objections put enormous pressure on Bob. I had to keep reassuring him and pumping up his spirits. I valued his experience and ability, and he was one of the few people I've met who could get on my wavelength in brainstorming ideas. He would come up with pronouncements like: "What I've found is that the things that count are what people have in common, not their differences." To me, that was a home run. But he topped it a few years later when I asked him if he remembered making the statement. He said, "Sure, that's my religion." Now, that was a homer with the bases loaded.

After Dick Mueller left and I regionalized operations, we finally worked out an arrangement to bring Cotman aboard full-time. He sold his interest in Group 243 to his employees and joined us as vice-president of operations. I thought his new status eliminated the conflict-of-interest question, but apparently some of the other executive team members didn't think so. When Bob resigned in 1985 to start a marketing firm with another former Domino's executive, one of the other team members told me he felt relieved because "I never knew whether I was talking to Group 243 Bob Cotman or to Domino's Bob Cotman." Nevertheless, Bob's departure was painful for me. I had appointed him senior vice-president in charge of marketing after Dave Black took over operations in 1981.

The period of explosive growth that started in that year was especially gratifying for me, because it proved the effectiveness of the management style I'd developed through trial and error during twenty years of building Domino's. Some of my management ideas had been working well for a long time. But to be unified into a functioning whole, my approach needed a solid organizational base, and this base was finally provided by the executive talent I assembled, beginning in 1978, and the structure we established with the help of Adizes.

I have no lofty theories about management. I take what Peter Drucker would call an empirical approach, and my only argument in its favor is to point to the results it has achieved in Domino's. But I believe my style would work just as well in any kind of corporation. The basic building block of management, for me, is goal setting. You must have a goal in order to know what direction to take. Whether you're managing a company, your own career, or a household, if you decide to just go through the motions and wait for something to turn up, you'll find your toes do it first.

Writing is the key to my system of goal setting; but goal setting sounds too ordinary to describe what I have in mind. What I'm doing is building exciting dreams. The goals must be exciting or people won't be motivated to strive for them. I carry a yellow legal pad with me everywhere I go. All my thoughts, my plans, my dreams, my analyses of problems—everything that comes into my mind, sometimes even a shopping list—are written down in my current pad. When that one is full, I start another; I sometimes have several pads going at once for different kinds of thoughts. I learned this method from my old friend Chuck Parsons, an Ann Arbor-based marketing consultant. Over the last twenty years I accumulated dozens of packing boxes full of these pads—I finally threw them away because they were taking up too much room, and I never look at them again once I'm finished writing, anyhow. The reason is that it's the process of writing that's important to me. It's the thinking that goes into writing, not the words that wind up on the paper, that makes the difference.

I set long-range goals, annual goals, monthly, weekly, and daily goals. The daily goals take the form of to-do lists. The long-range goals are dream sheets. But the other lists are specific and action-oriented. My goal list for 1980, for example, began with this entry: "500 units." To me, that meant we would have a total of 500 stores by the end of the year. This was a high goal at that point in our development, but it was attainable. The important thing about this goal, though, is that it was *specific*, it wasn't just "let's increase the number of units this year." It was *500 or bust!* If a goal is specific, it is easy to communicate it to others. This is important, because when you are dealing with a corporate goal, you have to *sell* it to the people who can help you achieve it: They have to understand exactly what the goal is, they must believe it can be done, and they must be convinced that it can be done by *them*.

Another important aspect of my goal setting is the time limit. A task is to be done by the end of the year, not just "in the near future." In 1979, my list for the coming year went on for four pages, 150 items, and covered not only business goals but phys-

ical goals—I wanted to get my weight down to 156 pounds, do
200 pushups in one session every other day, get my body fat and
cholesterol level down, and finish a marathon. There also were
personal items, including purchase of a third car and having a
meeting with Ray Kroc. Most of these goals were achieved. I fell a
bit short on some, including the big one: We didn't open our five
hundredth store until the following year. But falling a bit short
made me fight all the harder to attain that number.

When I talk of communicating my goal to other people and
selling them on it—making them believe in their own ability to
achieve—I'm not talking about hype. The process of building belief works on a strictly personal goal, too: when you tell someone
else what your goal is, it gives you reinforcement, added incentive
to accomplish it. I discovered this in 1962, when I quit smoking. I
told everybody I knew, "This is it. I have smoked my last cigarette." That helped give me the strength to follow through. If you
believe you're going to do something, and tell everybody else
you're going to do it, their belief will be a backstop for yours.

Books have been important in development of my own style
of management. I've selected useful techniques from a lot of
them. But I emphasize *selected* because I find many things in
books about management that would be poison for Domino's.
The best book I've found on management philosophy was *In
Search of Excellence* by Thomas J. Peters and Robert H. Waterman.
But I didn't really learn much that was new to me from it. That
book simply confirmed everything I instinctively believed. I was
already living its precepts. I found as I was reading it that I knew
the sense of what it was going to say next even before I read the
words.

For example, *In Search of Excellence* talks about how companies need to have a "bias for action." I'm an action guy. I've
always believed that the best plan is something you came up with

through trying and failing. Failure shows you how to do something right. You can try, fail, and try again while someone else is still reading textbooks to try and learn how to do something, probably less effectively than if he'd bumped his nose on failure a few times. Failure strengthens you because it teaches you to look for the seed of benefit that every adversity contains. I believe my greatest strength is the ability I've developed to turn adversity into advantage. Every time I suffer a setback, I find myself thinking instinctively, How can I capitalize on this?

Excellent companies stay "close to the customer," according to Peters and Waterman. As far as I'm concerned, everything in Domino's begins with the customer. I learned this rule by making at least a million pizzas and delivering a lot of them. The customer is boss.

Getting "productivity through people" is another major point of *In Search of Excellence,* and it has always been one of my operating principles. I realized right at the beginning that I had to do things through other people, and I always tried to hire people who were smarter than I was. There've been some who've been paid higher salaries than I took, too. But that's always been fine with me if it helped Domino's move forward.

The book's identification and reinforcement of these and other management principles was helpful. I was delighted when Don Vlcek gave his entire staff a day off to read *In Search of Excellence,* because it echoes everything I've been preaching in Domino's.

There are some personal approaches in management that I don't think I could have learned from a book. My method of making decisions is one of them. I don't know that it would work for anyone else. But here, for whatever it's worth, is how I do it:

I reach decisions by making lists on my yellow legal pads. Down one side of a page, I'll write all the reasons I can think of in

favor of a given course of action. On the other side, I list every
reason I can think of against it. Thinking of arguments for and
against a decision is where my ability to dream comes in handy. I
imagine the decision has been made. I see in my mind's eye how it
affects people and the way they react. If it's a complicated issue,
with many reasons for it and a lot of others against, I will break
each point down into sublists and assign them a kind of point
value so I can weigh them against each other.

Sometimes, as I learned from my experience with the proposal that we change our name to Pizza Dispatch, it's good to
consider future situations, too. In that case, my list of the benefits
of the name Pizza Dispatch were outweighed by the drawbacks of
giving up Domino's. But I concentrated on the immediate situation. I didn't ask myself, Okay, five years from now, when we
have more than two thousand stores and are in every state in the
Union, what will the pros and cons be then? Had I done so, I
would have made a better decision.

I also make lists as a way of brainstorming ideas with myself
on paper. This is a written version of what I love to do verbally on
the occasions when I can get on the same wavelength with another person. Doing it verbally is more fun because it's exciting to
share the exploration of ideas. But the written approach is absorbing, too, and it can be extremely fruitful.

At the outset I'm often unable to see a good idea because
there's a clutter of other things hiding it. There are roads through
the clutter, though, and I have to go down them until I find the
one that will take me up mentally above the clutter, to a point
where I can see a good idea on the horizon. The roads are propositions that I think up, write down on my list, and follow one by
one. A proposition might be stupid or obvious, but I take it anyway because I don't know where it will lead and what it might
connect with. I say to myself, Why don't we do this? Well, I see

that if we did that, it would allow us to do something else, and I just keep adding to it. If I don't go down those roads, I never get to the good idea, because there's a link, and I find the link by following something that may not work or is impossible.

I sometimes compare my brainstorming on paper to the drilling of oil wells. The only way to strike oil is to drill a lot of wells. My lists are wells, and every once in a while I hit a gusher. I'm working away, making lists, and all of a sudden something pops right out. I'll say, Hey, look at that!

Lots of times I'll be writing lists of things I want to do this year or next year, which I do just for the fun of it, and I'll find one item I want to think about some more. So I'll take a separate page, or sometimes even another pad, and start making lists of ideas about that particular thing. I expand on it, and who knows, maybe I'll find other things in *that* list that I want to expand on. It's like fishing. I never know what kind of idea I might catch.

I don't reject an idea just because it doesn't make sense, either. If you wait for something to make sense before you explore it, you'll never get anywhere with it. Take, for example, the idea of going into competition with ourselves as a way of expanding in markets that Domino's already dominates. Not only did this idea make no sense, it seemed like it might be a good way to shoot ourselves in the foot. But I began looking at it by making one of my typical lists.

If we did compete with ourselves, we could use the name Pizza Dispatch, which we already had registered and knew was a good name. There were lots of negatives surrounding the idea, but they were all predictable pitfalls; they could be foreseen and avoided. On the other hand, the positive propositions just kept popping out onto my yellow pages. Finally, I could see that if the program worked, we could offer it to franchisees who had developed their stores into maturity and filled all the nooks and cran-

nies of their areas. They could compete against themselves and—
if my theory is right, and I know it is—the competition would
make their existing stores stronger. But what if it didn't work?
Well, we'd never know if we didn't get into action and try it. We
could do this without threat to any franchisees' sales or personnel
programs by experimenting first in corporate-store areas.

We started by building a few Pizza Dispatch units. By the end
of 1985, we had eight of them scattered in Denver, Dallas,
Houston, Nashville, and Columbus. I wasn't very happy with the
way the stores were set up, because my concept was to make
everything exactly the same as Domino's except the name. I knew
from experience that the public would prefer one shop or the
other even if the pizzas were exactly the same. I'd seen it happen
when I was operating Pizza King and DomiNick's in Ypsilanti. The
product was identical, yet some customers at DomiNick's said
they preferred its pizza to Pizza King's and vice versa. The outstanding commercial example of this principle, of course, is Evin-
rude and Johnson outboard motors. They compete all across the
country, yet their engines are essentially the same, made of the
same parts by the same firm. Using Domino's products in Pizza
Dispatch stores and supplying them from our commissaries made
sense to me. But something got lost in the translation by our marketing department, and Pizza Dispatch came out with a different
product—a ten-inch pizza.

I'm reminded of something about my personal management
style that emerged in the Adizes sessions with Jerry Faust. He said
I had a tendency to abdicate rather than delegate jobs. This may
have been true early in my career—when I gave people jobs, I
expected them to take the ball and run with it. I didn't want to
interfere with them or inhibit them. I felt they would do a better
job if I simply stayed out of their way. That was wrong, and I've
learned that you have to check on what people are doing—this is
what Tom Peters calls "Management by Walking Around."

But I also believe in giving people responsibility, and I insist on letting them make their own mistakes. This practice isn't abdication and it isn't really delegation, either. It's the difference between a coach who lets the quarterback be the field general and one who calls all the plays from the sidelines. I believe in picking the right quarterback and letting him do it himself. I guess I tend to trust people more than others do. In baseball, I like to see a guy go all out and dive for the ball. If he misses, I say, "Nice try." The same thing applies in Domino's. I want my people to go all out. They'll make mistakes that way, but there's nothing wrong with making a mistake, providing you learn from it.

This philosophy is one reason I advocated naming our operating regions after the regional directors when I decentralized the company in 1981. There were six regions at that time—we now have thirteen, plus international. But my attitude is still the same as it was when I told those first six directors: "These regions belong to you, and I want you to make your own mark on them, just as I have with DPI."

Big obligations make good leaders. But good leaders also take on big obligations. They set standards for themselves that are above what's expected, and they hustle in response to what's inside driving them, not to who is out there pushing them.

We use a lot of sports analogies at Domino's because what we do in the pizza-delivery business is very much like playing team sports. We frequently use sayings like, *The team with the best defense wins.* It may be a cliché, but it's true. I'm a strong believer in defensive management.

Mark Latvala, a Domino's area franchisee in western Pennsylvania, coined the term *defensive management,* and he described it in an article he wrote for the *Pepperoni Press* in 1983. It recounted a visit I had made to his store when he first became a manager. He had sales of only $2,446 his first week, and he asked me for some advice. I told him, "Mark, at this volume, you can't afford to lose a single customer. You've got to make sure that every one is completely satisfied."

He said he thought about that and connected it in his mind to teamwork in pro sports. The team whose players know how to perform the fundamental defensive tasks day in and day out doesn't get scored on. So even if its offense scores only once, it will win.

The area of defense Mark stressed was one that's close to my heart—thirty-minute service. Suppose a store is delivering 95 percent of its pizzas within thirty minutes. Sounds pretty good. But let's look at that 5 percent of orders that are delivered late. Let's say it comes to fifty late orders per week. We know that more than 10 percent of late deliveries result in lost customers, which means that this store is losing, at minimum, five customers per week. If you multiply that out for the year, then multiply *that* by twenty-six, which is the average number of times a customer buys from us during the year, you get 6,760 lost orders. It would take a lot of time and money spent on advertising and promotion to bring in that many orders. And there's no way to atone for bad word-of-mouth from the disgruntled customer.

Defensive management means taking care of the business you have. I've always said that if you just take care of every single customer, your business will grow by 50 percent a year. Make sure every pizza gets there in thirty minutes, make sure every one is good—no burned pizzas and no raw pizzas—and don't skimp on the ingredients. That's it. You don't need any sophisticated marketing programs. The solution is simple, and it's right before your nose.

Mark said that after seven months in his first store, doing no advertising but practicing solid defense and striving to please every customer, his sales more than doubled, to $5,600 per week. That, he added, was just one of many instances that proved the

value of concentrating on the customers you have. Mark demonstrated this principle over and over again. When he got his own
store in Pittsburgh, his sales were phenomenal.

I'm a firm believer in keeping a business simple. I think the
only guy who was less complicated than me and put more emphasis on keeping it simple than I did was Ray Kroc. That's one
reason he was an idol of mine and why I was so intent on meeting him and telling him about Domino's.

Beginning in 1968, I tried to make appointments with Ray
Kroc. His staff would always ask, "Why do you want to see
him?" and I'd explain, "I feel that Domino's is about fifteen years
behind McDonald's; we're following the same path of development. McDonald's is my model, and Mr. Kroc is my idol." It
didn't get me to first base.

From 1972 on, I had someone call Mr. Kroc's office once a
month to try to arrange a meeting. There was always some reason
I couldn't get to talk to him. Then, early in the summer of 1980,
Helen McNulty managed to get me a tentative appointment with
him at his office in San Diego. Margie and I planned a vacation
trip to San Diego with our four daughters, and Kroc's assistant
said he'd do his best for me. Kroc was then seventy-eight years
old and in failing health, so his schedule was erratic. But if I
would call his office every day while we were out there, the assistant said, he'd see what he could do. After several fruitless phone
calls, while Margie and the girls were off visiting Sea World and
the San Diego Zoo, I finally was told that Kroc would see me, but
only for fifteen minutes.

Wow! I was so excited I could hardly stand it. I had to wait in
the lobby of his office for quite a while, and I began to worry that
he might cancel our meeting. But then I was ushered in—and
there he was, smiling that impish smile. I had brought along my
dogeared copy of his autobiography, *Grinding It Out: The Making*

of McDonald's, and I showed him how I'd underlined his precepts. He autographed the book for me, and we had a great chat. I was getting frustrated, though. I wanted to listen to him so I could learn from him, but he kept asking such great questions that I was doing all the talking. In no time at all, he understood the Domino's concept as well as anyone except me.

We talked for about two and a half hours. Finally, his assistant broke in and said we had to wind it up. Kroc nodded, leaned over his desk toward me, and said: "I'm gonna give you some advice. You've got it made now. You can do anything you want. The system you've got will give you all the money you can possibly spend. So what you should do now is slow down. Take it easy. Open a few stores every year, but be careful. Don't make any new deals that could get you into trouble. Get your debts paid off. Play it safe . . ."

I couldn't believe what I was hearing. It was the exact opposite of what I thought he believed in. Finally, I could take no more of it.

I blurted: "But that wouldn't be any fun!"

He stopped talking and just stared at me, kind of hurt-looking. Then his face broke out into a big grin. He lunged forward across his desk and pumped my hand.

"That's just what I hoped you'd say!" he laughed.

I guess I must have made some sort of impression on him, because that night I got a call from Mike Paul, who told me excitedly: "Hey, Tom, guess what . . . Ray Kroc just came into our store and ordered a pizza!"

BANKERS ARE THE KEEPERS of the keys to success for an entrepreneur. They can help you more than anyone else. They can also hurt you most, because all creditors and potential creditors check with the bankers first. A negative word from a banker can block all your plans. In times of trouble, it's doubly important to have a good relationship with your bank, because you must be able to write checks to stay in business.

But bankers speak the language of accounting and finance, and if you haven't been schooled in those mysterious tongues, as I was not, you can talk yourself blue in the face and they won't understand you. My inability to communicate with bankers was enormously frustrating to me. I always felt they were creating unnecessary barriers, trying to limit me.

Why? The only reason I could see was that I was too honest with them. I'd tell them what my problems were. I thought they'd appreciate my candor. My first inkling that this was not necessarily the case came after Doug Dawson joined us as chief financial officer and went with me to talk about arranging some financing. I told the banker the background of Domino's, including the Crash and how I got out of it. To my surprise, after we left the man's office, Doug asked, "How come all you talked about was all that negative company history?"

"I didn't think it was negative," I said. "I think the fact that I was able to get out of trouble is positive. Bankers always think, What's he going to do if we loan him money and he gets in trouble? They are trained to think about the worst that can happen, and the message I was trying to get across to him was that if we do get into trouble, we're going to make a lot more effort than others would to get out of it. We're not going to throw in the towel."

I still feel that way, but Doug's reaction certainly underscored the fact that I might have had an easier time getting money in the past if I'd not bothered to bring up a discussion of our problems. But I couldn't do that. I wanted to make sure the bankers understood that our company was honest, that the Golden Rule really was our operating philosophy.

I told Doug I wanted him to be sure and tell bankers the down side as well as the up about Domino's. I consider the truth cheap insurance. If we have problems, our banks won't be taken by surprise or panic on us because they lack information.

It's important not to take bankers for granted when times are good. We work hard at letting bankers know we appreciate them and at keeping them abreast of what's going on in the company. We have Bankers' Days, to which we invite a lot of bank officers; they come to Ann Arbor to play golf, tour our plant, and review our financials. Many of them represent banks we've never done business with, but we want a lot of banks out there to be familiar with us in case we need them. We pump them full of knowledge about Domino's.

The low point of my banking relationships was that time in 1970 when the president of the National Bank of Ypsilanti swore at me on the telephone and used barracks-room language to order me over to his office. I'd learned to use that lingo myself in the Marine Corps, and I gave it back to him in spades. That was a mistake because the resulting blot on our relationship was difficult to erase.

Part of the problem with my approach to bankers, I think, was that I was always begging for money. I'd go hat in hand, which probably gave them the impression I was weak. I can remember a humiliating discussion with another Ypsilanti bank president back in the early sixties. I wanted to borrow $250 to buy a used refrigerator for my DomiNick's store. I asked for the money in a very humble way.

"Nope," he said.

I begged and pleaded, but he just leaned back in his big leather swivel chair and tossed his head from side to side for emphasis as he slowly repeated, "Nope . . . nope . . . nope."

He gave me a long lecture about all these ratios, and what it amounted to was that I had to have $500 in the bank in order to borrow $250.

"If I had five hundred dollars," I asked, "why would I want to borrow two hundred fifty dollars from you? Why don't you take that refrigerator I want to buy as collateral?"

"Nope."

Needless to say, I switched banks at the first opportunity.

I couldn't help thinking of that Ypsilanti banker early in 1985, when Charles T. (Chick) Fisher III, chairman and president of NBD, the National Bank of Detroit, and his senior vice-chairman, Richard Cummings, came to my office and asked me to sit on NBD's board of directors. As I accepted, I thought, This is my revenge for being turned down on that refrigerator loan, and as Jackie Gleason used to say, "How sweet it is!"

Even as late as 1973, after we had recovered from the Crash and Operation Surprise was whittling away at our old debts, I was denied a bank loan. I'd been paying off notes with interest and hadn't borrowed any new money—I paid cash for everything. But I wanted to get two new Gremlins as delivery cars for $8,000, and I figured I could put half down and borrow the rest. So I explained my proposal to a vice-president of the bank, and his response was: "We don't need that kind of trouble." When the bank president found out about it, he called me up and got very diplomatic. He had good reason: Our average weekly balance was $100,000, and we were probably his bank's best customer. "You shouldn't be buying delivery vehicles with car loans," he said. "You should be buying a fleet of cars at commercial rates." I thanked him for his advice and paid cash for the two cars.

The financial guru who spoke the mysterious language of bankers and acted as my interpreter to them was John McDivitt, now president of TSM, Inc., and its divisions.

I met McDivitt in 1977 through a mutual friend who had retained his Financial Intermediaries, Inc., as a financial consultant. McDivitt's list of clients included some of the wealthiest people in Michigan, and I was impressed with his command of figures and the swift, aggressive way he dealt with issues. He was younger than me by about thirteen years, but we felt we had a lot in common, not the least of which was a strong religious background— my years in the orphanage and his growing up in a strict Irish-Catholic family. Anyway, we clicked, and John said he would help me figure out a better approach to financing Domino's operations. It must have been quite a contrast for him to leave the offices of a powerful industrialist in Detroit and walk into my Quonset-hut quarters. My desk was rickety, one leg propped up on a milk crate. I had a swivel chair with one caster that would pop out from time to time and drop me down with a jolt.

I'm not sure what John thought of Domino's potential, but I was fascinated by his response when I explained the hard times I'd had in dealing with bankers. He told me that when a company has difficulty raising money, it often means it has structural problems. Domino's certainly had such problems, and I was then in the midst of trying to sort them out. John helped solve one of these difficulties by recommending Doug Dawson. But his principal contribution was a penetrating financial analysis of our business and a presentation of it that allowed bankers to understand, for the first time, what a dynamic company they were looking at in Domino's.

John constructed an economic model of our business, demonstrating its organization from a single working unit, a store, through all the various levels of consolidation we had at that time. He analyzed the variable costs at the store level, showing how they changed and related to each other at differing volumes of business. These models became templates to overlay reports from the stores so we could interpret what was happening in them. I was fascinated by the logic of this exercise and how it clearly demonstrated the economic functioning of our stores as if they were machines with observation windows cut into them to show their working parts.

John then drew a numerical picture in which he channeled the cash tributaries produced by all our operating units into a single stream. Collectively, this grew into a broad river of money. I wasn't surprised. I knew what a powerful cash producer Domino's was, but this was the first time I had seen it depicted so objectively. Now I understood what John meant when he talked about explaining our business in economic terms.

No wonder bankers had failed to appreciate my passionate appeals for money. I might as well have been speaking Swahili, because the words I was using to describe our business simply weren't meaningful to them. The persuasive power of John's economic model was immediately self-evident.

Incidentally, this work was done before the widespread availability of mini- and micro-computers, and John constructed the whole model manually.

Unfortunately, although the model showed that Domino's was a well-oiled machine, which had never been demonstrated on paper before, and though it revealed our tremendous cash flow, this cash wasn't streaming into our pockets. It was going to all the various local banks around Michigan and Ohio where I had borrowed money to finance delivery vehicles and stores.

"Gosh, Tom, I can see how you got into this position by growing as you did," John said. "But you're going to have to change it now. You have all these loans with add-on interest that are making the banks rich and crimping cash flow to Domino's. You're paying interest of eighteen to twenty-one percent, and you should be borrowing at ten or twelve percent, tops. What you are doing is like credit-card borrowing instead of commercial credit."

"Okay, but how do we change it?" I asked.

"We consolidate your debt," he said. "We pay off all these smaller loans you've had to negotiate individually and get rid of all the separate payment books. We put them into a line of credit with a larger bank. You can't have a bank holding your equipment as collateral anymore. You can't operate a national account and want to hold on to a bunch of pizza ovens, one of which will wind up in Texas, another in Florida, and so on, and try to track them as loans."

I was eager to try his plan, so McDivitt made some appointments, and he and I went to put his economic model of Domino's under the noses of bankers. It was amazing the way their eyes lit up as they watched how cash was generated by that paper pizza machine. However, the big banks, whose officers understood John's model and were impressed by it, still considered us too small an account at the time to qualify for commercial credit from them. The officers we approached at smaller and medium-size banks didn't seem to grasp the potential in what he was showing them. It was frustrating.

The luck of the Irish was with McDivitt when he happened to be introduced to Bill Broucek, who had recently retired from NBD, where he'd worked in international banking while handling several major domestic accounts. Broucek now ran a "country bank," Citizen's Trust of Ann Arbor, and John was able to talk with him on a high level of economic sophistication about his analysis of Domino's. By this time John had expanded his presentation into a ten-year model, with five years of history and a five-year-forward projection. It showed that our stores were fully capable of paying off their own debts in five years or less, in most cases without outside assistance. Using the model, we could generate a complete life-cycle accounting from the store level up, plugging in different variables to demonstrate the results achieved in changing economic situations. Broucek liked what he saw, and after several months, McDivitt cut a deal with him for a $450,000 loan. I was delighted but also astonished. The biggest loan I'd ever obtained for Domino's was $200,000, and to get it I'd practically had to let the bank put a ring through my nose—pledging everything Margie and I owned in a personal guarantee.

Next, McDivitt helped me refinance Dick Mueller's operation in Ohio. At this time I was trying to persuade Dick to become vice-president of operations, and John was very helpful in cementing our financial agreement with Dick. We consolidated Dick's stores, in which we had 49 percent ownership, and got a loan for them equal to the one from Citizen's Trust from an Ohio bank. Then we bought Dick out for stock in Domino's instead of cash, and he came to work in Ann Arbor. Later, John and Doug Dawson consolidated the Ohio bank loan with the one with Citizen's and we established a line of credit, which within the year was for more than $1 million.

Although McDivitt's work was invaluable on the financial front, he was creating waves among members of my executive team. John had no axes to grind. He was simply looking at the system and suggesting changes to make it better. "I'm not interested in organizational charts," he told me. "I'm interested in key people and numbers. Just hand me your P&L and I'll tell you whether people are performing or not." And he did.

I could sympathize with some of the difficulties others had with his pragmatic, impersonal approach. I felt rankled by it myself when he told me we should get rid of our company plane. Our flying field-consultants program was no longer operating; it had become too expensive. "You need to increase your cash flow, put more stores in the field, and look better to bankers," John said. "The plane is a luxury you can't afford at this time."

That hurt. I wanted that plane! But I had to take my medicine like everybody else. So I gave it up. When Dawson reported the sale in the meeting, I turned to McDivitt and said, "Well, I hope you're happy."

He looked at me in surprise and replied, "Gee, I never thought of it on a personal level, Tom."

Within a few years, of course, we could justify several corporate planes—including a Hawker-Siddely jet and a Sikorsky S-76—and I made sure McDivitt handled the financing for them.

My earlier, unsophisticated approach to corporate finance was evident in our approach to budgeting as we began our rapid expansion in 1980.

I had always set up store budgets in terms of the level of activity I expected. Over the years, I filled page after page in my legal pads with sales projections for stores around the country, and I shared these expectations with the individual managers. But I resisted setting up budgeting procedures for the entire company for two reasons.

First: I was concerned that our people might think budgeting could solve all their problems. It can't.

But I soon realized that good budgeting could help us anticipate changes. If our budgeting had been better in 1980, we would have foreseen the immediate financial impact of winning the Amstar suit, and we might have dealt with it much more sensibly. We'd been paying legal fees of $30,000 to $40,000 a month for so long that we didn't even think of the money as part of our income anymore. The payments became automatic, like income tax. Once the suit was settled and those bills stopped coming in, whoopee! Suddenly we had a windfall, and all departments started finding things they needed to buy. I had to clamp down hard to eliminate all the new expenses that were creeping in.

Second: I feared that a formal budgeting system would foster bureaucracy in the company. Doug Dawson, however, developed a type of financial forecasting flexible enough to avoid that. We needed a system with enough latitude to allow for our galloping growth rate—we are doubling in size every two years. When you're growing that fast, the budget you set at the beginning of the year gets outdated pretty darn quick.

One use of budgeting I hadn't foreseen is as a training tool. What better way could there be for a manager to prepare to run his own pizza store than to be forced to sit down and figure out whether his operation is going to make money or not?

My reservations about budgeting and other formal accounting procedures were based largely on the fact that up until 1978, my experience with accountants had been mostly bad. I blamed accountants for a big share of the difficulties that led to the Crash in 1969. I once gave a speech for an association of accountants in which I told them, "I don't know why you invited me here. I'm an accountant's nightmare." It wasn't that I didn't value the numbers they came up with. In fact, I was keenly aware of the importance of those numbers; my frustration was that I never saw them in time to do anything about them. We were always playing catch-up. I said time after time that late P&Ls were worse than no P&Ls at all.

Finally, after Doug Dawson came aboard, I put my foot down and demanded that we get those statements on time even if we had to use air freight or charter jets—whatever it took to gather the information. There was a lot of moaning and groaning. Dick Mueller objected that I was putting too much stress on finance instead of operations, and others said it was impossible to get statements as fast as I wanted them. I was told that if they were done quickly, they couldn't be accurate. But I stuck to my guns, and that proved to be one of my better management decisions. We got that next statement on time, and we haven't had a late one since. We get thirteen of them a year now like clockwork. Getting timely statements cleared up a lot of potential problems in obtaining lines of credit, and they make possible our current ability to get out an audited annual statement before the end of January. Very few companies can do that. Our accounting went from being among the sloppiest in the country to being one of the best.

Doug Dawson, who is now vice-president of marketing and corporate treasurer, Tim Carr, our vice-president of finance, and John Samselle, our controller, oversee a group of dedicated accounting people who work on compiling our financial data, and their reports land on my desk every twenty-eight days without fail. The sources of these records are all our individual profit centers, including each of our corporate stores, each corporately owned commissary, our equipment and supply division, each regional office, and our corporate office. There are close to a thousand of these profit centers, and the number is growing steadily. Their individual reports funnel into the regional offices, where they are consolidated and sent to headquarters. Doug's office compiles all this information into a single report.

The first page of this master report lists our assets; the next shows our liabilities and equity; then comes a consolidated statement of income, year to date, compared with the prior year to date; followed by the same information for the current period, prior period, and current period in the previous year. Next is a statement of how our funds are distributed, showing any changes in equity position; then comes a page reviewing sources and use of working capital, year to date and for the period. This is followed by a page showing all our financial ratios under our key bank agreement, month by month for the last two years so we can see the trend, whether our situation is improving or deteriorating. Then come summaries of the number of stores opened in each region during the period, the sales in each region, and pretax profits. Following the summaries is a consolidation of the period's P&L statements for our store regions, for Domino's Pizza Distribution, Inc. (the commissary), and for Domino's Pizza, Inc.

This mass of numbers is a lot to chew on. Going through the statements carefully and noting the changes since the last report is sheer drudgery, but it has to be done. The comparative numbers are gauges, like the instruments on the dashboard of a car. They tell me how the engine of our business is running. The two key indicators I watch most carefully are the weekly average sales volumes for each store compared to the same week a year ago, and the stores' delivery times, which are plotted on a graph by our operations department. No machine runs perfectly all the time, especially one like Domino's, which depends on the energy and skill and pride of so many people. So I keep my eye on the gauges and take action to correct any problem the instant a red light goes on.

I learned the importance of reading financial statements from knowledgeable people like Eugene Power, whose use of financial data to pinpoint a particular trouble spot made a lasting impression on me. Doug Dawson gives the board a summary of our financial report each month. In 1978, these summaries were far less complete than the ones he does now, yet they were sufficient for Mr. Power to become agitated about the trend at our commissary in Kentucky. I was a little surprised at the tough stance Mr. Power took, because it was his first board meeting. The man who was running the commissaries at the time had a variety of excuses for the losses, but Mr. Power didn't buy them. He kept saying, "You'd better check out this situation. Somebody must be stealing from that commissary." Finally, we agreed to send Doug Dawson down to check it out and, sure enough, someone *was* stealing, by the truckload!

Very often a red light is anticipated because of problems I'm aware of in a store or commissary, so I'm not surprised when they show up on the financial reports. What I look for in each four-week period are the exceptions, the unexpected changes that indicate trouble we need to identify and eliminate. Watching the sales and profit for stores over the preceding thirteen periods shows the trend any one of them is taking. If a store is faltering, it's almost always a sign that management needs bolstering and may have to be changed. Sometimes, though, investigation indicates that no amount of effort will improve a store and it needs to be moved or closed.

Harold Geneen's book *Managing* contains the best discussion I've read on the importance of numbers in running a business. He says, "The ability to pay or refinance your debts as they come due is absolutely essential. The only irreparable mistake in business is to run out of cash. Almost any other mistake in business can be remedied in one way or another. But when you run out of cash, they take you out of the game." Domino's current debt ratio is about 2.1/1, liabilities to equity. Under our loan agreement we can go up to 3/1. This might be considered high in some businesses, but our cash flow is so strong that if we stopped growing, we could pay back our total debt in one year.

One of the financial moves I'm proudest of is TSM Leasing, Inc., which John McDivitt set up in 1982 as a financial services company for our franchisees.

I know from hard experience how tough it can be for an entrepreneur to raise money. It's toughest when you're only twenty-one or twenty-two years old and need $80,000 or $100,000 to open your own pizza store. Many of our aspiring franchisees are in that position. They've managed a store for at least a year. They've proven their dedication, their ability to schedule crews, handle the rush, and budget both their time and money well. But they have a hard time convincing a bank that they'd be a good risk for so much credit. The bank won't take a chance on them, but TSM Leasing does.

We finance from twenty-five to forty stores every month. Franchisees don't have to do their financing with us, and we don't attempt to give them the lowest rates. We just want to provide more dollars than anyone else will in a particular situation and give them the fastest service. Our goal is to be there if needed. If a franchisee can get a bank loan, we encourage him to do so, but if he can't, or if he runs into trouble in financing locally, we are there to help.

When a franchisee is approved and wants to get financing from us, he calls and sketches his plans in a telephone conversation. We fire off an initial letter and a packet of forms to him by Federal Express. The reason for the haste is that time truly is money when you're trying to open a pizza store, and we want to help the franchisee get in business within a month. Sometimes, with our help, a franchisee can open a store in twenty days.

The documentation furnished by the franchisee includes all the details on the proposed lease, location, and business plan. Once the lease is agreed to and we've approved the equipment package he wants, he can order his equipment. We start sending out checks, and the equipment is delivered to him. Then he's in business. Not all of TSM Leasing's customers are new starts, of course. About two-thirds of our franchisees use its services, and we have a lot of repeat customers—existing franchisees opening additional stores.

We want to be sure to do everything possible to help our stores, because they are our front line. Our average sales per store have been increasing 15 to 16 percent a year. Of course, some credit goes to our marketing staff, as public awareness of Domino's has grown through their effort and our tie to the Detroit Tigers. But the basic reason for our continued success is the excellent job done by the people in our stores, the ones who make sure that customers get a good product and those all-important drivers, who get the product delivered in thirty minutes or less.

THOSE ALL-IMPORTANT PEOPLE in our stores are supported by our operations department. Operations is the heartbeat of Domino's, which is why I say that the vice-president of operations has the most important job in the company.

Dick Mueller's return to franchising in February 1981 left a vacuum in that critical job. It had to be filled immediately, and I was the only person in sight who was qualified to handle it. Besides, I wanted to reacquaint myself with our operations and install some of my own ideas that Mueller had resisted. So I stepped in and took over that department in addition to my responsibilities as president and CEO. It was a big challenge because our surge of growth after the Amstar decision had added 130 stores, taking us to a total of 440, and I knew we were barely out of the starting blocks.

Most of our growth from 1978 to 1981 had been on college

campuses and near military bases—our experience in 1969 had made me wary of residential development—and while we now had strong stores, they were so spread out across the country that supervising them was murder. The constant travel it required was one of the things that had soured Mueller on the job, and his departure made me realize that it was ridiculous to continue to do all the supervision out of Ann Arbor.

Regionalization was the obvious answer. There were plenty of models for it in the franchise industry; McDonald's was the prime example. But our needs, as a delivery-only company with a commissary network, were so unique that none of the patterns in use by other companies could suit us. The closest thing we had to a working model was the decentralized organization of Domino's Pizza of Ohio.

Helen McNulty, loyal trouper that she is, has a story she tells to illustrate how fast I work. She says I asked her one Thursday evening for her opinion on how long it would take us to set up six regional offices around the country. Her answer was three months at least, maybe four. I called her at home that night, she says, and told her I had a decentralization plan and wanted to implement it the next Monday.

Well, that's true. But as much as I hate to spoil a good story, I have to point out that Helen wasn't aware that I had been making notes to myself about the plan and thinking it through for some time. Dick Mueller and I had discussed decentralization pretty thoroughly, and I began a separate legal pad on it—a white one, to distinguish it from my piles of yellow pads—in July 1980. I put our regionalization plan into action seven months later, shortly after Mueller left to become a franchisee again.

I had defined six geographic regions and made list upon list of store locations, sales volumes, and my estimation of their potential. So by the time I mentioned regionalization to Helen, I had a complete outline of how I wanted it to work. Fine-tuning that outline and assembling it into a finished plan was no more than a long weekend's work. I felt I had to move fast because I'd already talked about doing it. I couldn't wait to get in touch with the six people I had in mind to be regional directors. I could imagine their surprise and then the enthusiasm that would develop as I explained the dream job I was giving them.

Each would be in complete charge in his or her region (two of the six were women), responsible for setting up his own offices and hiring a controller. I wanted to name the regions after the directors principally to make it clear that they were the authority there, but I was sure this would give their self-esteem a boost, too. The regions would receive half of the royalties they collected from the stores in their territory. Incidentally, Domino's collects royalties weekly, not monthly, which I believe is unique among food-franchise chains.

I received a real shock that following Monday morning as I started calling the select six. Instead of elation, their reaction was confusion and reluctance. I had planned to locate the office of the Romano region in Dallas, but Joe Romano said he didn't want to move to Dallas. The Papineau region was to be headquartered in San Francisco, but George objected to moving there. The White region was to be centered in New York City, but Joyce White didn't want to live in New York City. Dave Black didn't object strongly to the prospect of moving to Atlanta, but he sure wasn't overjoyed about it. Dave Board was to remain in Ann Arbor and Sue Pagniano would remain in Columbus, so at least they couldn't complain about moving. But all the candidates objected to using their own names for the regions: They thought it would appear self-serving.

Surprising as these objections were, I didn't reconsider my plan, except to allow Papineau to settle in Los Angeles instead of

San Francisco. I knew that if I hesitated and tried to satisfy all the individual reservations, I'd never get my plan out of limbo. We had to charge ahead, and for the long-range good of the company the offices had to be centrally located in their regions. So I got tough and told each candidate this was it. Take it or leave it. They all went along.

The regional system has worked out exactly as I had planned. It gave us the long communications lines with tight controls at the working ends that we needed for rapid but well-orchestrated growth. Decentralization had a positive effect in corporate head-quarters, too. It reduced bureaucracy and freed me to concentrate on a few key areas. I found I could do a much better job when I had fewer people reporting to me. I had really been wearing my-self pretty thin. And it was satisfying to see my trimmed-down executive team begin cooperating, helping one another, and working for the good of the company as a whole rather than pro-tecting their own turfs.

Bob Cotman had taken over as vice-president of operations when he first came aboard. But Ichak Adizes, who was very big on theory of succession and continuity in a company, advised me that whoever I selected to be my second-in-command should be a marketing person. After careful thought, I decided Adizes was right. I would make Bob Cotman senior vice-president and give him responsibility for marketing. I had really considered it a coup when I got Bob to give up Group 243 and join us. I thought he was head and shoulders above any other candidates as my suc-cessor, so this move made a lot of sense.

Dave Black was my top candidate to succeed Cotman as vice-president of operations, and he took the job in October 1981.

Dave had started with Domino's in January 1972, working for Dave Kilby in Tampa. After three years as a manager there, he had built up enough equity in the store, through a bonus plan Kilby had instituted, to buy a franchise in Raleigh, North Carolina. I remembered Dave as a sincere kid who told me during a visit to Tampa on one of our motor home inspection tours that Domino's should forget about the rest of the country and build all our stores in Florida. He made the statement with tongue in cheek, of course. But his enthusiasm was genuine, and I liked that. "People here love Domino's Pizza," he said, "and you'd have no more sales problems if you just concentrated on this state."

Dave's service as a field consultant and regional director were important considerations in selecting him to head operations, but his best qualification, in my view, was that he's an extremely sensitive and fair-minded individual, a real "people person." Equally important was the fact that he was the only person in Domino's ever to be named Manager of the Year twice. The person who runs our operations department has to have his heart in the stores and pizza sauce in his veins. Theoretically, just about any other executive position in the company could be done by a competent outside consultant. But operations requires personal knowledge of the problems of delivery and mastery of the fundamental skills of pizza making and store management. Why? Because operations functions as a team, and just as with any sports team, the head coach has to know the game better than anyone else.

Individual jobs in a Domino's store require myriad complex arm-and-hand motions which, when performed rapidly, are as difficult to master as tennis strokes. The management skill that coordinates these activities and forms them into a smoothly working team is important. But the whole enterprise rests on the mastery of fundamentals by each member of the team. Domino's acknowledges the importance of basic skills in a variety of training programs, incentive promotions, and in our competitions for the

Two-Tray Times Award, which is the Domino's Olympics of pizza making. It measures the contestants' speed and ability in slapping out two complete trays of dough balls—twenty of them, eight large and twelve small—and applying sauce to them.

These two initial steps, slapping out the dough and applying sauce, are the most important in pizza making. Our dough is alive, it has yeast in it, and you can feel it growing in your hands as you stretch it from the ball form and slap it from hand to hand. Properly slapped-out dough will be perfectly round, snuggling up precisely to the periphery of the screen, and it will be uniform in thickness, with no thin spots. Incidentally, tossing or spinning dough overhead can create poor pizza because it tends to cause thin spots in the center of the pie. Saucing is a skill that some people master much more readily than others. I maintain that I can teach anyone to make a pizza and, if they have the desire, how to manage a store successfully. But there are some fine spots in the process at which relatively few people will excel, and saucing is one of them. We use one sauce-spoonful of sauce for a small pizza, two for a large, and it requires a very delicate touch to spread sauce smoothly, making it the same thickness over the entire pizza without any ridges. Our sauce is a rich mixture of tomato and spices that is crucial to the taste of the pizza. If it's spread too thin, the pizza will taste bland. If it's too thick, the spices will be overpowering. A master of saucing will spread the bright red mixture exactly to within one-half to five-eighths of an inch from the rim, so there's no gap around the edges, and it will look as smooth and level as a jewel in a Swiss watch.

Our Two-Tray Times competitions start at the store level each year, and winners advance up an eliminations ladder to the nationals, which are held in September in the training store in our new headquarters in Ann Arbor. Nine finalists slap out and sauce their twenty pizzas, trying to beat the current record of five min-

utes fourteen seconds, which was set in 1985 by Jeff Goddard of
Sault Ste. Marie, Michigan.

Cheesing the pizza is another art that's difficult to master. We
don't make it part of the competition, because it would be pro-
hibitively expensive, but I'd like to see a lot more attention paid
to proper cheesing technique. You have to be able to grab exactly
the right amount of cheese in your hand and distribute it on the
sauced surface of the pizza so it's uniform in thickness and covers
the layer of sauce completely, right up to the edge of the sauce.
During my days as a pizza maker, I perfected a hand motion for
cheesing that worked well. I'd roll my hand over, palm down to
palm up, like dealing cards. It was quick, easy, accurate, and
wasted no cheese. But Terry Voice was the best pizza cheeser I've
ever seen. He had a little flourish in his wrist motion that made
the cheese just flow like liquid and spread evenly over the entire
pie.

In a way, I would rather handle operations myself, because
my heart is really in the stores. I enjoy the daily contact with
franchisees and managers and the challenge of helping them improve their performance. The operations job gives you an opportunity to visit stores occasionally, and there's nothing I like better
than that and talking shop with a store crew. I have techniques of
pizza making that I think are faster and more efficient than some
of the methods used these days. For example, most oven tenders
now use a pizza cutter with a big wheel, three inches or so in
diameter, which I think is slow and inefficient. The big wheel
tends to wobble, so its hard to cut fast and keep your cut on a
straight line. I favor the old pizza cutter with a small wheel, about
two inches in diameter. It allows you to get down close to the pie
and zip right across it with a push-pull stroke. This was a natural
motion for me, like flicking a left jab. My arm moves from the
shoulder like a piston. I just grab the pizza and, zip-zip-zip, it's

cut and gone. Advocates of the larger wheel say the smaller one will sometimes fail to cut through the dough, causing it to ride up over the top of the pizza and plow up cheese. But that won't happen, I maintain, if you apply the right pressure in your stroke. The larger wheels came into favor mainly because they keep your knuckles away from the hot surface of the pizza. But I'm willing to put up with a little pain in exchange for speed and accuracy in cutting.

Since Dave Black took over operations, we have developed four area organizations to supervise the regions. The areas also are named after the executives who run them: Gale Ebert in the Midwest; Pat Kelly, West; Mike Orcutt, South; and Dave Smith, East. We also have reregionalized twice. In 1984, we expanded the six original regions to ten. Then, in March 1985, we added three more. The linkage of headquarters to areas to regions to stores has worked very well in extending our decentralization and keeping supervision close to the stores, which is what has allowed us to grow so fast.

Some other factors contribute to the speed of our growth, of course, including our corporate store-development department. We use a number of independent site selectors across the country, realtors who have been trained to evaluate store locations for us and are paid on the basis of leases approved, negotiated, and signed. Most of the construction work on new stores is done by one of eight major contractors, depending on geographic area, although there are four or five smaller firms we occasionally do business with. We like to stick with a few proven contractors because a Domino's store has specialized needs for exhaust, ventilation, and installation of equipment, and construction is faster when workers know our needs and standards. It's good for the contractors, too, because at the rate we're building—224 new corporate stores in 1985, plus remodeling or relocating existing stores—we keep them pretty busy. Our store-development people have become so good that when we decided to enter Hawaii, George Papineau was able to blitz the islands and open five stores at once so he could establish a commissary there immediately.

As I learned in 1969, however, growth for its own sake can be dangerous. Growth is healthy only if you practice defensive management and improve the operations you already have at the same time. Dave Black hit upon a way of doing this in 1981 by switching our attention from the best stores to concentrate on the worst performers. He called them the Dirty Thirty.

We assigned a task force to spend five hours each month studying the thirty stores at the bottom of our sales reports and brainstorming what could be done to improve them. The lower on the list a store was, the more attention it got. So the bottom ten got a lot of extra care. The task force would come up with a list of fifty or sixty possible actions. From that list we would select five or ten specific things we thought would work and implement them. Then we'd follow the stores' performance for a couple of months and push hard on improving it. The object was to move those lowest stores up into the middle of the sales pack. The bulk of them did move up, and overall quality improved each time.

There were a few bleeders that didn't respond to this treatment. These were bad apples that might spoil the barrel, and our solution in most cases was to move them to a different location. This happened to only one or two of each Dirty Thirty. We were growing so fast that new stores would appear on the list each month, but we kept at the program systematically and the performance of the low end kept gradually going up.

In 1984, Dave began shifting responsibility for the Dirty Thirty to the regions. Each regional office adapted the program to its own needs, and there are now thirteen versions in operation under a variety of names.

I'm sometimes asked why we don't get rid of our corporate stores and become strictly a franchise company. One of the main reasons is that corporate stores keep us in close touch with the business and the customer. Corporate stores also happen to be our biggest profit producers, so they're important in keeping the company strong. Besides, if you have franchised stores only, you will always be at the mercy of franchisees. So we intend to continue our corporate operations in about one-third of the total number of stores.

Domino's has fewer problems with franchisee relations than many chains, I think, thanks in large part to the fact that our franchisees have to come up through our system. They must prove themselves by managing a store successfully for a year before they can apply for a franchise. The last external franchise contract we signed was in February 1981. I then closed down that department, and Dave Kilby went off to other ventures. I think external franchising could work for us given the right circumstances, but there's always a tendency for externals to run to their attorneys whenever there's some situation they don't understand. I like our system, because our franchisees are Dominoids from the start. We don't have to sell them on buying a store; they have to sell us to get one. We do our best to make the business mutually beneficial.

I'm not saying our way of franchising is easy. Franchisees are human, and they're subject to human failings just like any of us. And since they're independent, entrepreneurial personalities, franchisees tend to have strong opinions, which they assert vigorously. I think it's important to get their input on corporate policies before we implement them, so we created the position of National Director of Franchise Concerns (NDFC), filled by a franchisee who agrees to serve in the post for one year. Any franchisee who is interested in serving puts his hat in the ring and is voted on by his fellow franchisees. The company pays the person as a consultant, but his or her allegiance is to the franchisees and their point of view.

The franchisee who takes the job as NDFC has to leave home and business behind and spend the year in Ann Arbor. This is quite a sacrifice, so we try to make the stay as pleasant as possible by letting them live at Snowflake House, a Frank Lloyd Wright home near Plymouth that I bought for this purpose in 1983. Giving me a convenient excuse to fulfill another dream. We also pay their way home for frequent weekend visits.

One thing NDFCs must have, of course, is someone to tend the store for them. The first two who served in the post, Ron Conkey in 1984 and Colleen Butterick in 1985, both had spouses who were very capable of handling the business. I think this year spent as NDFC can be a kind of sabbatical from the pressures of store operation. It should allow the appointee to return home with a fresh perspective on the business, a lot of insights into the workings of the corporation, and renewed energy for the compctitive battle.

Burnout isn't a problem among Domino's franchisees, but anyone can get distracted, and I insist that franchisees shouldn't take on outside duties that will divert time and attention from the business of running their Domino's stores. This applies particularly to getting into other types of businesses.

Passive investmcnts are fine. Many franchisees have a lot of money to think about, and I encourage them to use it to make more money. But I'm absolutely opposed to active investments that drain time and energy away from Domino's. This viewpoint, which I've stressed frequently, was questioned by franchisees when Ron Conkey was NDFC, and I addressed it at a board of franchisees meeting in Los Angeles.

One of the hazards of success in Domino's, I said, is that the grass tends to start looking greener on the other side of the fence. You start thinking you can do anything. I was that way back in the early days. I got into frozen pizza for a while, and it was a disaster. If I hadn't messed around with those frozen pizzas for the better part of a year, trying to sell them in bars and restaurants, Domino's probably would have had 5,000 or 6,000 stores by now. I robbed us of that year's potential by getting off on a tangent.

It amazes me how often owners of a restaurant will fail to exploit a successful business in favor of something different. I've seen it happen many times: A business is built up over a period of years and becomes a great restaurant. Then, instead of paying attention to all the details that made that restaurant great and building on them, the owners begin to look for other things they can do. They go into sideline businesses or start building other restaurants that drain attention and energy away from the first one. I went through this with Gilmore, and I learned my lesson— don't neglect the goose that lays your golden egg. The urge is always there to do something different. It happens to Domino's franchisees, and it's preposterous because there's such incredible market potential in one Domino's store.

I took time at that meeting to discuss once again franchisees' questions about why we serve just two sizes of pizza and why we won't permit stores to carry more than one kind of soft drink. The answers to these questions are vital; they are at the core of Domino's operations philosophy. In outlining why we want to stick with only two sizes of pizza, I shared some of my own experiences: how I started by serving five sizes, including the little six-inchers, and how every time I cut down the number of sizes, sales went up. The most money I've ever made in a pizza store was in East Lansing, when we had only one size, a twelve-inch pizza, and the simplicity of that operation was beautiful. I spoke from experience on the question of stocking only one beverage, too. I say a lot of our stores would be better off if they didn't carry any drink at all. I've tried carrying more than one kind of beverage, and no matter how many varieties I experienced with, Coke or Pepsi wound up accounting for more than 90 percent of my trade. Other brands did nothing but create confusion during the rush. I don't know how many times I delivered pizzas to college dorms and witnessed an argument about who ordered which drink. The customer is always right, so I'd have to return to the store and make a special trip back again with the drink they wanted. I didn't need too many experiences like that to see that carrying more than one type of drink was hurting us.

I expected to get a lot of flack for my next statements, but I thought the subject was important to the future of Domino's and I intended to hammer my points home and make them stick.

"If you feel the urge to get into some other business, then do what you love to do," I said. "If you are going to love that other business more than Domino's, then go to it. Sell out. The nice thing about Domino's is that there's always someone there ready to buy you out. Nobody is tying you here. If you don't like our policies, sell out!"

There were no protests, just an attentive silence, so I went on to outline another concern I have about temptations for franchisees.

"Because you're successful, people come to you with all kinds of deals, for limited partnerships and things like that. But for gosh sake, you're working your tail off in Domino's, and if you have any spare time you ought to get away from the pizza business and take care of your health and your family. There's more to life than making money.

"A lot of things in this world are more important than Domino's Pizza. We want well-rounded people as franchisees. We don't want one-dimensional people who get burned out after three or four years. We want people who take care of their health and have a good self-image. Generally, that's the type of person we have, that's the kind of person who is attracted to Domino's. But there's a tendency, as we get a little older and a little more successful, to lose some of our interest and enthusiasm. We get a little more defensive, a little more negative, and we lose our interest in learning new things, we lose our childlike enthusiasm. Don't fall into that trap!''

I had expected some moans and groans. Instead, I got a standing ovation. This meant that the franchisees and I shared the same vision of Domino's, and I was glad to learn that. I wasn't sure before my talk, because I don't know as much about what franchisees are thinking as I'd like to.

I long for the kind of communications we had back in the old days in Ypsilanti, when all of us would get together after work and hash out problems and share ideas over breakfast. I've tried to compensate for the loss of personal contact between me and the bright new people coming into the company by having telephone conference calls—phone-ins, we call them—in which we chat and they can ask me questions. I set aside an afternoon, from 2:00 P.M. to 4:00 P.M., and take calls from anyone in the company on a first-come first-served basis. I probably learn more from these monthly sessions than the callers do, and if nothing else, they help me reinforce my concern for customer service and concentration on the basics.

Franchisees who are just starting out in the company these days are concerned that larger franchisees are going to gobble up all the remaining territory in the country. I don't have much to say personally about how the space is allocated. That decision is handled by the regions. However, I believe we are far from our saturation point. I've said many times that if General Motors can have ten thousand dealers, then Domino's should be able to have ten thousand stores.

When we reach the point where all store service areas have been filled in nationwide, we'll strengthen stores by moving them—a strategy that follows from the natural tendency for business areas to change over time. What was a hot area five years ago is likely to be on the fringe tomorrow. We can use this phenomenon to advantage by staying alert to trends everywhere we have stores and, when the time is ripe, splitting an area, moving the existing store into the center of one half, and building a new store in the center of the other half. This strategy works even when there isn't much change in an area, because a new Domino's store always makes sales in an existing store stronger. The idea is very simple to grasp: Just visualize a pizza, representing a delivery area, with one piece of pepperoni in the center, representing the existing store. Cut that pizza in half; move the piece of pepperoni to the center of one half and put another piece, representing a new store, in the center of the other half. That's the concept: divide and conquer—move your service closer to the customer.

The Pizza Dispatch program might someday improve business in truly saturated situations by allowing us to compete with ourselves. But Pizza Dispatch is still experimental. There's a lot we can do right now to improve our existing business. I point out to franchisees that almost always there are several other pizza places in their areas, and these places are doing business that Domino's should have. I'm not talking about grasping at someone else's customers or hurting the competitor; I'm talking about defensive management, increasing business by becoming better. If a Domino's operator will keep track of his deliveries every day for six months, I'm sure he will find that 75 to 80 percent of his business is done within the first three-quarters of a mile of his store. That means he is only delivering to half of his potential customers. He doesn't need to look elsewhere for them—he may not realize it, but like the man in Russell Conwell's famous story "Acres of Diamonds," he is sitting on a treasure in a single Domino's store.

Since Domino's is a company built on wheels, its history could be envisioned as a parade of all the cars we've driven and fondly remembered for the last twenty-five years. But nice as nostalgia is, delivery cars have always been a source of aggravation for me. Cars can have many kinds of problems, and I'm sure I've dealt with all of them, from dead batteries on sub-zero nights to mechanical rigor mortis due to the steady stop-and-go driving of pizza delivery. Our cars get hard use. It's not that they're driven fast, it's just that they get worn out by the short-run, stop-start nature of delivery driving and the number of different people with different driving styles who operate them. Our drivers open and slam doors continuously and leap in and out of the seats at every stop. That kind of treatment would wear out a Sherman tank.

I used to think it would be great to have a big fleet of Domino's cars, and we've taken a stab or two at it over the years. But it's never worked very well. Maintenance of the cars has always taken time and attention away from the mission of making and delivering pizzas. The only time I ever had good maintenance on a regular basis was when my uncle Dan did it for me in 1966. In 1968 and again in 1970 I contracted with different mechanics for delivery-car maintenance, but each time, after promising starts, they'd wind up with a backlog of cars in the shop and we'd have to go begging and borrowing cars to make deliveries. I've tried all kinds of cars, too, including Checker cabs. But the reality has always been that most of our drivers deliver pizzas in their own cars and we pay them mileage. Some franchisees maintain fleets, but as of 1986, the corporate requirement is merely that each store must own at least one delivery car.

I think it's inevitable that someday we'll have a fleet of special Domino's delivery vehicles. Maybe they'll be electric cars. My brother, Jim, talked about electric delivery cars on the first day we started in business. He thought they'd be great for us because they have so few moving parts. During the energy crisis of the seventies, Jim and Towny Beaman did a lot of experimental work on electric cars at Towny's old stone village on Vandecook Lake.

Towny was a very unusual man. A big, robust outdoor type, he'd studied engineering at the University of Michigan, taking a year each of mechanical, civil, chemical, and electrical to get a broad background. Then he went to Washington, D.C., and got a job in the patent office while working on his law degree at night at National University. He returned to Jackson to set up practice in the early thirties. He and his wife, who was a writer, made a Beaman family compound of the stone village, which some eccentric had built about a hundred years earlier. They had a theater for their daughter, who was interested in drama, an art studio for one son and a machine shop for another. Their third son, Duncan, also became a patent lawyer and went into partnership with his father.

Towny was in his late sixties when I met him, but he was very active. After joining Domino's board of directors, he did a lot of tinkering in his machine shop on improved hot boxes for pizza delivery. One day he brought all the board members out and showed us a charging-coupler bumper he and Jim had designed for the electric car they had been working on. A lot of other inventors have also struggled with the electric car, with no more success than Jim and Towny had.

Domino's does have ten little "aerocars," called Tritan A2s, built by Doug Amick, of Ann Arbor. These low-slung plastic--

hulled machines that look like wingless miniature jet planes run on small gasoline engines and are nice showpieces for grand openings of stores and other events, but they create too many insurance problems to be used for day-to-day delivery.

I love cars—I have stacks of books on them and read them avidly—so I went along with our marketing department's idea of buying an Indy race car: Domino's Pizza Hot One. Our marketing department and many franchisees feel it's been a terrific promotion for us, especially in 1985, when driver Al Unser, Jr., and Domino's Pizza Team Shierson overcame a series of mechanical problems and ended the season in second place in the Indy Car competition, with ten top-ten finishes and eight top-three winner's circle finishes. The most exciting race I've ever seen was when our driver lost out to his father, Al Unser, Sr., with five laps to go in the last race of the year. The comments of the father-son competitors afterward brought tears to my eyes.

Racing has been good publicity for Domino's; all eighteen races on the circuit are nationally televised. We've had many corporate meetings scheduled around events like Indy and the Domino's 500 in the Poconos. The turnout on these occasions made clear that many of our franchisees are fanatical fans of auto racing. But I guess this shouldn't have surprised me, since auto racing is the second-largest spectator sport in the world.

Our marketing department calls the shots on the race-car program, and I try not to second-guess them. I don't want to get too emotionally involved in the races because my feelings might start swaying decisions on Domino's advertising. Besides, I'm not so much interested in automotive speed or mechanical sophistication as in design excellence. My passion is for the styling of classic cars.

THE PLAY'S THE THING.''

    I often repeat that line to myself to help me focus on the action at hand. No literary reference is intended. I simply take the words Shakespeare penned for Hamlet and give them my own meaning. When I was working in a store, "the play" to me meant *the rush,* and handling it was the *only thing,* the all-important task.

I wanted our commissary to apply the same active attitude in its service to our stores. But the play never became the thing in the commissary until 1978, when Don Vlcek took over. Until then, in fact, I felt like the commissary was a tar baby I'd created myself. I wanted to let go of it and have it stand on its own feet as a separate company. But it kept having problems that made it stick to me, demanding attention.

The commissary concept seemed simple enough: Take the backroom work out of the stores and consolidate it in a manufacturing operation to allow the store manager to concentrate on his main task—getting pizzas out. Theoretically, consolidation of backroom work would allow us to take advantage of bulk purchasing and lower our cost of raw materials. At the same time, if the commissary concentrated on just a few things—making dough, chopping cheese and toppings, and shipping them to stores—we should have better quality control. But theory and practice often parted company at the commissary door. Complaints from stores about commissary service and product had become pretty alarming by 1978. Our stores aren't required to buy from the commissary, although most of them do because backroom work is tedious and detracts from the main mission. In addition, when it's run right, the commissary provides a superior product at a better price. If stores choose to do the job themselves, of course, they have to meet our standards for purchasing and making all the ingredients, and that ain't easy.

We had seven commissaries and an eighth was under construction when I hired Don Vlcek in September 1978. I told him his mission was to get control of the organization and make it capable of supporting the growth of our stores. To do that, though, he'd first have to stop the bleeding—I had just received a P&L for the commissary division that showed a year-to-date loss of three hundred thousand dollars!

The loss was bad enough, but in addition, the division was the laughingstock of the company. Anytime something went wrong, people would joke, "That must have been done by the commissary." It was a touchy situation, and I wasn't sure at first whether Vlcek had the kind of temperament that could deal with being the butt of jokes from all sides. Guys in the meat business, where he'd been trained, tend to be tough and quick to take offense. But fortunately, Don had a kind of transformational experience in a board of directors' meeting not long after he joined us. He says it gave him a valuable perspective on Domino's and how to approach his job.

I had invited Don to the meeting so I could introduce him to the board, and he was awed by the presence of men like Towny Beaman, Mr. Power, and Robert D. Ulrich, a prominent Ann Arbor attorney. A discussion developed over whether we should change the price of our pizza, and Bob Ulrich just sat there quietly puffing on his pipe and listening. Finally, he put down his pipe and said, "You know, Tom, I think I've finally figured out why you asked me to be on this board. I don't know anything about this pizza business. I don't know how you make one, I don't know how you price it or how you sell it. All I know about a pizza is how to eat it. So I see that what I can offer you is my ignorance. I'll be able to ask dumb questions that maybe no one else here would think of asking."

Don says this statement hit him like a thunderbolt, because in his previous companies ignorance was considered shameful. Even if you didn't know something, you had to pretend you did or you would lose face. Ulrich's observation that ignorance might be a positive contribution gave Don the courage to be forthright about his own lack of knowledge of our operation. His commissary managers and our franchisees all responded to his honesty with offers of help.

I liked the way Don took charge. He wasn't afraid to challenge the way we were doing things. For example, the commissaries were still using the VCM to grind cheese, make dough, and mix sauce. Apparently, the machine was regarded as a sacred cow because I was the one who had discovered it and made it a standard in the industry. But that had been nearly fifteen years earlier, and Don knew that there were better machines available now. So he came to me with a gleam of heresy in his eye.

"Tom, I have figured out what the intitials *VCM* stand for," he said.

"Oh yeah?" I replied. "What's that?"

"They mean: *very crappy machine.*"

He went on to tell me exactly why the VCM was outmoded. The Ohio commissary had three eight-hour shifts working six days a week grinding cheese with the VCM. He said he knew of a machine called a Urschell dicer that was designed specifically for dicing cheese. It could produce the same volume of cheese the Ohio commissary was turning out using only one eight-hour shift working two and a half days.

Another problem with the VCM, Don said, was that our cheese was ground to varying specifications in it, depending on who was running the machine. He showed me the results of a survey he'd taken among both commissary managers and store operators to determine what the standard cheese grind should be. Their ideas varied all over the place—from big chunks to powder. This meant we simply weren't providing a consistent product. With cheese diced instead of ground, he pointed out, we'd automatically have absolute consistency.

The major drawback to using the VCM for mixing dough, Don continued, was that it had no timer. "We're pouring in twenty pounds of flour and adding the water, sugar, salt, and yeast, closing it up and running it so many seconds at one speed, so long at another speed. It's a waste of time. We need a machine that will meter the water automatically and then go through the phases in sequences timed to the split second. What we do now is have someone keep an eye on the wall clock, trying to remember whether he started at five minutes to three or five minutes after."

If Don was expecting a big argument from me in defense of the VCM, he was disappointed. I was glad to see him suggesting creative changes. I knew about the machinery he was proposing to use, of course. I kept up with all the latest developments in the industry, and if I'd been running the commissary, I probably would have been advocating the same changes. I always favored new ideas, but I rarely had a commissary manager who could come up with them on his own as Vlcek did. It didn't do any good for me to have ideas if the commissary managers resisted them.

But he had a tough time making his innovations stick, particularly the switch to diced cheese instead of the granular product of the VCM. His customers, our store operators and franchisees, had to be convinced that diced cheese would improve their pizza. They finally accepted it, though. He also got them to accept cheese packaged in fifteen-pound cryovac bags—plastic bags from which the oxygen is removed as the diced cheese goes in. A shot of nitrogen gas is added to keep the particles from solidifying back into a block. This method gives complete protection from contamination and extends the shelf life of the fresh cheese to thirty days.

Don also invented a device he called a dough rounder. Our raw dough has to be rounded into a ball before it's sent to the stores or it won't develop a good skin. Rounding by hand is very slow, but it was the accepted method. One day I was walking through our Michigan commissary and noticed that some small roller bars had been attached to the conveyor belts that led from the dough-dividing machine. As the portions of dough came along, they were pinched by the roller bars to form a perfect ball. I got as excited about this innovation as a kid seeing his first toy choo-choo train.

Changes such as these were just the beginning of what has become a continuous process of improving our machinery. Companies like Bernier Equipment Manufacturers of Holland are constantly studying our needs and trying to come up with more sophisticated and more powerful mixers, dividers, and rounders. We account for about 10 percent of Bernier's business, so they birddog our account pretty well. And they're so proud of what they've done for us that they dubbed themselves "official suppliers" to our Domino's Pizza Distribution Olympics.

When young doctor Vlcek started examining the sick division he'd taken on, it turned out that much of its bleeding came from a number of small wounds. For example, our North Carolina commissary reported laundry bills ten times higher than those in our Ohio unit. When Vlcek probed into it, he learned that Kelly Hannan, the old pro who was running the Ohio commissary, managed to make his tray-drying towels last a week before sending them to the laundry. At the end of a shift, he'd have his crew put a little soap in the sink and toss the wet towels in to soak overnight. Next morning, they'd be rinsed out and hung up to dry for reuse. Don got all the units to adopt Hannan's system and the commissary laundry bills immediately dropped from 2 percent of sales down to .5 percent.

Then there were commissary managers who weren't taking advantage of bulk purchasing. One guy was buying cheese from a local distributor at forty-five cents a pound over the block price, which is the cost of raw ingredients and manufacture as set weekly by the cheese industry. Our national supplier's price was twenty-five cents over block. Why didn't he buy from the national supplier? Poor planning. The manager was scared off by the national supplier's 1,500 pound minimum order. He knew he was running through 2,000 pounds of cheese every ten days, but he didn't realize that if he asked his customers what their needs would be instead of merely waiting to *react* and fill their orders, he could regulate his purchasing and save twenty cents a pound on his cheese.

One by one, Don found and treated all those wounds. The bleeding stopped. Within seven months, the commissary was current with its payments of bills and was able to start taking advantage of discounts from suppliers.

At the same time, Don made some major advances in the quality of the food we were supplying to our stores. One of the biggest changes was his move of the mixing of our sauce out of the individual commissaries and into the tomato packer's plant. I am a stickler about our sauce. It's made from my own recipe, developed through a lot of trial and error, and it's probably the main thing that distinguishes Domino's Pizza from all the rest. But the way we were making sauce in the commissaries, mixing a batch at a time and stirring in a special prepackaged blend of spices, resulted in a certain lack of consistency.

Don switched all sauce preparations to a central packing plant in 1979. The sauce was made to our specifications by a predecessor of our current supplier, Tri-Valley Growers near San Francisco, and we bought 50,000 cases of sauce that first year. In 1986 we were up to nearly 2 million cases. The tomatoes used in the sauce are specially grown for us on 2,800 acres, which in 1986 produced 84,000 tons of tomatoes destined for our sauce. The centrally prepared sauce gives us great consistency, and our packaging costs are dramatically lower than they were with the old system, in which we got everything—tomatoes and paste and packets of spices—in separate containers.

In general, I was happy with the way the commissary was coming together. But I wondered why its growth was being delayed. Don had opened four commissaries that were already on the drawing board when he joined us, giving us a total of twelve. But then he said he needed a six-month moratorium on new ones so he could get his management ducks in line. I okayed that. After the six months were up, however, he kept holding back. I didn't make an issue of it. I had faith in his promise that he would get back on the program as soon as possible. But I was beginning to question him after another six months had passed and still no new commissaries had been started. Many of the new stores we were opening were performing their own backroom work, and I didn't want that. But I also didn't want to issue any directives. I don't believe I've given Don more than one or two direct orders in all the time he's worked for me.

My philosophy of management is to let my executives do their job their way. I express my point of view, but decisions are up to the person in charge. I believe that the best people work well with this approach, perhaps because I've always had my own methods for doing things. In math classes in school, for example, I'd always get the right answers to problems, but I seldom followed the rules in arriving at them. I don't like to lay down operating rules at Domino's.

My approach worked well with Vlcek. When he was ready, he launched his building program, and it was a doozy. He built a commissary a month for the next eight months, taking us from twelve units to twenty. That's Vlcek for you.

Building commissaries in 1986, when we had grown to thirty-two units, was a far different ball game than it was even in 1980, when we could put up a modern facility for $300,000. In 1986, the cost of a new commissary was up to $1.3 million. Newer commissaries have tons of complex machinery. They have one new feature, the flour silo, that alone costs $100,000, a pretty staggering figure when you consider that ten years earlier we could build an entire commissary for $8,000. Of course, we were growing so rapidly by 1986 that the new commissaries had to be three or four times larger than the old ones. The main reason commissaries cost so much more today, though, is that we're no longer remodeling old warehouses but building our own units from scratch. This means we now can bring the commissaries up to the level of quality projected by our modern store facilities.

To handle the new commissaries and other real-estate development, I had John McDivitt establish TSM Properties, Inc., as another division of my holding company. TSM Properties acquires sites for commissaries, builds them, and leases them to the Domino's National Commissaries Division of the company Don Vlcek heads, Domino's Pizza Distribution, Inc. In some cases the commissary mortgage is held by an insurance company; in other cases we sell bonds to finance the construction. Owning commissaries is a good investment for us because it requires no more management than leasing the same buildings. The construction requires more net worth and more expertise up front than leasing, of course, but it pays off in the end, because even if changes in delivery patterns made it necessary to change a commissary location in the future, we could get our money back out of the building. Commissary buildings have pretty basic structures with a wide variety of possible applications in light manufacturing, and we locate them mainly in good industrial parks.

TSM Properties also owns Domino's warehouses and is responsible for the development of our new headquarters, Domino's Farms.

The idea of having my office on a farm has roots in my boyhood experiences, of course, but it was not a dream born full-blown. It came into focus slowly as Domino's grew and as the problem of providing for its future needs required plans of ever increasing scope.

I had always wanted to have offices in buildings with architectural merit. The house that had burned on Cross Street in Ypsilanti had had eye-pleasing lines. Even our tacky office in the Quonset huts had had possibilities. I made a lot of sketches of the place and came up with a design for trellises and covered walkways that would have turned it into an oasis in the midst of an urban wasteland.

The offices on Boardwalk that I was so proud of became overcrowded in less than two years. Then I had an opportunity to buy the old Hoover Mansion in Ann Arbor, a majestic French château of limestone with a heavy slate roof. It reminded me of the *Reader's Digest* headquarters in Pleasantville, New York, which had been featured in a story in the fortieth-anniversary issue of the magazine, in February 1962. The *Reader's Digest*'s gracious Georgian-style building, suggestive of colonial Williamsburg, surrounded by broad lawns, gardens, and orchards, appealed to me because its elegance retained an air of rural informality. I thought I'd be able to achieve something like that with the Hoover Mansion. However, the selling price was $216,000 and it took me a year to arrange the financing. By the time I bought it and started planning how we would use the various rooms for our offices, I discovered that we'd outgrown it! I was dismayed.

Mr. Power found a fine building for us on Research Park Drive, on the south side of Ann Arbor, and this was to be Domino's first major real-estate investment. The price was $1,050,000, so it was a big step, but I figured such a purchase would give us impetus to further growth. The land around the building might also be purchased for expansion. But even though I thought bigger than others in the company, I'd still been thinking too small. We sold the Hoover Mansion to Bob Cotman's Group 243 for what we had paid for it, and moved into the Research Park Drive building in 1979. It seemed huge at first—we used only part of the space—but within two years, we had filled the whole building and our people were tripping over each other once again.

Beginning in the late sixties, when I happened upon Charley O. Finley's farm while driving through northern Indiana, the idea of having our headquarters on a farm had been taking shape in my mind. I suppose the idea would have come to me anyhow, because I had a great curiosity about farms and how they were laid out, but the Finley farm really crystallized the notion in my mind. I thought the Finley farm was beautiful; it reminded me of one of my favorite books, Louis Bromfield's *Pleasant Valley*. I had a similar feeling about the Darby Dan Farm near Columbus, Ohio, which I also came upon by chance sometime later.

The concept of Domino's Farms was different from most of my dreams because there was nothing specific to visualize. Most of the time I can focus on a particular object and create a mental picture of attaining it. Just as I put Shakespeare's lines to my own self-motivating use, I can utilize an illustration as a visualization tool in ways that have nothing to do with what the artist or photographer intended. For example, if I come upon a picture of a particular car that's on my wish list, say a Ferrari Daytona roadster, the Spyder, and it's in the Ferrari red, I'll put it up on my office wall as a reinforcement of my desire to own that car. I'll imagine myself driving it. Every time I look at that picture, I'll imagine I own a car like that. I still don't have one, but I'm visualizing it in my garage as I write this, and one day it will be there. In contrast to this, my usual approach, the idea of Domino's Farms began with just a hint here and there, like pieces from a jigsaw puzzle without a clue to the final picture they would form.

One day in 1973, I was driving through the Chelsea area near Ann Arbor and spotted a barn roof behind a hill. Curious, I drove in and found a beautiful farm tucked into the hills with a little lake and white fences running all around the property. I could imagine our headquarters situated here, with administrative offices in the house and various departments set up in the barn and outbuildings. All the interiors would be remodeled, of course, made comfortable and businesslike inside, but the exteriors would retain their farmstead character. It was a terrific vision! I dreamed about driving through the countryside from my home to my office on that farm. To my joy, the site was for sale, and I made a good offer—$200,000—but I must not have looked like a

buyer to the real-estate agent who was handling the property. He
acted like he thought I was a kid who was getting a little too big
for his britches. At any rate, I didn't get the place.

There was one thing about the Finley farm that the Chelsea
farm lacked: visibility from a major highway. Finley had OAKLAND
A's and a baseball bat and ball painted in white on the green roof
of the barn, and I thought that was a little garish, but otherwise it
was beautiful. So in 1974, I started looking for farms with expressway exposure. In the next few years, I visited every single
farm that was visible from the expressway between Ann Arbor
and Chelsea. One near Grass Lake had a big beautiful barn, and I
talked the owner into selling, but his children wouldn't go along
with the deal. Another place near Ann Arbor looked like a Cur-
rier & Ives print. It had neat white buildings and a picturesque
pond where ducks swam. But the farm included only fifteen
acres, and I wanted more land.

Then my need for more space forced me to abandon the farm
idea for a time. I found a sprawling modern office complex tucked
into berms and surrounded by open, rolling land. Situated near
Green Road, next to the University of Michigan's North Campus,
the building had great expressway exposure. Nothing indicated
that it was for sale, but I thought, Nothing ventured, nothing
gained. The owner, whose not-for-profit company occupied the
building, flinched when I asked him if he would sell. He said he
would, but he didn't want anyone to know it because people
might think his firm was in trouble. He said the property had
been appraised at $4.5 million, which knocked me back a few
steps. But I thought the location was too good to pass up. The cost
of this property scared everybody on our board and my executive
team. Even Doug Dawson thought that if we bought this complex
we'd be biting off more than we could chew. He was afraid that
even though it would be purchased by TSM Properties, Inc., and

not Domino's, a purchase that big might endanger our line of credit, which we needed to build stores.

I got busy with my legal pad, and the conclusion I reached was that not only were we *able* to buy the Green Road property, but adequate planning for the future dictated that we *must* buy it. I was uneasy about the objections I'd heard—Dawson's vote against the purchase was especially worrisome—so I made my first offer at only $3.2 million. It was rejected. Others in the company probably sighed with relief at that, but I was really upset. We had to have that building! I was afraid I'd messed up my chances of getting it. According to my calculations, we would need only 20 percent of the office space and could rent the remainder to the seller—so we'd acquire the space we needed for growth and have someone else pay for part of it. We would take over the entire space over the course of three years.

I said to myself, "I need this place and I'm willing to pay what it's worth. I'll give him the appraised price, $4.5 million." We put $800,000 down, $500,000 of which was borrowed from our Ohio commissary, thanks to my old friend and franchisee Harold Mitchell, who owns 41 percent of that commissary. Arthur Andersen worked with Doug Dawson to structure the deal, and when they got finished with it, I hardly recognized it. The sellers' not-for-profit status provided us with several tax advantages; as a result, we wound up paying less than $4 million for the property.

We moved into the Green Road building in 1982, and we grew so fast that our three-year program of expansion was compressed into a single year. We then set about acquiring adjacent property. But there seemed to be no way to get all the land we needed to provide for future growth. I talked this problem over with Larry Brink, a local architect who was trained by Frank Lloyd Wright and has done a lot of work for me. "Well, Tom," he said, "I guess you're just going to have to build the Golden Beacon."

That remark hit me like a sledgehammer. It was the perfect idea! I knew Wright's drawings for the building very well. He'd designed it in 1956 for a Chicago real-estate developer named Charles Glore, but it was never built. The Golden Beacon was to have been an apartment tower, and it would have culminated Wright's tall-building designs, which included Price Tower in Bartlesville, Oklahoma. I could picture the Golden Beacon on our property so clearly, I just knew it would some day stand there. It would give us all the space we needed, it would be a great tribute to my idol Frank Lloyd Wright, and it would be an ornament to the area, visible for miles on the expressway. I immediately began negotiating with William Wesley Peters of the Frank Lloyd Wright Foundation's Taliesin Associated Architects to have the tower design adapted for Domino's.

Then, on the heels of that terrific idea for building the Golden Beacon came one that was even better. I learned from a consultant named Doug Rader about a 224-acre site just across the expressway from our Green Road office and I thought, There I can have the farm! Suddenly all the pieces in that jigsaw puzzle started coming together. I could picture a long, low Frank Lloyd Wright-style office building, with the Golden Beacon adjacent across a reflecting pond and a cluster of working-farm buildings nearby. Wright's words about his love of farms and animals came back to me, and I remembered his idea that "a tall building or high-rise should not be thrust into a crowded city, where it would function only as a landlord's expedient to extract more rent from a given plot of land, but rather should stand free, preferably in semi-rural surroundings." Domino's Farms would be a perfect tribute to him!

Our building at Domino's Farms is being done in phases. We moved our administrative offices into the first phase in December 1985, just in time to celebrate the company's twenty-fifth anniversary there. The second phase was completed in November 1986.

Meanwhile, my decision to pay the full appraised price for the Green Road property began to pay off handsomely. The seller says our $800,000 down payment helped him save his company, and he rebuilt it to the point where he was able to lease the entire building back from us when we got ready to vacate. Incidentally, the property is now appraised for $9.6 million.

One of the exciting things about Domino's Farms is that I'm hoping to raise crops on the Booker T. Whatley farm. If we can get this project established, it will occupy a little over a hundred acres of our property and be a model of Dr. Whatley's concept for saving the small farm in America.

In 1983, I read a story in the *Wall Street Journal* about Dr. Whatley and his ideas for a "pick-your-own" farm that would allow a farmer with only twenty-five acres to gross more than a hundred thousand dollars a year. Dr. Whatley's credentials, which the *Journal* story said kept him from being "dismissed as just another back-to-the-land idealist," were impressive. He earned his Ph.D. in horticulture from Rutgers University and taught plant and soil science for twelve years at Tuskegee Institute, the school founded by his namesake, Booker T. Washington. Before he retired in 1981, Dr. Whatley had developed five varieties of sweet potato and fourteen varieties of muscadine grapes. My own studies of farming told me he was dead right in his observation that "the trouble with today's average small farm is that it's nothing but a scaled-down big farm. It's probably got corn and soybeans, a few cattle, a lot of debt, and an owner with a job in town." But what really made me sit up and take notice was his description of the working of his ideal small farm, which should be situated near a city, where the farmer can sign up members for his pick-your-own club. Members pay a modest annual fee and have the right to pick fresh fruit and vegetables at a cost that averages 40 percent below what they would pay for the same produce at the supermarket. I thought, My gosh, wouldn't it be great to have one of these farms on Domino's Farms? It would add a real agricultural flavor to the place. Besides, Dr. Whatley could be a great adviser on crops we would raise on the farm, like green peppers and onions for use as toppings in our stores.

I called Dr. Whatley's home in Montgomery, Alabama, and learned that he was going to be lecturing at Michigan State University, so I made arrangements to attend and meet with him afterward. He gave a fascinating talk, illustrated with a big chart showing his model twenty-five-acre farm.

I was completely captivated by this sixty-eight-year-old black man. He came on like Bill Cosby imitating Uncle Remus; he had the audience in stitches, but he never cracked a smile while making sly jokes based on farm folklore and taking pokes at the U.S. Department of Agriculture. He has a low opinion of farm bureaucracy.

"The small farmers have got to let the big boys grow soybeans, cotton, hay, peanuts, beef cattle," he said. "We've got to concentrate on the high-value crops."

He outlined five criteria a small farm has to meet to be successful with his plan: First, it must have a balance of crops that will provide year-round weekly family income. On his model, which he said was being followed by about fifty farmers in Alabama, strawberries provided cash flow from mid-April to mid-May, then in the following months, the farmers harvested blackberries, then blueberries, then grapes, followed by collards, mustards, southern peas, sweet potatoes, and turnips. The progression of crops underscored his second point, which was that harvests should be staggered so they don't compete with one another. Third, each crop must produce at least three thousand dollars in annual gross income per acre. "That's what I mean by high value," he said. Fourth, the farm must provide full employment year-round. The twenty-five-acre model "requires a family to run it—a man and wife and three teenagers who work after school." His fifth and final point was that the farm has to be within twenty-five miles of its you-pick market. "Ideally, it will be on a paved road, and the nearby city will have a population of at least fifty thousand," he said.

After his talk, Dr. Whatley sat down with me, and I explained my concept for Domino's Farms and my hope for a model Whatley Farm on it. He seemed very interested, and this first conversation developed into a continuing dialogue. In addition to his awesome scientific knowledge, Dr. Whatley has a keen sense of promotion and could see the potential publicity his ideas would receive if there was a Booker T. Whatley farm in the midst of Domino's office and farm complex, virtually in the shadow of the Golden Beacon skyscraper.

In October 1985 Dr. Whatley, who by this time was a close acquaintance of mine—known fondly around our office as Booker T.—came up to Ann Arbor and gave me his proposal for a farm on our property. The Ann Arbor climate required different types of crops than his southern model, so he had substituted cauliflower for collards and beans for southern peas, for example. But he maintains that sweet potatoes will grow in Michigan. In addition to the pick-your-own crops, we'd have other benefits for our club's members. Another of Dr. Whatley's ideas for the farm is a twenty-acre pond, which would be stocked with varieties of fish recommended by the Michigan Department of Conservation. The pond's operation would be catch-your-own, with hook and line, rather than a pick-your-own. We couldn't guarantee the fish harvests, of course, but we could promise fun. We'd also raise quail, pheasants, rabbits, and lambs for sale to club members as dressed meat, and we'd have lots of honey for sale—two acres have been set aside for bees. It's a terrific dream, though it will be difficult and, maybe, impossible to achieve. But I still hope to pull it off.

Although my boyhood love of farm life probably was the main reason I decided that Domino's headquarters should be a farm, my sympathy with Frank Lloyd Wright's idea of integrating architectural forms with a rural countryside had a lot to do with it, too.

I think there's also a strong correlation between my insistence on simplicity in the operation of Domino's and the integrity of good design as Wright saw it. I feel I understand Wright's ideas at a gut level. My experiences, though quite different from Wright's, share a certain similarity of effect with things that happened to him.

According to Finis Farr, one of Wright's biographers, Frank Lloyd Wright was given a set of blocks in 1876, when he was seven years old. These blocks were clean-cut maple cubes, spheres, and triangles, which happen to be the basic shapes architects work with. Wright played with the blocks tirelessly, arranging them in all kinds of formations, and he later said, "Those blocks stayed in my fingers all my life."

I feel something similar happened to me when I was growing up in the orphanage. I got the feel for doing work with my hands quickly and well from ironing hundreds of shirts and pairs of pants. I prided myself on being the best and fastest ironer in the orphanage. That dexterity stayed in my fingers and came out in my ability to make pizzas fast.

I see Domino's delivery system as excellence in design, a thing of beauty, and I can't stand to see its structure violated. The concept of delivering a hot tasty pizza in thirty minutes or less is pure and needs no embellishment any more than a Frank Lloyd Wright design might need a gothic tower grafted onto it.

To go one step further, I believe that if Domino's is to survive the pizza wars as a privately held company pitted against the corporate might of Pizza Hut and the assembled strength of thousands of independent pizza shops that are delivering against us, it will be due to the integrity of our basic design and our dedication to customer service.

WHEN I CAME to a big fork in the road back in 1960, I chose the path that led to the pizza business instead of architecture. But I've been blessed with a wife who tolerates my passion for the art of Frank Lloyd Wright, so over the years I've been able to explore at least part of that road not taken.

In 1973, Margie and I bought a house in Barton Hills, a prestigious residential area just across the Huron River, north of Ann Arbor. Living here fulfilled a dream I'd had since high school. I'd often driven through the area admiring the houses and their spacious, wooded settings. We settled on this particular house because it was one of the few I'd seen with lines that had something of Wright's style about them. I was looking forward to putting more of Wright into the place by designing changes with the help of Larry Brink.

Because Brink was trained by Frank Lloyd Wright, he is as

familiar with all of Wright's houses as I am, and we can beam our thoughts on the same wavelength. It's really exciting to brainstorm architectural ideas with Brink. He has the technical training to articulate my inspirations, and we often express an idea merely by mentioning a detail of Wright's work or the feeling projected by one of his rooms, a system of reference that's simplified by Wright's habit of naming his houses for clients or giving them nicknames like Falling Water. My favorite Wright design has always been the McCormick House, which much to his dismay and mine, was never built.

Visiting Wright houses is my idea of a super vacation, and the year after Margie and I bought the Barton Hills house, we went on the first real vacation we'd had since our honeymoon. We packed our four daughters in a motor home and took off to tour most of the Wright houses in the Midwest. I had a fantastic time, because just standing in a Wright room is an emotional experience for me.

Although Brink and I talked a lot about possibilities in the Barton Hills house, I made no major changes until after Domino's won the Amstar suit. Margie wouldn't let me do any work on the house at all unless we paid cash. But in 1980 I began a series of alterations that kept growing in scale until the property just wasn't big enough to accommodate our plans. We started with installation of a light shelf in the living room ceiling and antique Mexican tile floors with the look of old leather in the kitchen and entryways. Then I changed the woodwork to notch-pattern oak and redid the fireplace in Wrightian style, at the same time creating an open kitchen with a work island. Next came the incorporation of what had been a screened-in porch into a rumpus room off the kitchen. Later we drafted plans for new wings, and since the lot wasn't large enough to triple the size of the house horizontally, we planned to do so vertically, accentuating the rather steep natural slope of the lot by excavating to create four additional stories. The remodeling would have cost about two million dollars. I thought about buying up the surrounding homes and creating a Monaghan family compound, like the Kennedy compound, where my daughters could live after they married. Margie wasn't too keen about the idea, however.

I thought I was creating a work of art, but complaints from community officials and their refusal to let me build beyond the zoned setbacks were frustrating. Actually, the complaints were minor, but they hit me at the wrong time. I had the feeling I couldn't be as free as I wanted with the design. Margie had reservations about my plans, too, and I think they were valid—my proposal had gotten out of scale for the site, and if I went ahead with it, we'd probably be unable to sell the house. I'd known from the beginning, though, that I'd never be able to get my money back for the improvements. That wasn't important to me, because this house was to be an expression of what artistic abilities I have. But the community's restrictions finally caused me to drop my plans and call off further construction.

I was reluctant to stop building. I'd already put more than I'd originally paid for the place into garage, deck, and gazebo additions, unified by a new overhang for the roof and a band of large windows looking out over the deck along the entire length of the living room. Crews had started putting a copper roof on the new garage, but I had them remove it. I made up my mind that it would be far easier and a lot less expensive to buy a suitable site and start from scratch on the dwelling of my dreams, the one that had been the inspiration for many of the changes I wanted to make in the Barton Hills place: McCormick House.

Larry Brink sent for a book of drawings of McCormick House, and he and I began working on adapting them to a setting John McDivitt was lining up for me in the vicinity of Domino's Farms.

Wright had designed the house in 1907 for the heir to Cyrus McCormick's reaping-machine fortune, Harold McCormick, and his wife, Edith, daughter of John D. Rockefeller. It was to have been situated on a bluff overlooking Lake Michigan at Lake Forest, Illinois, thirty miles north of Chicago. Finis Farr describes it as "a marvel of a house—or rather, a complex of connecting houses—with the bluffs reinforced by retaining walls to make a running base for the entire composition of pavilions and galleries. There was magic and wonder in his conception—one can imagine how it would have looked from the lake at night. And no imagination is needed, when looking at Wright's drawings, to see how his galleries would have framed the changing vistas of the lake."

The house was never built. Edith Rockefeller McCormick was seized by what Farr describes as a "demon of indecision" and "at the last moment decided not to approve Wright's plans. Instead, she went to New York and engaged Charles Adams Platt, an accomplished designer in the Palladian style. The resulting Villa Turicum, though correct and elegant, and handsomely set in formal gardens, has long since been torn down."

Wright believed McCormick House was the greatest residential work he'd ever done. Loss of the commission came at a time when he was troubled both financially and psychologically, and I think it probably was the main reason he left Chicago and his family. At any rate, Mrs. McCormick's memory is scorned because she robbed the world, and Frank Lloyd Wright, of this building. I've often been angered about her lack of taste as I studied Wright's drawings. I think I probably have looked at those plans more than anyone else in the world except perhaps Frank Lloyd Wright.

I feel immense satisfaction in being able to vindicate Wright's design now, on a site that slopes down to the edge of a lake. It will appear to float on the water instead of perching on a bluff high above the water as the original McCormick House would have. But it will bear out Wright's original concept completely, and in doing so it will echo Goethe's observation: "The fate of the architect is the strangest of all. How often he expends his whole soul, his whole heart and passion to produce buildings into which he himself may never enter."

One of my goals for Domino's Farms is to have more Frank Lloyd Wright buildings together in one place than anywhere else. We need nine—Florida Southern University in Lakeland, Florida, has eight. We already have a start toward this goal since I bought a Wright house at an auction in New York in 1984 for $117,000. This house, one of the most significant of Wright's two-bedroom Usonian designs, was one of his later ones. The Usonian houses came after his Prairie houses and the name was taken from Samuel Butler's 1872 novel *Erewhon*. Wright put a lot of time into designing this particular house because he knew it would be seen by thousands of people as part of a Guggenheim Museum exhibit of his work in 1953. The house had been dismantled after the exhibit and stored at the home of one of Wright's friends for thirty years.

I want to have a Frank Lloyd Wright chapel at Domino's Farms. For several years we've had a chaplain come to our headquarters each workday morning to say mass. And while this practice occasioned a snide comment in a magazine story in one of the Detroit newspapers, which characterized it as a "conference room service for about fifteen faithful, doling eucharists from a Tupperware tub," the spirit of the voluntary religious exercise is an important part of our company's attitude and I see no reason to be ashamed of it.

I have my eye on several other Frank Lloyd Wright buildings, and our office structure on Domino's Farms—flanking the site where the Golden Beacon will rise—was designed along Wright-ian lines by Gunnar Birkerts, the man I consider to be the world's greatest living architect.

Beginning in 1983, Birkerts and I agreed on a working arrangement. I was to deal directly with him, not one of his assistants, and he would design our offices in the spirit of Wright's prairie style. He said his aim was "to project Frank Lloyd Wright into this century, using some of the vocabulary with a different syntax to say contemporary things." His syntax, to my way of thinking, was often too different from Wright's, and we had a series of creative clashes about his renderings. I simply rejected his first effort completely, as the plans were too high tech, not reflective of Wright's prairie style. This first design was within the letter of my criteria but not its spirit.

The final plans were beautiful, but I had to fight with Birkerts to keep him from adding unnecessary touches. His basic design was what I wanted—a building that could have been designed in 1907 or 1986 and would retain its appeal for another hundred years or more. A building will not become dated if it's simple and graceful, even when, like Domino's Farms, it is a large commercial structure. The more I work in Birkerts's building, the more I like it. I think I like it better than any building I've ever seen, including Wright's own. Return on investment was not a major consideration in its design but art was, because I knew that if it was an artistic success, it would automatically become a financial success. Only the most sophisticated banker would understand this logic.

At times during the designing, both Gunnar and I had moments of doubt that the outcome would suit us. He told me I was the most opinionated client he'd ever had. A client who was so emotionally and passionately involved in what he was doing was a new experience for him. He also said he'd never had a client who made up his mind so quickly on what he liked or disliked. At the dedication ceremony of the building, he addressed the assemblage of employees and guests in his lofty, professorial manner.

"My relationship with Tom has been very interesting," he said. "I can draw parallels in it to the Medicis and Michelangelo or the Fuggers and their architect." This drew appreciative snickers, and he beamed and embellished the point.

"It was easier for Michelangelo . . . he preceeded Frank Lloyd Wright." The room rocked with laughter, and when it died down, he continued.

"Tom has the image of Frank Lloyd Wright's formidable genius very clearly in mind, and we had to work within that image. The way I did it was to work with his alphabet and his vocabulary, but I think we wrote our own story. It is a story that's unprecedented in the world because we have taken Frank Lloyd Wright's work and paraphrased and adapted it to the future. It is put in the context of today's economy and methodology."

Working with Gunnar on the basic design of the building was fun, but the most fascinating part, and one of the most enjoyable experiences of my life, was designing my own office. We had agreed that my office was the only part of the interior on which I would get involved in details. I viewed this as a once in a lifetime opportunity. If I messed up the design, it would be my problem. No one else would have to live with it. Working with Gunnar on the details and seeing how this great architect's mind tackled problems was fascinating. What emerged from our collaboration was an office that's unique and, very possibly, the finest in the world.

My office occupies the top two stories at the north end of the building, and I gave Gunnar the opportunity to go far beyond anything he'd ever been able to do in choosing his materials. We both had to compromise in places. I wanted wood ceilings, and his response was, "You've got too much wood in there already." He put in a raw silk ceiling. He wanted bands of mirrors. I like mirrors, but I wanted more wood. The leather tile for the floor was his idea, but I liked it. Neither of us had ever seen leather tile on a floor before, so that choice was venturesome, and it may be a failure; I knew for sure it would be slippery. Part of the area is carpeted, and we argued about the kind of carpet to be used. The one I wanted wasn't made anymore, so we had to have it specially loomed. Gunnar really got carried away in his ideas for colors—he wanted orange and purple, which I abhorred. But I finally gave in and let him use those colors as accents behind the bookcases that line the open stairway between the first and second floors of the office. I'll just fill those shelves with books, and you won't see those colors at all.

What I learned from working with Gunnar is that he's an incredibly good listener. Somehow, he got into my brain and came up with plans to create what I was visualizing. He took elements of my favorite architectural designs and put them together in a way that I find immensely pleasing. He refined my ideas and made them work. For example, I pictured Wright-style board-and-batten walls in my office. Instead, Gunnar used wood paneling with thin horizontal strips of bronze. I thought the bronze detailing was ridiculous, but he was determined to have it, and I had learned that when he was convinced something would be right and argued strongly for it, I'd be pleased with the result. I probably wouldn't feel that way about any other architect.

I got so completely wrapped up in the artistic aspects of the office that I had no idea what it was going to cost. I would have guessed three hundred thousand dollars. I wasn't thinking of creating something expensive; I was thinking about making it beautiful. I got carried away, and that was a big mistake.

At one point I asked Gunnar, "What kind of pictures do you want to put on the walls?" He gave me a blank look and said, "We don't need anything on the walls. The room itself is art." And so it is. But this piece of art, when all the costs were added up, came to two million dollars!

Even though that two million dollars was paid by TSM Properties and not by Domino's, I felt the office was far too grand to be limited to my personal and business use. After all, art is worthless unless it can be seen and appreciated. So I decided to make my office available to the community for various kinds of meetings and charitable functions. I entertain guests and have meetings there as well, of course. But my real working office is a nearby, windowless area measuring ten by fifteen feet. Here, I can concentrate in complete seclusion, and I have deep, floor-to-ceiling shelves all around to hold my stacks of current paperwork.

Even with only the Birkerts building completed and the Golden Beacon yet to come, Domino's Farms is spectacular when viewed from the adjacent expressway. An estimated 70,000 cars pass our location daily, so in addition to our employees and visitors to Domino's Farms, perhaps 140,000 people have a passing opportunity each day to enjoy the majestic, eye-pleasing lines of our building, which is more than a third of a mile long (when complete, it will be six-tenths of a mile long) and has the largest expanse of copper roof in the world.

One of the most impressive aspects of the whole Domino's Farms project, though, is the real-estate deal John McDivitt put together to give us the site. I signed my name more than five hundred times on the documents needed to assemble the property. The papers came in several large briefcases and made a stack three feet high. Given the various problems that arose in assembling the land, it seems like a miracle that it all came together. Authorities have told me it was the most complicated real-estate deal in the history of Michigan. Only a year before we moved our offices into the building, we had not even owned the land on which it stands. Thanks to John, this land was acquired and changed from a cornfield, and not a very good cornfield at that, into office space that rents for twenty-four dollars a square foot. When the Golden Beacon is erected, on the opposite side of a lake we're creating immediately west of our office structure, its tower will house one of the world's finest conference centers, in addition to a sports-medicine facility run by the University of Michigan Hospital and offices leased to outside tenants. And even though this is the most expensive office space in the state, it is oversubscribed, indicating that major tenants appreciate quality and architectural inspiration. Our timing looks pretty good, because Ann Arbor is being rated higher each year as a center of employment and economic growth. In the next ten years, it will be among the top ten metropolitan areas in the country in technological development. In 1984, the U.S. Census Bureau ranked Ann Arbor thirty-first in the nation in income and population growth, and by 1994, it is expected to rise to fifteenth place. John Naisbitt, author of *Megatrends*, predicts that Ann Arbor will become the number-one environment for business in the Midwest.

None of my ideas in architecture—including my new house or my plans for the farm—means a thing, though, if Domino's Pizza, Inc., doesn't do well. It's the goose that lays our golden egg. So my test for any undertaking is: How will it benefit DPI? There has to be linkage, some benefit to the pizza business, or the program or investment I'm considering is not good for us. Ideally, I'm looking for *synergism*, a term I learned from Adizes, which he defines in one of his training manuals as: "cooperative action between two different organizations in which the total effect of the combined effort is greater than the sum of the two parts operating independently." The way I put it is: "Synergism is when two plus two equals five."

To me, a prime example of synergism is the connection between Domino's and the Detroit Tigers. It was a great day for me personally when I bought the team, but it was also a home run for Domino's in the synergism league. There was no doubt in my mind that my connection with the Tigers would sell pizzas, and it has. It also established my status in the business community and opened a lot of doors for me socially.

Of all the dreams I've had, buying the Tigers seemed to be the least likely to come true. Owner John Fetzer had said repeatedly that he had no interest in selling the team, which he bought as a member of a twelve-man syndicate in 1956 for $5.5 million. He later bought out his partners and became far and away the greatest owner in the history of baseball. Although Mr. Fetzer was getting on in years (he was born in 1900) and it was clear that age would force him to sell in the not-too-distant future, it also was clear that competition for the privilege of owning the club probably would be intense. So my hopes had a lot of if's and but's attached.

When I visited Ray Kroc in 1980, I mentioned to him in the course of our conversation that I'd like to buy the Tigers someday. I guess he wasn't too happy about the way his San Diego Padres were playing at that point, and he was on the verge of losing Dave Winfield to the Yankees. He looked at me like I was crazy and yelled, "Why would you want to do that? Baseball is the craziest business I've ever gotten into in my life. You don't own anything! It's more frustrating than the hamburger business. If I were you, I'd forget it." I explained my lifelong love of the Tigers, my memories of listening to Harry Heilmann broadcast their games on the radio, and my gratitude to the Knights of Columbus, who used to take us boys from the orphanage to Tigers games once a year. That had been the high point of the whole year for me.

"The Tigers wouldn't be an investment for me," I said.

"There's no logic to it, it's just something I've always wanted to do. I can remember looking at newspaper pictures of Walter Briggs sitting in his box like a king. The caption said: 'owner of the Tigers.' And I thought, 'That's what I want. Someday they'll write that about me.'"

Mr. Kroc just looked at me, and I don't think he wondered anymore whether I was crazy. He was certain of it.

My daughter Susie is nearly as big a Tiger fan as I am, and as a reward for her high marks in school in 1982, I took her to visit the team's spring training camp in Lakeland, Florida. We walked into the Tigertown office near the stadium, and I recognized Jim Campbell, the club's president, as he sat in the cafeteria. I introduced myself and told him what a big fan I was. I also mentioned Domino's Pizza.

"Oh," he said. "You wouldn't by any chance be the guy who gave Bo Schembechler the pizza place in Columbus, Ohio, would you?"

He was referring to an incident that took place a year earlier, after Bo had accepted a seat on Domino's board of directors. Texas A&M, which was panting to acquire Bo as its football coach, launched a major campaign to entice him to leave the University of Michigan. For weeks, Bo was the main topic of conversation around Ann Arbor and Detroit. Every edition of the newspapers and TV sportscasts had updates on the pressing question "Will Bo Go?"

As the deadline neared, it looked very much as if Bo *would* go, and I was heartsick. I felt a responsibility to keep him in Ann Arbor if I could. Bo had once mentioned casually that he'd like to own a Domino's store. We had two corporate stores in Columbus on the campus of his Michigan football team's archrival, Ohio State, and in a flash of inspiration, I decided I'd give one of these stores to Bo. As it turned out, he had already made up his mind to stay at Michigan before I arrived at his house with my news, but I gave him the store anyhow.

There was a big press conference when Bo announced his decision, and he mentioned that one reason he was staying was that I'd given him a Domino's Pizza store at Ohio State. So we got some great publicity out of it.

When I responded affirmatively to Jim Campbell's question, he beamed, saying he was a good friend of Bo's, and he offered to give Susie and me a private tour of Tigertown. We jumped at the opportunity, of course, and we had a great time. That chance meeting, on March 14, 1982, turned out to be the start of my negotiations to buy the Tigers, although neither Jim Campbell nor I realized it at the time. I told him I would be interested in buying the team, and he said a lot of other people were as well, but he knew Mr. Fetzer was not interested in selling. So that was that.

The following March, I went back down to Lakeland to relax in the sun with my family for a few days and indulge in two of my favorite hobbies: watching the Tigers and visiting Frank Lloyd Wright buildings. The Wright buildings on the campus of Florida Southern University aren't my favorites, but I like to look at them anyhow. I telephoned Jim Campbell and asked him if I could make an appointment to talk to him and give him my biographical sketch and personal financial summary. I wanted Mr. Fetzer to know I was serious in my desire and ability to buy the team. Campbell was cordial, and he agreed to pass the material on. He said he'd try to arrange for me to have an introductory meeting with Mr. Fetzer. But he added again that the club still was not for sale.

I didn't find out until much later, after I bought the Tigers, that following his chat with Susie and me, Campbell had telephoned Ann Arbor and asked Bo to "level" with him about me. It must have been a good report, because Campbell told me, "When I next talked to Mr. Fetzer, I mentioned that I'd found a man of the sort he said he would look for if he ever decided to sell the club—a young person who could carry on some of the traditions he'd established."

I made a third visit to Tigertown in 1983, and about two weeks later, on March 31, I flew back down to Lakeland for a meeting Jim Campbell had set up with Mr. Fetzer. Clearly, this was going to be a critical session, and I did a lot of scribbling on my legal pad in preparation for it. My notes indicate the tension I was feeling: "1st job is selling Mr. Fetzer on selling," I wrote. "Don't talk too much . . . listen . . . don't argue . . . I'll be nervous, so pray . . . Be humble, remember he doesn't want to be forced into anything . . .

"This would be a very emotional thing for him. He has no family; put yourself in his shoes, he's owned this club for 25 plus yrs. it's part of him & where he's got all his recognition & press & public respect . . . I am custodian/steward of his legacy." I wrote down all the negative impressions he might have of me. The timing might not be good, with the season about to start. He might feel that Campbell was pushing him. He could feel resentful that I was trying to steal his child. He could easily see me as too green. He might think I look too much like a kid and not too bright. I had a whole page of possible negatives, and once I had them written down, I decided that all I could do was try to be myself and persuade him that I am honest and sincere. It was very unlikely that he would make a snap decision. Mr. Fetzer was known as a deliberative person.

As Campbell and I drove to the Hilton Hotel for the meeting, he cautioned me that Mr. Fetzer wouldn't have anything to do with anyone seeking publicity in regard to the sale of the ball club. "This meeting is confidential," he said. "If anything leaks out about it to the media, it will kill any hope you have of ever owning the team.''

I was too nervous to remember exactly what Mr. Fetzer and I talked about after Jim Campbell left us together. I told him how I'd always dreamed of owning the Tigers and said I admired the way he ran the team and had made it a viable business. He told me about his own emotional attachment to the team, and he said he wanted to be certain he didn't create a messy succession like Tom Yawkey had with the Boston Red Sox. When Yawkey died, he thought he'd left the club in good hands, but it wasn't long before his wife and the associates he'd appointed to run the team were squabbling about it in the courts.

Mr. Fetzer suggested that I go to the ball game that afternoon with Jim Campbell's secretary. He wanted to chat with Jim. Later, Mr. Fetzer drove me to the airport and told me that if and when he ever decided to sell the Tigers, he would sell them to me. I was elated. I could hardly believe my ears. After that, though, I talked to Campbell on the phone several times, but there was no indication from Mr. Fetzer of a willingness to sell. I thought my chances were evaporating.

Then, five months later, Campbell called me to set up a meeting at the Westin Hotel in Detroit on August 25, when the Tigers were to play Chicago. "Oh my gosh," I said. "That's my wedding anniversary!" I was really in a bind. Margie and I had never missed celebrating on our anniversary. I went ahead and made the appointment, though, and Margie understood—she knew how much this deal meant to me.

Bowie Kuhn had announced his resignation as commissioner of baseball on August 3, and that, Mr. Fetzer said, was what triggered his decision to actively consider transferring ownership of the franchise. He was only *considering the possibility*, he emphasized, and he wanted to know in detail what deal I would offer if he *should* decide to sell.

I left that meeting thinking we were in general agreement on the terms of a sale. But then the lawyers on both sides started adding conditions and provisions that got so tangled up I could no longer tell who was on first. Nobody was satisfied, and it looked like the whole deal was off. I was saddened, but thought maybe the sale had been too good to be true.

Then I got a call from Mr. Fetzer. He said, "Y'know, Tom, if you and I sat down together without any attorneys, I'll bet we could work this out."

"When would you like to do it?" I asked.

"How about right now?"

We agreed to meet in Battle Creek, which is near his home in Kalamazoo. He let me bring along my tax expert, Bert Carlson, because I needed to know the tax consequences of what we were doing, but he and I made the contract amically, hammering it out line by line, putting it in language we could understand. When we finished, Mr. Fetzer said he would give it to his attorneys and ask them to write the final documents.

More than a week went by without further word, and I was getting more tense with every hour that passed. I'd pace the floor until Margie told me I didn't need to buy the Tigers, I was turning into a tiger myself.

Then I got a phone call from Jim Campbell and he said, "Well, my boy, you did it!"

"Did what?" I asked.

"You bought the Detroit Tigers. I never thought anyone would be able to do it!"

Jim started outlining the schedule of arrangements. We were supposed to meet Mr. Fetzer and fly to Chicago on October 8, so I could be introduced to Bowie Kuhn, Lee McPhail, the president of the American League, and Edward Bennett Williams, who owned the Baltimore franchise and was a member of the league's financial committee. Then, on October 10, there would be a press conference to announce the sale. As Jim recited these details, the incredible truth sank in: I *had* done it! I had bought the Tigers!

The next morning when I went out to jog at dawn, I was sick with tension, and I released it by vomiting uncontrollably in the bushes.

Everything came off as scheduled. At the meeting in Chicago, I was introduced to Jerry Reinsorf, chairman of the White Sox. He said, "If you're okay by John Fetzer, you're okay by me."

So far, not a word of the sale had appeared in the newspapers, which made me very happy because it pleased Mr. Fetzer. All our meetings had been supersecret; we covered the logo of our plane when we flew to meet with Mr. Fetzer, and we used code names when we called each other. But as we worked out the deal and lawyers and bankers got involved on both sides, there must have been a hundred people who knew about the sale. So it was amazing that there'd been no leaks. We did have one close call when Jack Moss, a friend of mine and columnist for a newspaper in Mr. Fetzer's home town, the *Kalamazoo Gazette*, called me just after my meeting with Mr. Fetzer in Marshall. He said he wanted to talk to me.

"What about?" I asked.

"About your interest in sports in general," Jack said.

He had quoted me several times in the past about my interest in buying the Tigers, and I just *knew* he'd gotten wind of the deal. I was worried that if he printed something about it, Mr. Fetzer would call the whole sale off. But if I refused to talk to him, he might print something anyway, so I agreed to see him and he came to my office. Sure enough, he asked whether I was buying the Tigers. I told him that was still my dream and talked vaguely about how I didn't think I'd ever be able to afford them. Domino's was growing so fast that I didn't have time to think about the Tigers much. When he left, he said, "I'm going to see your friend Bo."

Oh my gosh, I thought. He's going to tell Bo something that will make Bo think I let it out and Bo will confirm it. So I called Bo and said, "What the heck do we do?"

"Listen, Jack's a good guy," Bo said. "I know Jack. I'll just tell him off the record and he'll keep it secret."

So Bo told him, and Jack Moss didn't print the story. Of course, he was the first one I called about our press conference. I couldn't be specific. I just said, "Jack, I think it would be in your best interest to be there." Other papers didn't pay much attention to our notice, so Moss got a beat on the story.

I called my executive team together the day before the announcement and filled them in on the details. They knew the general outlines already, and Doug Dawson knew everything, of course, because he'd handled all the financial arrangements with Richard H. Cummings, senior vice-chairman of the National Bank of Detroit and Vern Iscotk, my favorite banker, who handled all the details. I told them that they were going to hear some mighty big numbers tossed around in connection with the sale. We couldn't disclose the actual price immediately—it was $53 million—but I rationalized the cost by saying the purchase was going to be worth at least $5 million a year to Domino's in advertising and publicity. Considering the way the Tigers played in the '84 season, I don't think that figure was too far off.

That 1984 season contained enough great memories to last a lifetime. I can close my eyes and replay Jack Morris's no hitter, tremendous hits by Kirk Gibson, and great catches like the one Chet Lemon made by turning all the way around. The exhilaration I felt as champagne was poured on my head—not to mention a five-gallon bucket of ice water dumped on me by Gibson—when we won the World Series is unforgettable. But the emotional high point of the entire season was what might be called a nonevent. We were in first place all year, but Toronto was always right on our heels. On September 17, we had to win and Toronto had to lose in order for the Tigers to clinch the pennant. We beat the Brewers 7–3, and Boston was beating Toronto. It looked like we'd clinched the pennant for sure. I felt a tingling all over my body. Manager Sparky Anderson had four and a half cases of champagne on ice in the clubhouse, and it looked like we were going to start popping those corks. We went down to the locker room and turned on the radio, and I'll be darned if Toronto didn't put on a big ninth-inning rally and pull it out. I was a basket case.

My disappointment released all the tension that had built up during the season and took some of the edge off the next night, when we actually won the pennant.

I made sure Mr. Fetzer stayed involved with the team that first year, and he kept me from making any foolish mistakes. I did anger some of the other owners after the season by saying in a magazine interview that I thought the policy of not sharing financial statements with players was stupid. My policy at Domino's has always been to be very up-front about how the company is doing financially. We put out annual reports, even though as a privately held company we aren't required to do so. I thought the same policy should apply in baseball, and I was amazed to learn that Jim Campbell didn't even share the financials with Sparky. It seemed unusual not to let your manager in on financial information. So I shot off my mouth and got my ears pinned back by the other owners. But I didn't take it personally. I learned a lesson: Baseball traditions are as rigid among owners as among players.

I can't call baseball a hobby. My interest is more serious than that, but I am never going to get more intimately involved in running the team. I leave that up to the professionals. In this I differ from some other owners. Ray Kroc used to let his frustrations show in public, and he interfered with the management of the Padres and undermined it. I don't want to do that. I just want to keep informed enough about what's going on with the team so I can hire and fire the president. That's my only job as owner.

Ownership of the Tigers, of course, is a very special privilege. I love going to spring training and rubbing elbows with players and coaches. I get to play in pickup games with the clubhouse staff after practice—and can you imagine the thrill for this dyed-in-the-wool Tiger fan in going into the batting cage with Al Kaline and having him give me batting practice! I like to go down to the instructional-league games in Florida in November, too. In that relaxed atmosphere I can talk about plans for the next season with Jim Campbell and our general manager, Bill Lajoie. It gives me a chance to see the best young talent that's coming up in our farm system, too, and to get insights on them from our scouts.

But one of the most enjoyable aspects of owning the team is hosting gatherings in my box like the Monaghan family reunion in June of 1985. Forty-two people were there, and after the game we went aboard Domino's yacht, *Tigress*, and cruised down the Detroit River to have dinner at Grosse Isle. It was terrific to have my mother there with my brother, Jim, along with relatives I don't get to see as often as I'd like, such as my aunt Aggie, aunt Peg, and uncle Dan, and my cousin Maureen. Maureen and her husband, Bill Dobbs, live in Kalamazoo, where he's an optometrist, and we had a good time reminiscing about the old days, when I would crash at their house after checking on pizza stores. I was like a phantom, they recalled, because I'd arrive after midnight, and when they got up the next morning, I'd be gone. My uncle Dan reminded me of some of the foolish things I did as a boy, such as working like mad to save twenty-five dollars so I could buy a MacGregor baseball glove. I was so proud of that glove that for a long time I used it for a pillow. I could have bought a Wilson glove that was less expensive and just as good, maybe better. I admitted that was true, but I had wanted to buy the one that cost the most. "Well," Uncle Dan said, glancing around at the gleaming wood and brass of *Tigress*. "You haven't changed a bit, Tom. I hope you never do."

T HE SHOT HEARD 'round the pizza world was fired on October 8, 1985, by Arthur G. Gunther, chairman of Pizza Hut. He told *USA Today* that his company would open 1,300 new stores in 1986 and 1,000 of these would be delivery-only units. He was aiming at Domino's, of course, and he could have been speaking for every single pizza chain in the country. They all appeared to be planning to get into delivery, confronting us with an unavoidable series of competitive battles. It was time for pizza wars!

The next morning, I read Gunther's statement to a meeting of our board of franchisees in Las Vegas. I emphasized his reference to us. "I think Domino's represents our major threat right now," he had said, and my response was, "Well, I should hope so." This got a big laugh from the crowd of franchisees. "This is what we wanted," I told them. "We wanted to be in the spotlight. And now that we *are* in the spotlight, we are a big target. Everybody is taking shots at us.

"You've heard me saying for years that we've got a great concept; that Domino's has the potential to be the largest pizza chain in the country, and possibly the largest restaurant chain in the world. Now everything you read in the trade journals indicates that delivery is the wave of the future for pizza. And not only for pizza, it's also the wave of the future for fast food in general. Virtually every chicken and hamburger chain is experimenting with delivery. They're all talking about it; so you Domino's franchisees should feel proud. You're the ones who started it.

"Having everyone in the country coming at you can be awfully scary. Or it can be awfully exciting. I happen to think it's awfully exciting. As most of you know, I've been expecting this. We have the organization and the people to handle it."

One of our strategies in preparing for pizza wars has been to get out in the marketplace and rigorously test our product. The results are not always things we enjoy hearing, but they help us make our product, which 90 percent of our customers think is very good, even better. For example, we learned in 1984 that customers thought our dough wasn't as thick as that of some of our competitors. We worked on this in our lab and came up with a formula for adding 15 percent more dough to each pizza.

The switch to increased volume in our dough had a major impact on the commissary. Many procedures in dough production had to be modified. Crews had to be retrained. Machinery had to be changed to handle the heavier dough balls. The result of these alterations was that costs began to get out of control, which created problems for Don Vlcek. He spent a lot of time putting out fires during 1985.

However, instead of imposing budget restrictions and becoming cautious and conservative, Don reorganized Domino's National Commissaries to make it less centralized and began a series of "Let's Get Revolutionary" meetings throughout the organization. When I asked about this program, Don told me, "People don't seem to understand how much freedom they have to come up with ideas. I want to inspire radicals throughout the company.'' This program seems to be working. Ideas are exploding in the commissary like firecrackers on the Fourth of July. Some of these inspirations are appealing though unworkable, like the proposal to equip delivery cars with an aroma machine that would waft the scent of fresh pizza through neighborhoods as they drive along. However, some of the ideas are ingenious. For example, one employee suggested we pay the commissary drivers who deliver food products to our stores a commission for selling Domino's merchandise to store employees. The commissary's Emporium department carries a range of clothing items such as jackets, caps, running shoes, and belts in our colors, imprinted with the company logo. It also has a large selection of Domino's accessories, from ashtrays to a go-cart replica of our Indy race car for kids. The plan to have commissary drivers sell these items instantly increased the Emporium's sales force from 9 to 509 at no expense.

This kind of energy is why we welcome pizza wars. Competition makes us sharper, keeps us looking for new answers, and prevents us from getting complacent and thinking we know it all. Of course, our twenty-five years of experience in pizza delivery has taught us what most of the problems are. So maybe we make delivery look easy. Maybe we've given some of our competitors the idea that it *is* easy. If so, they're in for a heck of a shock.

Our experience gives us a big edge, but it also helps our competition. We know they watch every move we make. In the past, we've seen some of them pawing through our garbage. And we see every innovation we make pop up immediately in the stores of our rivals. For example, when we went to Ferris-wheel ovens back in the late sixties, it wasn't long before one Detroit-based chain had every one of its stores equipped with Ferris-wheel ovens.

The pressure to keep up with advances in kitchen technology has never relaxed in our business. Ovens continue to be a major focus of Domino's research and development, even though the ovens our stores are equipped with today are far faster and more efficient than the old models. We use infrared or gas-convection conveyor ovens that heat the product rather than the surrounding air. They don't bake a pizza much faster than a conventional oven (we gain one or two minutes at most), but these ovens provide a real advantage in handling the rush. When it gets busy, cooking time in a conventional oven increases from seven minutes to fourteen or fifteen minutes because you're opening the door constantly to put pizzas in or take them out. The oven loses heat each time you open the door, and it doesn't recover rapidly. With infrared or convection, there is no heat loss. The big advantage of the conveyor is that it's loaded in a single place, so your oven tender doesn't have to run back and forth from one oven to another. But best of all, with the conveyor you don't have to worry about burning a pizza or sending one out raw. Domino's managers have perfected some operating tricks that help make the baking uniform. For example, if you have two pies going into the oven at the same time, one loaded with toppings and the other plain cheese, how you place them on the conveyor belt is going to make a big difference in the finished product. The plain pie gets shoved way in at the start. The loaded one goes on right at the end of the conveyor belt to give it maximum exposure time in the oven as the belt proceeds.

Pizza wars have made us extend research and development into many new areas, including the speed of pizza making. The most critical period in a Domino's store occurs between the time the phone is hung up and when the pizza goes into the oven. This is true whether it's just a single order or the phones are ringing off the hooks. I want to have time-and-motion studies done on pizza making, because there must be ways to speed up the action without sacrificing quality.

Our test kitchen is studying a whole exciting range of product improvements. For example, we need better ways to handle green peppers. Slicing them is too slow. One of our commissary workers competing in the regionals of the first Domino's Pizza Distribution Olympics in 1985 came up with a homemade gadget he called a pepper corer to extract the pulp with one stroke. But this tool hasn't been perfected yet. The biggest single challenge facing our test kitchen is finding a way to keep bubbles from forming in the dough. Dick Mueller invented a plastic roller with blunt spikes on it, called a dough docker, for this purpose. It works fairly well, but I'm opposed to it for two reasons. First, because it's a partial solution; it doesn't prevent bubbles in the dough, it just reduces their size and frequency. I want to see us spend more time finding a way to eliminate the problem from the dough itself. Second, the dough docker adds an extra step to the process of making a pizza. We need to eliminate steps, not add them.

I could write a whole book about improvements that need to be made in our equipment. A chapter or two would be devoted to ovens. Our conveyor ovens are good, but the way they are ventilated leaves a lot to be desired. And we need to solve the problem of bubbles that are formed in the pizza as it's baking. These bubbles are different from the bubbles we are trying to eliminate from the dough. When a bubble rises in the pizza as it's cooking, everything melts off that location and you get a bare spot that burns and turns black. When the oven tender sees a big bubble forming, he needs to be able to pop it with a fork or a knife, and with some of our oven designs, he can't.

The hot boxes in our delivery cars need improvement, too. I thought the answer would be an electric hot box that could plug into a car's cigarette lighter socket. We tried it and drivers didn't use it, apparently because it drained their cars' batteries too much. The insulated pouches our drivers use to carry pizzas have helped keep the product hot and they've made hot boxes virtually unnecessary except in cold weather. But there's room for improvement in the pouches, too.

Another book I could write—maybe I should—is on the training of store managers. When you see a good manager in action, it's clear that he has trained his drivers to handle every job in the store. At the least, they know how to serve walk-in customers, how to cut a pizza and box it, how to chase supplies, how to keep enough pizza boxes folded ahead. These skills can be learned in an hour, and they should be taught in a driver's first day on the job. It takes longer to learn the art of making pizzas and how to tend the oven, but the good manager is a good teacher, and he takes every opportunity to pass on his knowledge.

When a store is running at peak efficiency, it has a minimum number of people inside; the rest are on the road. A good manager will have three people inside and five on the road. A great manager will have one person inside and seven people helping him in turns as they pass through to pick up orders and hit the road again. This is possible when the drivers are well trained. They start answering phones and making pizzas as soon as they come back in; everyone is doing at least two jobs in the store, and the manager directs traffic. He stays flexible and never lets himself get pinned down alone in the store. Busy periods have a certain rhythm, and a great manager knows how to flow with the rhythm so he has enough people inside when the tempo is hottest there. Then he sends everybody out on delivery.

Great managers don't come along too often, but we have a number who are heading in that direction, and pizza wars will give them the opportunity to distinguish themselves.

More and more, our competition will be international, which

I think is an exciting prospect. I see no limit to the popularity of pizza or the expansion of the Domino's concept. When we announced plans to open Domino's stores in West Germany—Dick Mueller is our first franchisee there—people said, "But Germans don't eat pizza!" Well, maybe not, but they're doing something with an awful lot of pizzas. We heard the same reservation about Japan, Hong Kong, England, and Australia, and Domino's Pizza is catching on in those markets, too.

Our drive to become the largest and best pizza chain in the world—which was launched in 1980, when we won the Amstar suit—has gained momentum every year since. That momentum comes from the Dominoids throughout our system. When I wrote my President's Letter for our 1983 annual report, I concluded with a list of our goals for 1984 and stated, "We intend to meet these lofty goals and have more good news to report next year. Until then, I thank all of you great people in Domino's Pizza for creating such an exciting company." Then I had a second thought and crossed out the final word. In its place I wrote *family.*

I truly feel that Domino's is a family. I also believe we would not be making any progress if we didn't have a lot of excited people striving upward. Many things contribute to our growth, but the underlying power of our organization is the desire of our people to satisfy our customers. When I look out the window of our magnificent building at Domino's Farms and consider how far we've come, I feel the presence of a lot of people who have helped push us along.

Some of these individuals, like Towny Beaman, didn't live to see the dream of Domino's Farms come true. Towny died of a heart attack in June 1983. I'll never forget that big smile of his and what a rock he was even when things looked darkest during the Amstar trial. Bob Ulrich also died in 1983, and his wisdom has been sorely missed.

Jim Gilmore is dead, too. I felt sorry for him, despite all the trouble he caused me. He was an unforgettable character, and in his own strange way he did make a contribution to the growth of Domino's.

Some of those who contributed a great deal to the company have moved on. A few of them left with hard feelings toward me, which I regret. I'd like one day to sit down with Chuck Gray, for example, and Russ Hughes, and apologize for the harsh things I said about them. They contributed to our success, too, and I want them to know that I respect them.

Most of my past associations in Domino's have been happy ones, and it's always gratifying to be able to renew them. Larry Sperling, who went through hell for me in exchange for miserly fees in the old days in Ypsilanti and played a major role in the development of the company, has joined the firm that is Domino's principal legal consultant (now) Pear Sperling Eggan & Muskovitz. His move hasn't meant that Larry and I get to see each other any more frequently, but it's comforting to me to know that he's there handling our business again.

One of my fond memories of Sperling is of playing basketball against him in a men's league that met in a school gym one night a week. He told me he had a theory that you could determine a person's true character if you played basketball or cards with him. We never played cards much, but we had frequent encounters on the basketball floor. Sperling was small and quick. He thought he could fake me out and drive around me—I was heavier then than I am now—but I was always able to get to him and prevent him from taking a shot. I once knocked him flat on his face while blocking him, and as I helped him to his feet, he said, "The trouble with you, Monaghan, is that you don't know when you're beaten."

I liked that. It reminded me of a story about Knute Rockne,

the famous coach of Notre Dame, who is one of my personal heroes. Rockne used to do a lot of speaking at banquets and sales meetings, according to his biographer, Francis Wallace, and he often told about a professional game in 1919 in which he played against the herculean Jim Thorpe. Rockne portrayed himself as a mosquito end who had been annoying Thorpe by tackling him repeatedly. "Finally," Wallace relates, "the colorful Indian ran the little end down as a truck might demolish a bicycle. On his way back from the touchdown, he paused to help Rock to his feet with this consoling remark: 'That's a good boy, Rock. You let Big Jim run. The people pay to see Big Jim run.'"

Unfortunately, business competition lacks that sporting congeniality. More often than not, the attitude toward direct competitors is the one expressed by Ray Kroc: "It's rat eat rat, dog eat dog. I'll kill 'em . . . I'm going to kill 'em before they kill me." Much as I admired Kroc, I don't share that philosophy.

I believe everyone has a right to exist in the market space they can carve out for themselves with price, product, or service. Let the consumer be the judge.

I'm not predicting an easy victory for Domino's in pizza wars, because the combined forces of all our competitors is formidable. But I think we have a good shot at coming out on top because not everyone in the pizza-delivery business is willing to hustle as hard as Domino's does or to stress quality as much as we do.

There aren't many competitors who are ready to go as far as Domino's does in guaranteeing fast service. My old friend and steadfast competitor Jerry Liss of Bowling Green, Ohio, believes I place too much emphasis on thirty-minute delivery. "Most of our deliveries are done in thirty minutes, but I don't demand it," Jerry says. "My motto is: Our delivery is fast no matter how long it takes." Maybe he'll change his tune when he reads my thoughts on defensive management.

Another important element in our ability to compete is the support furnished by Domino's suppliers. We have a fine group of suppliers, and we work hard to make our association with them mutually beneficial. I'm particularly sensitive to the importance of suppliers because they helped me a great deal over the years. I learned a great deal about business from them, but most of our chief suppliers were major Domino's creditors, too.

Doing business was fun when you could deal with people like Eldon Huff, Barney Barnes, Howard Miller, Arm Leone, Frank Fata, and Jerry Garber. Another terrific supplier was Ira Nevins, president of Bakers Pride Oven Company. There is a lot of back-biting in the wholesale end of the pizza business, and Nevins stood out as an exception. He fortified my belief in being nice to people.

I also had a great working relationship with Warren Reuther of Bay Corrugated. He pumped up his company's capacity for Domino's and, as a creditor, he helped see me through some mighty tough times.

Then there was Andy Smith, an electrical contractor in Ypsilanti. He was a gruff old guy with a heart of gold. He came over to our Quonset-hut headquarters one time to chew me out because I was behind on paying his bill. He gave me a good going over. But as he was leaving, he said, "This driveway of yours is in terrible shape. You ought to fix it. I'll send over one of my tractors." Sure enough, a few days later one of his tractors rumbled up and graded our drive, and there was no charge.

I wonder what some of those old-timers would think of our new headquarters. I wish I could give some of them a tour of the place. Towny Beaman would have been enchanted by my office with its sophisticated electronics, operated from a control panel at my desk that regulates the lighting, temperature, and communications, including a TV set that pops out of a wall at the push of a button.

With his engineering bent, however, Towny probably would be much more interested in our service area, which connects the two segments of our building through a continuous lower-level corridor one-third of a mile long. At the extreme south end of our building, the end opposite my office, are the commissary and warehouse with loading docks concealed by landscaping. Although they share a roof with the rest of the building, they are separated from the northern segment by a central breezeway, through which will pass a road that will lead across the lake to the entrance of the Golden Beacon.

On that lower level of our headquarters, and directly beneath my office area, is another feature I'm very proud of—a modern, working Domino's Pizza store. When we dedicated the building on December 9, 1985, one of the events most meaningful to me was making the first pizza in that store. Since there was no rush and I had a huge crowd of Domino's employees and guests watching me, I had to give them a bit of a show, flipping the dough in the air and catching it behind my back. Then I showed Michigan's governor, James Blanchard, and the other dignitaries how to slap out dough for themselves, and they all made pizzas. This store is used mostly for training purposes, but I like the way the smell of pizza wafts up through our offices, and I enjoy the symbolism of being close to a Domino's store again.

I find it's more difficult to follow my principle *have fun in the work you do* as CEO than it was when I was working in stores myself. But one of the things I have fun doing in my job is coming up with incentives to motivate our people. We have lots of sales contests, and it's a Domino's tradition for me to make awards of things I'm wearing—ceremoniously removing my necktie or taking the watch from my wrist and handing it the recipient. That's fun. I don't know how many seventy-dollar Hermes neckties and two-hundred-dollar DuPont pens I've given away over the years.

I started giving away watches in 1977, when I wore a Bulova with our Domino's logo on its face. A franchisee asked what he had to do to get that watch from me, and I told him, "Turn in a twenty-thousand-dollar sales week." He did it, and for the next few years I gave away several Seikos and, after that, hundreds of $800 Rolex watches.

In 1979 I bought a wristwatch I'd long yearned to own, a solid gold Swiss Patek Philippe. That moved the prize into the $12,000 class, so we established a whole new level of competition. We have two divisions in the contest now. One is for our store in Myrtle Beach, South Carolina, which enjoys fantastic business each year when college students flock to the area on spring vacation. In 1985, they pushed gross sales for that one week to $80,837. Our other division is for the rest of the country, and the record there stood at $48,047 in 1985. Since our Myrtle Beach franchisee, Chris Strong, and his manager, Loyal Smith, have both won watches from me—a Patek Philippe and a Piaget—the prize for exceeding their own record will be a platinum diamond-encrusted lady's Patek Philippe for their wives. During the Myrtle Beach store's record-breaking week in 1985, it averaged nearly 75 pizzas per hour of operation, and its busiest single hour saw 180 pizzas go out the door! In 1986 Palm Springs, California, did the seemingly impossible and beat out Myrtle Beach with a sales week of almost $83,000.

Some of our other incentives include meetings aboard our yacht, *Tigress*, and trips to our hunting and fishing lodge on Drummond Island in the Upper Peninsula of Michigan.

I could spend virtually all my time attending sales meetings and other organizational functions for the various departments of the company, and in the future that's probably what I'll do. Margie may have to give up her job in our accounting department so she can travel with me then, though I'd hate to see her stop her regular payday ritual of walking through every office at head-quarters, passing out checks to all our employees. It's a nice personal touch.

I'm envisioning Domino's five years down the road, when we have ten thousand stores and our management has naturally evolved so that someone has emerged to take over as president. I'll be chairman then, and I'll be able to devote almost all of my time to visiting stores and attending corporate and franchisee meetings.

The Golden Beacon will be completed. Margie and I will be in our new lakeside home, and living there will be a constant source of pleasure. Domino's will own a bigger plane then, too, one on which Margie and I can set up housekeeping for our travels. I'll still be relatively young—fifty-four—and there are all kinds of things I want to do. . . . I'd better stop here or this page will turn into one of my typical long lists of dreams. I don't want to think beyond five years right now. I want to concentrate on the immediate future and the challenge of the pizza wars.

 s a boy, I was upset by the biblical proverb "It is easier for a camel to go through the eye of a needle than for a rich man to enter the kingdom of heaven." When I asked the nuns in the orphanage to explain it, they told me it means that a rich man ought to be poor in *spirit*. A person should be humble about wealth and want to do good deeds with money, never anything morally wrong. I thought that was a pretty good guideline.

I expect some criticism of what I do with my money. I'm certainly no Solomon and I may not always use my money in the wisest way, but I always try to avoid doing anything wrong. I don't mind the criticism except when it implies that I'm stingy. That hurts, because I enjoy giving things to people. I don't think I've ever been miserly. In fact, I've been criticized more often for being too lavish.

The year I bought the Tigers, I gave Mr. Fetzer a twelve-hundred-dollar eight-ply cashmere cardigan sweater for his birthday, March 25. I was told that some people thought the gift "too ostentatious." Well, March 25 happens to be my birthday, too, and I bought an identical sweater for myself. I don't consider that purchase ostentatious; it was something of a private joke in self-defense—after a ribbing I took at the hands of Bo Schembechler and George Griffith when I showed up at a neighborhood party wearing a favorite old sweater with a big hole in one elbow.

I like old objects, weathered things, leather that's worn from use. I used to carry my jogging gear in a gym bag that some of my employees had given me, and over the years it got beaten up and stained. Finally the zipper broke, and when we were in San Francisco for the All-Star game in 1984, Jim Campbell scowled at that bag and said, "For God's sake, Tom, you ought to buy a new bag. You're a millionaire—look like one, dammit!" I went out that day and bought a new bag, but I made sure it was big enough to carry my old favorite one inside it.

This affection for old possessions may seem at odds with my emphasis on owning the best. But it's not. To my mind, age improves good things, and sentimental value can't be purchased. My favorite coat, for example, isn't a costly tailored vicuña but a rugged brown corduroy with a sheepskin lining that dates back to Christmas 1968. My employees shocked me at our office party that year. They grabbed my old coat, which I'd worn since I'd started in the pizza business, poured lighter fluid on it, and set it on fire! I was as burned up as the coat. I thought this was the worst practical joke I'd ever seen. True, that old coat was shabby, but it was the only one I had. Before I exploded with outrage, though, the gang revealed their present to me—this brown corduroy coat, then new and beautiful. It's gotten too fragile and disreputable looking for me to wear anymore, but I treasure all the memories it has rubbed into its torn and faded fabric, along with the residue of pizza sauce from delivery runs.

I couldn't deliver a pizza now; I no longer have a driver's license. I didn't bother to renew it because a security man drives me everywhere. The need for security is tiresome, but like any other negative, it also has a positive side, which for Domino's is the wide range of duties handled by our security staff. This unit was organized by Thomas R. Minick, our divisional vice-president of special services. T.R. and I were classmates at St. Thomas High School, where we shared an interest in sports and physical fitness. He later bought a home near Barton Hills and we often jogged together at dawn. He's an ex-Marine, too, and he had an outstanding career with the Ann Arbor police department and as sheriff of Washtenaw County. T.R. and I would often talk about Domino's security needs during our early morning runs, and it became evident to both of us that he should come to work for the company. He resigned as sheriff in April 1984, and has built a security force for Domino's that's probably the finest of its type in the country.

Among his many jobs, T.R. has helped arrange for the care and transportation of the classic cars I've been collecting. My interest in cars, coupled with my love of good design and high-quality workmanship, makes it perfectly logical to me that I should have a passion for classic cars. But apparently it came as a surprise to a lot of people, even those who have worked for me for years, when I paid a million dollars for a Duesenberg dual-cowl Phaeton. I guess they had me pegged as a nut about architecture and hoped that was it.

Anyhow, even though I didn't talk about it around the office, I've always been crazy about classic cars. I'm a long-time subscriber to *Hennings*, the bible of car buffs, and I've long planned to build a collection of cars. I want to display classic cars at our headquarters and use them in parades and promotions.

Owning a Duesenberg was a dream of mine for many years, because the Doozy embodies the whole spirit of the classic-car mystique. It was the best car in the world, and to me, it's far superior to a Rolls-Royce or Packard or Lincoln or Cadillac. The one I bought from Richard G. Gold of Minneapolis, many experts think, is the finest Duesenberg in existence. It won the Triple Crown of the Classic Car Club of America in 1974. Its coachwork was done by LeGrande, and it is one of the few Duesenbergs with an original supercharged engine and dual carburetors. The engine is rated at 320 horsepower and can reach 95 M.P.H. in second gear, with a top speed of 130 M.P.H. The car was built in 1934 for John L. Given of the H. J. Heinz family.

After I bought my Doozy, on September 24, 1985, I got wind that a Bugatti Royale would be auctioned from Harrah's collection in Reno, Nevada, the following year. So I went there to get the lay of the land. Another Duesenberg, a handsome black 1929 Murphy-body Model J convertible roadster, was auctioned. Although I hadn't planned on bidding, I decided to go after it. This Duesenberg wasn't as fine a car as the one I already owned, but the Murphy-body roadster was one of my personal favorites of all the Duesenbergs and this was the best preserved of all the original Doozies. The bidding was spirited, and I got into it hammer and tongs. I'm well aware that I can get carried away in a competitive situation, so when I'm bidding on a car, I always jot down the top price I'm willing to pay on a little piece of paper and keep it in the palm of my hand. Once the stakes get high and the adrenaline is pumping as the auctioneer urges the contestants on, I keep glancing at my price chit so I'll know when to stop. In the bidding for the Murphy-body roadster, the figure on my chit was $1 million.

One by one, the other bidders dropped out as the price passed $500,000. Then there was only one other bidder against me, and he called it quits at $975,000. I guessed that the undisclosed reserve price would be $1 million, which was also the limit I'd set for myself, so I bid the extra $25,000 and my hunch proved right. I got my second Doozy for $1 million. Ironically, this purchase received a lot more attention in the press than my previous one, because it was said to be the highest price ever paid at auction for a car.

I enjoyed the auction; it really got my juices flowing, so I started going to more auctions and talking about cars until it gave Margie a doozy of a headache.

It's impossible to underestimate my wife's interest in cars. Maybe that's good, because for years she had to drive whatever junkheap of a delivery car I happened to park in our driveway. But she is a good sport about my sudden enthusiasm for buying classic cars. She even went along with me to some of the auctions. In the fall of 1985, we had a great trip to Earl Clark's Dutch Wonderland Auction in Lancaster, Pennsylvania. I wanted to buy her a cute little '55 Thunderbird, but she didn't like the car's color. I did buy $127,500 worth of cars, including a rare 1920 center-door Model-T Ford and a 1942 Buick Roadmaster convertible. The Buick is the only one of its kind in the world and had been given a total frame-up restoration, so it was a real buy. It isn't precisely the Buick I had in mind—I've always wanted the '46 Roadmaster convertible, because it was my favorite car when I was a kid—but this one is virtually the same car, and I love its sweeping fender lines.

I'm concerned that some of our franchisees may think I am blowing money on classic cars. That's not the case, because I am following a very cautious investment process. I am buying quality cars at good prices, and machines like these have proven to be among the best investments of recent years.

Our classic cars have great public relations value, too. We send them to represent the company in parades and other events around the country, and when we celebrated Domino's twenty-fifth anniversary by moving to our new offices at Domino's Farms, we had nine classic cars to lead a parade from our old headquarters. The parade was headed by an original Peep, the predecessor of the World War II Jeep. Then came our massive dual-cowl Duesenberg Phaeton, with Governor Blanchard riding in it beside Margie and me. Following us, in addition to the Buick convertible and the center-door Model-T—one of only three in the world—was an Isotta-Fraschini; a 1938 Lincoln K convertible, one of only seven in the world; a 1937 Cadillac bus that had been used for sightseeing tours in Yosemite Park; a Model-T bus carrying Domino's board of directors; and our 1906 San Francisco Trolley Car on a bus chassis carrying the Red Garter Band, which played Dixieland jazz all the way to Domino's Farms. Our big blue commissary semis brought up the rear, blowing their mighty air horns. As we entered the farm property, a pair of flag-bearing horsemen in black uniform on jet-black steeds, part of our crack security force, galloped up to take the lead. Then our "Pizza Ponies" hitch of six high-stepping miniature horses—they're Falabellas, the smallest breed of horse in the world—pulled their wagon in behind the flag bearers. Overhead, our red, white and blue helicopter swooped and hovered. It was a blast!

I hope the parade and the publicity we got out of it helped demonstrate some of the value in our classic cars. I have been offered big prices for a couple of them, which I've turned down, because these cars are important to the image of Domino's: a company built on wheels whose emphasis is on quality and service.

Among the cars in Domino's permanent museum collection are two that weren't purchased by me, at least not in their present condition. In fact, I was astonished to see them. They were presented to me by my employees at the dedication of Domino's Farms. The first surprise was a 1959 Volkswagen Beetle like the first delivery car we ever had—the one I gave to my brother in payment for his half of the business. It was presented by the people in Domino's Pizza Distribution. Next I was given the Fleetwood Cadillac Talisman I had been so proud of when I bought it new in 1976. This was a limited-edition car, one of only about eight hundred built, and has the nicest interior of any car I've ever owned. It had been passed along to many other Domino's executives in the ten years between my original purchase and its return to me, beautifully restored. I could hardly believe my eyes, because the car had been so battered the last time I saw it, I had thought it beyond restoration.

All the publicity these exciting and expensive old cars generate is great for Domino's. But the press coverage becomes annoying when it plays me up as a big spender. I cringe at articles about how much money I have, which is interesting since people who are accustomed to wealth tend to shun publicity while the newly rich seem to enjoy being in the limelight. I fall somewhere in the middle: My wealth is new as far as the public is concerned, but not to me. My feelings are more like those of someone who inherited money, because I've always known I'd be a multi-millionaire. I never doubted it for a minute; the only question was *when*.

Since my personal net worth has become the subject of speculation in national magazines, I've been criticized from time to time for not being more philanthropic. But the truth is that I take the subject of philanthropy far too seriously to give money away in a scattershot or superficial manner. I want my contributions to be made in the most meaningful way possible.

Eugene Power, our senior board member and my mentor, is one of the country's greatest philanthropists, and I've studied his philosophy of giving. He is living proof that giving can provide the most lasting satisfactions. Mr. Power has made some suggestions, among them a program for home nursing care for elderly and terminally ill people. This might prove to be the right kind of project for Domino's, and it's one of the ideas I'm investigating with the help of Sam Fine.

Sam is another former associate from the early days of Domino's who has returned. He took over as vice-president of marketing in 1985. Sam is the man who designed the first logo for Domino's. He also created our first advertising campaigns. Then he moved on to the big-time advertising and public relations game in Washington, D.C. I kept in touch with him through the years and always wished I could hire him, but I simply couldn't afford him. Then, on the very day Bob Cotman resigned, while I was wondering what the devil I was going to do about getting someone to take over Bob's marketing chores, who should telephone me but Sam Fine! He said he was thinking about moving back to the Ann Arbor area and would be looking for a job. In less time than it takes to make a pizza, we had a deal.

One of the things I value in Sam is his compassion and his understanding of how to organize and mobilize major programs of a benevolent social nature. I would like to see Domino's Farm provide help for senior citizens that would be on a par with McDonald's Ronald McDonald Houses for parents of hospitalized children. I'm not sure yet what shape this idea will take, but I know we'll come up with a great plan.

The most fascinating charitable project I've become involved with is supporting a Catholic mission in Honduras. This came about as a result of meeting Father Enrique Silvestre in 1984. He is a Passionist priest who had come to Ann Arbor to study English with the Word of God Servant Ministry, an ecumenical evangelical group. He told me how he had gone to Honduras from his native Toldeo, Spain, in 1971 to build a church in the mining town of El Mochito, about seventy miles south of the city of San Pedro Sula.

It was clear that El Mochito must have been a hell town when Father Enrique arrived. The main street of its principal residential district was lined with bars and brothels. Apparently it's common among the poorer classes in that culture for a man to introduce his sons to drinking and using prostitutes when they are about fourteen years old. But in less than ten years, Father Enrique completely turned the place around. Most of the bars were closed and the prostitutes all left town or were converted to Christ. The men who work the zinc and silver mines began attending church with their families. Officials of Hispanic missions who visited El Mochito from time to time said the transformation in the town was a minor miracle.

That was only the beginning for Father Enrique, though. He had a lot of plans for improving the everyday lives of his parishioners, including construction of a hydroelectric plant high in the mountains to bring electricity to the isolated village of San Juan de los Andes. The energy and enthusiasm with which he talked about the project made it obvious to me why his friends call him "Father Firecracker."

In 1985 I made the first of a series of trips to Honduras to visit Father Enrique's parish. I learned, as every first-timer traveler to the area does, that the five countries of Central America—Honduras, Guatemala, El Salvador, Nicaragua, and Costa Rica—really are geographically in the backyard of the United States. Our flight from Ann Arbor in Domino's corporate jet took less time than a typical trip to Los Angeles.

That first visit gave me a vivid impression of what the dry statistics I'd read about extreme poverty in Honduras mean in terms of human misery. The sight of such widespread need in a country so beautiful and so rich in natural resources is heartrending. I made up my mind that I would do something to help Father Enrique change the situation.

My first action was to buy a four-wheel-drive pickup to replace his skinny old mule. Father Enrique was delighted, because not only would the truck allow him to visit all the villages of his parish in a single day—a circuit through rugged mountains that often required three days on mule back—he could also use the vehicle to haul supplies and provide emergency transportation for the villagers. I also gave Father Enrique some money to buy a generator for the hydroelectric plant he wanted to build for San Juan de los Andes.

I went back to Honduras in February 1986, this time with a group of men including Dr. Joseph Kosnic, an emergency room specialist at an inner-city hospital in Detroit, and Dr. Walter (Wally) W. Niemann, who has been my dentist for many years. These two made a survey of the medical and dental needs in Father Enrique's parish.

There is a medical clinic in El Mochito, but few of the natives can afford to be treated there. They frequently suffer from dysentery caused by bad drinking water and a general lack of sanitation, and the disease is often fatal because the folk remedy for it is to withhold fluids, which results in dehydration.

Wally Niemann didn't have the equipment he needed to treat dental problems on that trip (he took plenty the second time he went down a few months later), but he was able to pass out a lot of toothbrushes to children, giving them a pantomime demonstration of how to brush their teeth. They loved these gifts, and it was delightful to see them happily brushing away as they walked down the road.

I was eager to see what progress had been made on the hydroelectric plant in San Juan de los Andes, but first we were to observe mass in the little tin-roofed church Father Enrique had built in that peasant village, which has a population of about two thousand. I wasn't quite prepared for the emotional impact the service would have on me.

The interior of the church was unlike any I had ever seen. The wooden rafters were concealed by a ceiling of brightly colored crepe paper cut in geometric patterns. The entire ceiling seemed to float, undulating gently in the breeze from the paneless windows. This festive flutter overhead contrasted sharply with the stark white altar, a bedsheet draped over a rough wooden trestle table. The concrete-block wall behind the altar was covered with shiny white plastic from which were suspended swags of cloth in lurid greens and purples. The effect was magical.

Although the church building itself was plain, it was by far the most substantial structure in the village, and it demonstrated the strength of faith among these impoverished people, because every part of it, from the concrete floor to the delicate paper ceiling, was so obviously the work of many caring hands.

What made the service there so powerfully affecting for me, however, were the ragged children who filled the rough-hewn benches that served as pews. It was a Saturday afternoon, so most of the adults of the village were at work in the fields. Two of our group, Father Robert Lunsford of St. Thomas Church in Ann Arbor, and Father Patrick Egan, who is chaplain at Domino's Farms, assisted Father Enrique in performing the mass. The children were captivated by these two North Americans ministering to them, and I was captivated, in turn, by the kids. I hadn't felt that kind of spiritual identification with a group of youngsters since I left the orphanage.

After mass, some of the headmen of the village led us down a jungle path to the site of the hydroelectric plant. The generator was covered by a plastic tarp because the concrete-block building that would house it was not yet completed. There had been some difficulty, it seemed, in lining up the six-inch pipe to carry the water down a steep slope from a dam on the mountaintop. But the major holdup seemed to be a fear among the villagers about a pond that would be created below the plant. They thought that since the water in the pond would have passed through the turbine, it would be *full* of electricity!

Father Enrique, who is well acquainted with native superstitions, just smiled ruefully and shrugged his shoulders as one of the headmen explained the villagers' fear to him. I had no doubt that he'd manage to persuade them that the pond wouldn't electrocute their children or livestock. However, his hope of using its waters to grow fish and of teaching the villagers to eat the fish to supplement the meager protein in their diet may take a lot more time.

My experience in Honduras has motivated me to learn Spanish. I enjoy my lessons, especially the informal sessions I've had with members of Father Enrique's church. They gathered around and had a great time helping me build my vocabulary and improve my pronunciation.

I'm not yet sure what form my involvement in Honduras will take. One thing I'm trying is a small experiment in Honduran capitalism—starting a sewing industry in El Mochito. John McDivitt and I have developed a pilot project that has provided some sewing machines and is teaching a few of the people to operate them. For starters, they're working on the relatively simple task of stitching Domino's uniform aprons. But our hope is that as the workers become more proficient, the business will expand to making more complicated garments for Domino's and other clients.

If we can get sewing established as an industry owned and operated locally, it might have a reverse-domino effect as other communities learn capitalist techniques from El Mochito and follow its example. Whether such an outcome is possible depends on many factors outside our control, not the least of which is the unpredictable political situation in Honduras and throughout Central America.

Another idea I want to pursue is bringing baseball to El Mochito. I think those Honduran kids would be good at the game. I tossed a ball to one of them in the compound at Father Enrique's church, just to see what would happen. He caught it and tossed it back as though he'd been playing catch all his life. Other kids came running to join in, and they all seemed to have a natural throwing motion. I've thought about building a diamond somewhere near the church, if we can find enough level ground, and having some Latin players from our minor-league clubs go down there and teach the kids how to play. Maybe if the sewing industry gets started, the local seamstresses could make baseball uniforms for the kids and we could have teams from several villages play each other.

I have a feeling that I may find a purpose in Honduras that will be stronger than Domino's or the Tigers or anything else I've done so far. I hope that somehow I will be able to make a difference in whether this pivotal part of the world eventually becomes a stronghold of free enterprise or goes over to Godless communism.

Father Enrique inspires me with his energy and sense of mission. His work reminds me of things I've read about the priests in Ireland in the fifth century and how they literally Christianized all of Europe. Father Enrique is setting up a lot of little groups that are studying the Bible and going out and multiplying throughout the Honduran countryside.

For myself, I feel a strong sense of wanting to be a good Christian and wanting to help convert the whole world. But as a businessman, I have a fear of turning people off. People don't like to be preached to, and if you bring up the subject of religion outside church or some ceremonial situation, they will tense up. They don't want to confront religion or deal with it.

When I was in the seminary I told myself that when I became a priest I would find a way of preaching a sermon and relating to people that would be different. Many priests give sermons that are dry and dull. They talk way over people's heads, and they don't relate their message to things in everyday life like Christ did. I told myself, "There's gotta be a different way," and I think I'm beginning to find it. I always try to stress the importance of spirituality when I give a talk or am interviewed by the press. I keep it low key; I don't want to turn people off; I just want to plant a seed.

I also try to spread the good word by example. I don't hide the fact that I go to mass every day—maybe that fact alone will get someone else thinking that it's not a bad idea. I know I was inspired when I read that a guy I admired a lot, Miami Dolphins' coach Don Shula, went to mass every day. I was even inspired by Mayor Daley of Chicago, though I didn't admire him. I had associated him with crooked politics and payoffs, but when I read that he went to mass every day, it gave me a whole different perspective on him. I told myself, "The guy can't be that bad." Because you can't go to mass and take Communion with a mortal sin on your soul; it's simply not possible.

My point, as I close this final chapter, is that I believe there's something in life that's a lot bigger and more important than Domino's. I have faith that God will help me find it, and that He'll show me the way to my ultimate goal, which is to go to heaven and take as many people as possible with me.